Close Air Support

Case Studies on the Integration of Air Power on the Battlefield

Edited by Harry Raffal & John Alexander

Helion & Company

Helion & Company Limited
Unit 8 Amherst Business Centre
Budbrooke Road
Warwick
CV34 5WE
England
Tel. 01926 499619
Email: info@helion.co.uk
Website: www.helion.co.uk
X (formerly Twitter): @Helionbooks
Facebook: @HelionBooks
Visit our blog at helionbooks.wordpress.com

Published by Helion & Company 2024
Designed and typeset by Mach 3 Solutions (www.mach3solutions.co.uk)
Cover designed by Paul Hewitt, Battlefield Design (www.battlefield-design.co.uk)

ISBN 978-1-804515-35-8

British Library Cataloguing-in-Publication Data.
A catalogue record for this book is available from the British Library.

Contents

List of Illustrations and Maps

List of Contributors

John Alexander

John Alexander is researching for a PhD by publication on the beginnings of British joint air-land operations as operational art between 1918 and 1944. He has published in the *Air and Space Power Review*, the *RUSI Journal*, *Asian Affairs*, the *Journal of the T.E. Lawrence Society*, and the *Journal of the Royal Air Force Historical Society*, and edits the latter two. He won the 2021 'Two Air Forces Award' for the best historical research article by an RAF or USAF service person. As an RAF officer, he initially specialised in air-land integration, beginning in the Falklands in 1982, subsequently with airborne and commando forces, in Oman, as a corps headquarters Chief Air, and in various Middle East campaigns. He has written operational doctrine for the UK MOD, the RAF and NATO, and spent six years in Afghanistan and Pakistan in various roles. He now heads the UK Permanent Joint Headquarters J7 branch. He has degrees from Newcastle, the Open (two) and Cambridge Universities, and the National Defence University, Pakistan, and was twice selected as a Chief of the Air Staff Fellow.

Sebastian Lukasik

Dr Sebastian H. Lukasik is Associate Professor at the US Air Force Air Command and Staff College at Maxwell Air Force Base, Alabama. He received a PhD in Military History from Duke University. His research and teaching interests include the history and theory of airpower, combat motivation in modern warfare, and military culture in the North Atlantic world in the nineteenth and twentieth centuries. He is currently working on a book project on the emergence of combined-arms warfare in the US military during the First World War.

Fergus Macdonald

Squadron Leader Gus Macdonald joined the RAF in 1989, training as a navigator and qualifying on the Tornado GR1. Posted to No. 617 Squadron from 1991–95, operational flying included Operation *Jural* and Operation *Warden* (Iraq No Fly Zone). He then qualified as an instructor serving in Dhahran on secondment to the RSAF. In 1999, he returned to the UK and converted to the Tornado F3, serving on 43 Squadron in the Air Defence role and deploying on Operation *Resonance*, again in the Iraq NFZ. In 2007, Macdonald returned to the Tornado GR4 on 14 Squadron at Lossiemouth, conducting CAS in Operation *Telic* in 2008 and Operation *Herrick* in 2009, where he was part of the initial Tornado Force workup and handover team, deploying to Afghanistan in March 2009. In 2016, he returned to the Tornado Force for three final years of constant deployments on Operation *Shader*, operating from RAF Akrotiri in an anti-ISIS CAS role over Iraq and Syria. Staff appointments included Fast Jet Air planning at Northwood HQ and instructional duties in the Tactical Leadership Programme at Albacete, Spain. He retired from flying in March 2019 and now works in London as a staff officer within the MOD Saudi Armed Forces Programme. He completed his MA in Airpower Studies as part of the CAS Fellowship scheme in 2013.

Mike Meech
Mike Meech has written several articles on First World War aviation, including Contact Patrols, Air-Tank and Air-Cavalry cooperation and communication systems between aircraft and ground forces, these have been published in *Cross & Cockade International Journal*, the *Journal of the Society for Army Historical Research* and the RAF Museum's *First World War in the Air* publication. He has been a volunteer at the RAF Museum since 1993. Previously he had spent 10 years in the RAF followed by eight years in the Intelligence Corps, before undertaking a BA (Hons) Degree at the University of Southampton in Archaeology and History.

Samuel Oyewole
Samuel Oyewole is a lecturer at the Department of Political Science, Federal University Oye-Ekiti, Nigeria, and a post-doctoral research fellow at the Ocean Regions Programme, Department of Political Sciences, and the African Centre for the Study of the United States (ACSUS), University of Pretoria, South Africa. His research interests cover aerospace, defence and security strategies, science and technology policies, crisis management, African and Global South affairs, International Relations, and development studies. His articles have appeared in many journals, including *Astropolitics*, *Australian Journal of Maritime and Ocean Affairs*, *African Security*, *African Security Review*, *African Conflict and Peacebuilding Review*, *Defense and Security Analysis*, *Defence Studies*, *Democracy and Security*, *Geojournal*, *Journal of Asian and African Studies*, *New Zealand International Review*, *Politikon*, *Politeia*, *RUSI*, *South African Journal of International Affairs*, *Strategic Analysis*, and *Studies in Conflict & Terrorism*. His the author of *Utilitarianism in Outer Space: Space Policy, Socioeconomic Development and Security Strategies in Nigeria and South Africa* (Springer, 2024), and co-editor of *Power Politics in Africa: Nigeria and South Africa in Comparative Perspective* (Cambridge Scholar, 2020), *Boko Haram's Campaign of Terror in Nigeria: Context, Dimensions and Emerging Trajectories* (Routledge, 2021), *Armed Banditry in Nigeria: Evolution, Dynamics and Trajectories* (Palgrave Macmillan, 2024), *The Political Economy of Kidnapping and Insecurity in Nigeria: Beyond News and Rumours* (Springer, 2024).

Bill Pyke

Bill Pyke is an independent air power researcher who has focused on the role of the RAF in areas of policy, intelligence, and operations both during the Second World War and the Cold War. He completed an MA in Air Power studies at the University of Birmingham in 2016 under the guidance of Air Commodore (retd.) Peter Gray. He has subsequently written in the RAF's *Air Power Review* and his new biography of Marshal of the RAF Sir John Slessor was published in 2022. He has given presentations on various Cold War themes at conferences and talks at King's College, London, and at the RAF Museum. Pyke previously had a 42-year career in the oil industry. He has always maintained his keen interest in the role of air power.

Harry A.N. Raffal

Harry Raffal is the Head of Collections and Research at the Royal Air Force Museum. He holds a doctorate from the University of Hull for his thesis on the operations of the RAF and *Luftwaffe* during the evacuation of Dunkirk. He is a committee member of the Royal Air Force Historical Society and the British Commission for Military History, and is the Vice-Chair of the Royal Aeronautical Society, Aeronautical Heritage Group. Raffal has previously published research articles on 'The Royal Air Force in the Battle of France', *Nacelles*, 'The Royal Air Force in the Third Afghan War', *Journal of the Royal Air Force Historical Society*, and 'Tracing the Online Development of the Ministry of Defence and Armed Forces Through the UK Web Archive', *Internet Histories*. He has presented research papers at conferences across the world, including on 'Air Forces in a Conflict of Political Systems', 'British Historical Memory and Reference to MRAF Sir Arthur Harris', 'Émigrés, Refugees and Volunteers in RAF Service, 1939-1945', 'Online Commemoration and Memory', and 'Virtual Reality and Historical Understanding'. In 2021, Bloomsbury published his work *Air Power and the Evacuation of Dunkirk*.

Clive Richards

Clive Richards is an independent scholar. He previously served on the staff of the Ministry of Defence Air Historical Branch between 1996 and 2008. On leaving the Ministry of Defence he has continued to research and write on air power matters, and in December 2017 he was awarded an MA in Air Power: History, Theory and Practice by the University of Birmingham. Richards is a member of the British Commission for Military History and has delivered papers at conferences held by the BCMH, Royal Air Force Museum, the RAF Centre for Air and Space Power Studies, the Royal Air Force Historical Society, and the Polish Historical Society. His account of the early development of military aviation in India and the creation of the Indian Air Force appeared in *The British Indian Army: Virtue and Necessity*, edited by Dr Robert Johnson (Cambridge Scholars Press, 2014). He is the author of a COMEC Occasional Paper and has contributed to several other publications, including the *Journal of the Royal Air Force Historical Society*, *Air Power Review* and *The Aviation Historian*.

Michael Terry

Michael Terry is an English Literature graduate and early career researcher currently writing a PhD thesis for the Open University on the Representation of First World War Aerial Combat in Literature. His work aims to highlight the significance of this under-researched genre of writing. He examines how this body of work confounds our general expectations of what First World War literature should be like, and how it helped form a mythology about early aerial combat that persists to this day. He has presented a series of lectures for the British Commission for Military History and the Royal Air Force Museum discussing his work, and he is the winner of the 2023 Royal Air Force Museum Doctoral Bursary. He is an academic advisor to the Great War Aviation Society, for whom he presented the annual Leaman Lecture in 2024.

Geoffrey Vesey Holt

Lieutenant Colonel (Retired) Geoffrey Vesey Holt MBE was educated at the *Lycée Français de Londres*, Durham University (Upper 2:1 Class in Modern History) and the French Staff College. A career officer in the Royal Tank Regiment (RTR) until 2010, he also served as an instructor and operations staff officer and then on the Challenger 2 (he was awarded the MBE for his efforts), the Multi Role Armoured Vehicle and the even more convoluted Future Rapid Effect System programmes. He supported the RTR's First World War commemorations including some of the battlefield tours and wrote two articles in Volume 1 of the Battlefield tour guide. He has written a variety of other articles and is writing the two 1918 volumes of the history of the Tank Corps in the Great War (the 1916 volume by Stephen Pope has just been published). He also runs pro bono battlefield tours, gives lectures and walks regularly; surprisingly for a retired RTR officer, in the hills of Sussex Weald and other places.

This edited volume originated from a Royal Air Force Museum and British Commission for Military History conference on Close Air Support held at the RAF Museum, London in March 2023.

The editors would like to thank the Royal Air Force Museum and the British Commission for Military History for their support.

Abbreviations and Acronyms

AA	anti-aircraft
AAA	anti-aircraft artillery
AAP	allied administrative publication
ABDACOM	American-British-Dutch-Australian Command
ACE	Agile Combat Employment
ACM	airspace control measure
ACMED	Allied Command Mediterranean
ACTS	Air Corps Tactical School
AD	air defence
ADM	Admiralty file (TNA, Kew)
AFA	Aerial Field Artillery
AFB	Air Force Base (US)
AFC	Australian Flying Corps
AFC	Air Force Cross
AFM	army field manual
AGM	air-to-ground missile
AH	attack helicopter
AHB	Air Historical Branch (RAF)
AI	air interdiction
AIF	Austrailian Imperial Force
AIM	air interception missle
AJP	allied joint publication
ALG	advanced landing ground
ALI	air-land integration
AOC	Air Officer Commanding
AOC-in-C	Air Officer Commanding-in-Chief
AOIC	Air Officer in Charge
AOP	aerial observation posts
AP	air publication
ARA	Aerial Rocket Artillery
ATP	advanced targeting pod
ATP	allied tactical publication
AWM	Australian War Museum
BAI	battlefield air interdiction
BCMH	British Commission for Military History

BCT	brigade combat team
BEF	British Expeditionary Force
BGGS	brigadier-general general staff
C-in-C	Commander-in-Chief
C2	command and control
CAOC	combined air operations centre
CAP	Counterattack Patrol
CAS	close air support
CAS	Chief of the Air Staff
CBSO	counter-battery staff officer
CBU	cluster bomb unit
CD	confidential document (RAF)
CDS	Chief of Defence Staff
CG	commanding general
CGS	Chief of the General Staff
CIB	Central Information Bureau
CIGS	Chief of the Imperial General Staff
CLFFI	Commander Land Forces Falkland Islands
COIN	counter-insurgency
COMAW	Commander Amphibious Warfare
COS	Chiefs of Staff
CTG (or F)	Commander Task Group (or Force)
CTTO	Central Tactics and Trials Organisation
CW	continuous wave
CWS	Central Wireless Station
DEFE	Ministry of Defence Files TNA, Kew
DFC	Distinguished Flying Cross
DH	de Havilland
DMS	dual mode seeker
DOD	Department of Defence (US)
DS	directing staff
DSO	Distinguished Service Order
EA	Enemy Aircraft (First World War RFC/RAF)
ECOMOG	Economic Community of West African States Monitoring Group
EPII	Enhanced Paveway II
FAC	forward air controller
FI	Falkand Islands
FK	Frederick Koolhoven
FLOT	forward line of own troops
FM	field manual
FO	forward observer
FPV	first person view UAS
FSCL	fire support coordination line
FSCM	fire support coordination measures
FST	fire support teams
FW	fixed wing
GCAS	ground alert CAS
GF	British First World War call for artillery to engage a fleeting target

GHQ	General Headquarters
GOC	General Officer Commanding
GPS	Global Positioning System
GR	ground attack/recce
GSO	General staff officer [followed by grade]
HF	high frequency
HMS	Her/His Majesty's Ship
HMSO	Her/His Majesty's Stationary Office
HQ	Headquarters
HU	Helicopter utility
IISS	Institute of International Security Studies
IJAAS	Imperial Japanese Army Air Service
IJNAS	Imperial Japanese Naval Air Service
IP	initial point
IR	infra-red
ISAF	International Security Assistance Force
ISIS	Islamic State of Iraq and al-Sham
ISR	intelligence, surveillance, and reconnaissance
ISTAR	intelligence, surveillance, target acquisition and reconnaissance
IWM	Imperial War Museum
JDAM	joint direct attack munition
JDP	joint doctrine publication
JFACTSU	Joint Forward Air Controller Training and Standards Unit
JFC	joint fires cells
JTAC	Joint terminal attack controller
JTF	joint task force
LFFI	Land Forces Falkland Islands
LGB	laser-guided bomb
LIC	low-intensity conflict
LL	British First World War call for all available batteries and bombing squadrons to engage
MAAF	Mediterranean Allied Air Forces
MAC	Mediterranean Air Command
MACAF	Mediterranean Allied Coastal Air Force
MACV	Military Assistance Command, Vietnam
MANPADS	man-portable air defence system
MASAF	Mediterranean Allied Strategic Air Force
MATAF	Mediterranean Allied Tactical Air Force
MEND	Movement for the Emancipation of Niger Delta
MISREP	mission report
MOD	Ministry of Defence
MRAF	Marshal of the RAF
n. d.	no date
NAF	Nigerian Air Force
NATO	North Atlantic Treaty Organisation
NCO	non-commissoned officer
NDLF	Niger Delta Liberation Force
NDPVF	Niger Delta Peoples Volunteers Force

NFZ	no fly zone
OAS	offensive air support
OKH	*Oberkommando des Heeres* (upper command of the [German] Army.
OP	observation post
PGM	precision-guided munition
PSO	peace support operations
PWII	Paveway II (III and IV)
RA	Royal Artillery
RAAF	Royal Australian Air Force
RAF	Royal Air Force
RAFM	Royal Air Force Museum
RCAF	Royal Canadian Air Force
RE	Reconnaissance Experimental
RFC	Royal Flying Corps
RN	Royal Navy
ROAD	Reorganization Objectives, Army Divisions
ROE	rules of engagement
ROVER	Remotely Operated Video Enhanced Receiver
RPAS	pemotely piloted aircraft system
SAA	small arms ammunition
SAS	Special Air Service
SDB	small diameter bomb
SEAD	suppression of enemy defences
SF	special forces
SNEB	*Société Nouvelle des Etablissements Edgar Brandt*
SOP	standard operating procedure
SOS	save our souls
SS	Stationary Services
SS	Steam Ship
TAC	Tactical Air Command (USAF)
TACP	tactical air control party
TGRF	Tornado GR Force
TIC	troops in contact
TM	Tank Museum, Bovington
TNA	The National Archives (Kew)
TRADOC	US Army Training and Doctrine Command
TTPs	tactics, techniques and procedures
UAS	unmanned/uncrewed aircraft system
UH	utillty helicopter
USAAF	United States Army Air Force
USAF	United States Air Force
USCONARC	United States Continental Army Command
VC	Victoria Cross
VC	Viet Cong
VCAS	Vice Chief of the Air Staff
VHF	very high frequency
VKS	*Vozdushno-Kosmicheskiye Sily* – Russian Aerospace Forces

Foreword

This excellent study of the century-long struggle for the optimum application of aircraft to the land battle is the result of a conference jointly sponsored by the RAF Museum and the British Commission for Military History. The participants review the often-controversial history of the subject from the First World War to the twenty-first century and these case studies highlight one of the perennial issues affecting air power throughout the period: namely, is air power best applied at the point of contact between the troops fighting for their lives below; or is it better directed at the immediate hinterland of the battlefront to disrupt supply and reinforcement and command headquarters. For understandable reasons related to their own personal survival in battle soldiers have tended to the former viewpoint, whereas airmen have been inclined to point to one of air power's key characteristics in its ability to reach beyond the battle and thus have largely favoured its capacity to interdict. There is, of course, a fundamental, indeed foundational, issue underlying these differing perspectives and that is the issue of control. The soldier would like to exercise the maximum control of the supporting aircraft, and close air support at the point of battle is necessarily heavily dependent on direction from the person in contact on the ground. The air commander likewise wishes to be in full control of the air assets available and direct them to best effect during the campaign as a whole and thus tends towards the much broader application of air power.

There is no perfect solution to this near-perennial issue though it is legitimate to point out that close air support is principally effective only as a tactical tool whereas conversely interdiction is most effective at the operational level and when exercised over time and before battle is joined. In this respect history has some interesting lessons. The pivotal Battle of Amiens in 1918 is referred to several times over the following pages. The RAF planning for the battle was largely formulated on the basis of the Army's plan and when, belatedly, the RAF realised there was an opportunity to interdict the river crossings behind the German front the subsequent ad hoc effort largely failed. There are other examples from history where a failure to produce a properly joint plan has produced less than optimum results: a plan with 'Air' as an annex to a largely Army plan is not a joint plan. That said, however, as Clausewitz pointed out long before aircraft were invented, the first step is to identify the nature of the war itself. Interdiction in a counter-insurgency campaign where an enemy may be far less dependent on traditional supply lines or headquarters is far less likely to be the answer. A flexible approach is key and where air power is in plentiful supply, as in the battle of Normandy in 1944, an overall plan combining the two produces a powerful synergistic effect.

As these cases studies clearly show, air superiority is essential before air power can be effectively applied whether at depth or in close battle. Air support requires appropriate training, aircraft and weapons systems as well as targeting intelligence. It especially requires good communications and a familiar and appropriate machinery. Pre-planned operations are often more effective than an ad hoc application, but to reiterate air forces must be an intimate part of the planning process from the start of campaign planning and must not merely be an annex to a ground plan. Of note, in any but a benign environment, it is potentially expensive in lives and hardware.

Sebastian Cox
Head of the Air Historical Branch (RAF)
President of the British Commission For Military History

1

Introduction

John Alexander and Harry Raffal

The greatest development in land warfare since 1914 has been in the coordination between air forces and armies in military operations. In January 1943 shortly after his victory in the Second Battle of El Alamein, General Sir Bernard Law Montgomery wrote any 'officer who aspires to hold high command in war must understand clearly certain basic principles regarding the use of air power.'[1] In 1945 he listed air power as the first principle of war.[2] Yet the provision of close air support by integrating air power on the battlefield was and remains controversial. Situated at the seam of land and air operations, the priority close air support should be given relative to other air power roles, and who decides this priority, has been a point of frequent argument between armies and air forces. This continues to be the case. Army and air force attitudes to close air support are also episodic, as the United States Air Force (USAF) historian Benjamin Cooling's *Case Studies in the Development of Close Air Support* reminds us; quickly ranging from pivotal contributions to a campaign, to the most bitter inter-service disagreements. Independent air forces often prioritised independent strategic bombing over directly supporting armies while armies judged air forces on the close air support they could see immediately in front of them. Furthermore, the success or failure of close air support in each situation has depended upon factors such as operational capabilities and military effectiveness as much as doctrine.[3] The quality, quantity, and type of aircraft as well as personnel, command and control arrangements, air-ground communication systems, and air-ground training, are as important as theory when providing close air support. The case studies in this collection further highlight the challenge of close air support.

1 The National Archives, Kew (TNA): WO 201/2390: 'Notes on High Command by General Montgomery', Tripoli, January 1943.
2 Field Marshal B.L. Montgomery, *High Command in War* (21st Army Group, 1945), p.4.
3 B. Franklin Cooling, *Case Studies in the Development of Close Air Support* (Washington, DC: Office of Air Force History, US Air Force, 1990), pp.1–2.

Before introducing the case studies, it is important to understand the doctrinal terms used as they have evolved over time and to avoid teleology. The current definition of close air support used by North Atlantic Treaty Organisation (NATO) and partner armies and air forces is 'air action against hostile targets which are in close proximity to friendly forces and which require detailed integration of each air mission with the fire and movement of those forces.'[4] The US Army and USAF first used an almost identical definition in 1950, the Royal Air Force (RAF) has used this exact definition since at least 1963 and the term close air support was first used in US doctrine in 1946.[5] The other counter-surface force mission currently defined by NATO is 'air interdiction': 'air operations conducted to divert, disrupt, delay, or destroy the enemy's military surface capabilities before it can be brought to bear effectively against friendly forces, or to otherwise achieve objectives that are conducted at such distances from friendly forces that detailed integration of each air mission with the fire and movement of friendly forces is not required.' From the 1970s until 1990 NATO defined an intermediate form of attack called battlefield air interdiction (BAI).

In the First World War the British used fighters (often called scouts) for low-level attack on the battlefield, and the RAF's first air operations manual simply refers to the use of single-seaters to attack ground targets with machine-guns.[6] Whereas the German air service, the *Luftstreitkräfte,* had, by late 1917, created *Schlachtstaffeln* (battle flights) of armed and armoured, two-seat, ground attack aircraft used for pre-planned attacks. In retrospect, the First World War indicated a divide was already growing between proponents of aircraft designed and dedicated for battlefield air support and interdiction, and those who favoured utilising air superiority fighters to fulfil this role.[7] During the Second World War the British separated 'air support' into 'indirect air support' and 'direct air support'. Indirect air support was 'support by air action against objectives other than enemy forces involved in the tactical battle' – what would be air interdiction today. Direct air support was 'intended to have an immediate effect on current land or sea operations'. Direct air support included close support 'in close proximity to our forward troops' – today's close air support.[8]

4 Allied Joint Publication (AJP)-3.3.2(A), *Allied Joint Doctrine for Close Air Support and Air Interdiction* (NATO HQ, Brussels: NATO Standardization Office, 2009); Allied Tactical Publication (ATP)-3.3.2.1(E) Version 1, *Tactics, Techniques and Procedures for Close Air Support and Air Interdiction* (NATO HQ, Brussels: NATO Standardization Office, 2019); Office of the Chairman of the Joint Chiefs of Staff, *DOD Dictionary of Military and Associated Terms* (Washington, DC: The Joint Staff, 2021), p.35.

5 *Joint Training Directive for Air-Ground Operations* (Fort Munro, VA: Langley AFB, VA: Army Field Forces/Tactical Air Command, 1950), p.6, p.193; TNA: AIR 10/5589: AP1300 RAF Manual of Operations, Fourth Edition, 1957; United States. War Department, *FM 31-35 Air-Ground Operations* (Washington, DC: Army Department, 1946).

6 Air Ministry, *CD22 Royal Air Force Operations Manual*, Provisional (London: Air Ministry, 1922), p.91.

7 Richard P. Hallion and Richard Mason, *Strike from the Sky: The History of Battlefield Air Attack, 1910–1945* (Tuscaloosa, AL: University of Alabama Press, 2010), pp.16–7, p.37.

8 AHB, *Air Publication 3235. The Second World War, 1939–1945, Royal Air Force, Air Support* (London: Air Ministry (AHB), 1955), p.7.

This book adds fresh insights to our understanding of close air support, adding to Cooling's *History of Close Air Support* which comprises case studies outlining the development up to 1939, on the Allied and predominantly US Second World War experience in North Africa, Italy, North-West Europe and the Pacific, the German and Soviet experiences, and Korea, Vietnam, and the Israeli-Arab wars. The relatively limited recent literature on close air support, much of it American and dating from the late 1980s, perhaps reflects the view of many air power theorists and practitioners that close air support is an inefficient and costly distraction from more worthwhile air operations, or, from a land forces perspective, that the air forces are often unwilling to provide such support.[9] Furthermore, the historiography is also episodic, often reflecting on the need to relearn the forgotten practice of close air support, a common theme in the book.[10] Case studies considering close air support in specific operational circumstances have sought to determine the combat advantage that close air support provides to ground forces.[11] Moreover, broader works on tactical air support have considered the wider evolution of air support theory, and the development of the aircraft and arms to enable theory to be put into practice.[12]

There remains, however, a notable absence of works that unite both the developmental pattern of close air support, reflecting on its ebb and flow, with its battlefield effect. As a result, the historiography frequently references the contentious nature of close air support, but the existing scholarship considers close air support through examples that are frequently analogous. This lack of diverse study, with the analysis and evaluation typically structured around 'lessons' that might inform effective applications of air power in the future, has limited the study of close air support. This work provides a broader range of examples of close air support, from the First World War to recent operations in Afghanistan and contemporary operations in Africa, and through differing disciplinary approaches including historical analysis, representations in literature, political science and an aircrew practitioner's perspective.

Combined, the chapters within this edited volume provide the means to examine how, and when, close air support can influence the battlefield. A recurring theme is that in a contested air environment, tactical air power – both air interdiction and close air support – depends on clear, limited and achievable goals to affect the ground situation. Coordination is essential, as is expectation management; if the air force claims it can do too much, or the ground force believes more is possible than can be achieved, planning becomes disconnected from reality. Air forces are not artillery. Their tactical effect is distinct and unique. The combined works also show that close air support is

9 Peter A. Costello, *A Matter of Trust: Close Air Support Apportionment and Allocation for Operational Level Effects* (Air University Press, 1997).

10 See for example Wing Commander H. Smyth DFC, RAF, 'From Coningham to Project Coningham-Keyes: Did British Forces Relearn Historical Air-Land Cooperation Lessons During Operation "Telic"?', *Defence Studies*, 7:2 (2007), pp.258–86.

11 Ian Gooderson, *Air Power at the Battlefront: Allied Close Air Support in North-West Europe, 1943–45*, Cass Series: Studies in Air Power, (London: Frank Cass, 1998), p.2.

12 Hallion and Mason, *Strike from the Sky*.

just one air power mission and that it is dependent on other roles, most notably control of the air and reconnaissance. It also requires air and ground forces to cooperate and communicate effectively. Close air support is one mission in the interconnected whole and, as the authors demonstrate, when we discuss close air support it is necessary to look at the wider environment in which an air force is operating.

Close air support in (and beyond) the First World War

The first three chapters provide fresh insight into British close air support in the First World War. As Wing Commander John Slessor was to write, the focus of air power in the First World War was army cooperation, albeit all four roles of air power recognised in contemporary air power doctrine were developed rapidly in the war: intelligence, surveillance and reconnaissance (ISR), attack, control of the air and mobility.[13] By 1918 air power was essential to what Jonathan Bailey calls the birth of the modern system of warfare, which transformed the linear battlefield of 1914, familiar to Napoleon or Wellington, to the three-dimensional battlefield of 1918, recognisable to us now.[14] The use of indirect artillery, guided by artillery observation from the air and ground and by aerial photography, was the key element of this revolution, although the major powers also used aircraft for ground attack and the interdiction of lines of communications. The British, for example, used fighters for ground-strafing in defence, attack and pursuit, with great effect in attack at Cambrai in 1917, in defence during the German Spring Offensives, in attack during the Allied Hundred Days' Offensive, and in pursuits in Italy, Bulgaria and Palestine in 1918.

One of the British Army and RAF's lessons from the First World War was because of the extreme loss rates amongst ground-strafing aircraft it should only be used in extremis. Slessor cited the example of No. 80 Squadron RAF which lost an average of 75 percent of its pilots every month when it was employed for low-flying attack from March 1918 until the end of the war, some 168 officers from just one squadron, whose established strength was 20 pilots.[15] The first post-war edition of the Army's *Field Service Regulations* stated:

> Once aerial superiority has been established offensive action against the enemy's troops and transports by means of machine gun fire and bombs, by low-flying machines under the protection of high patrols, becomes feasible, and must be

13 Wing Commander John Slessor, *Air Power and Armies* (London: Oxford University Press: Oxford, 1936), p.1; Ministry of Defence, *Joint Doctrine Publication 0–30, UK Air Power*, 3rd edn (Shrivenham: Development, Concepts and Doctrine Centre, 2022), pp.25–45.

14 Jonathan B.A. Bailey, 'The First World War and the Birth of Modern Warfare', in MacGregor Knox and Williamson Murray (eds), *The Dynamics of Military Revolution, 1300–2050, 1st edn* (Cambridge University Press, 2001), pp.132–53.

15 Slessor, *Air Power and Armies*, p.100.

> vigorously undertaken. Whenever possible machines must be specially detailed to deal with anti-tank guns … Attacks by low-flying aeroplanes, however, are expensive in machines and causalities to personnel. They should be restricted, therefore, to occasions when really favourable targets are presented.[16]

The book's first chapter examines RAF fighter pilots' attitudes to low-flying attack with Michael Terry's insightful perspective as an early career researcher of English literature into the fighter-dominated cultural representations of First World War aerial warfare. Terry has found that close air support rarely features in this literature. One exception is No. 46 Squadron Royal Flying Corps (RFC)/RAF and the subsequent representation in literature of Arthur Gould Lee, later an air vice-marshal, Donald MacLaren, the war's highest-scoring Sopwith Camel ace, Sydney Philip Smith, a short-lived ground attack enthusiast, and Victor Maslin Yeates, who depicted many of No. 46 Squadron's close support missions in his 1934 novel *Winged Victory*. Their literature reveals a resentment by fighter pilots at being exposed to the perceived random dangers of ground-attack work, as well as a cynicism as to whether such work achieved anything, and a lack of recognition for it, which explains why it is largely ignored in subsequent cultural representations. As Terry examines, the historiography suggests that the unpopularity of the role shaped the RAF's inter-war attitudes, although one historian has recently questioned the loss rates that informed this doctrine, citing Nos. 8 and 73 Squadrons supporting the Tank Corps, examined in our fourth chapter.[17]

Mike Meech's chapter highlights a little-known overlap between ISR and attack. The Counter-Attack Patrol (CAP) of the RFC/RAF Corps squadrons was developed in 1917 as it was difficult for Contact Patrol machines to both maintain contact with advancing friendly troops and to warn of German counterattacks. The CAP machine could call in artillery fire by wireless telegraphy if within range, attack the German troops itself with its bombs and machine-guns or call-in other aircraft by firing a red Very light. In August 1918 a wireless Central Information Bureau (known as the CIB) was established at Villers-Bretonneux to coordinate CAPs although it was soon realised, as Meech shows, CAP machines were calling in air attacks on targets within range of friendly artillery, providing an early example close air support being regarded as 'flying artillery' and of the need for the integrated prioritisation of close air support and artillery.

In the final chapter on the First World War, Geoffrey Vesey Holt highlights the success of the dedicated air support provided to the Tank Corps in 1918, using Nos. 8

16 The War Office, *Field Service Regulations, Volume II, Operations, 1920 (Provisional)* (London: The War Office, 1920), p.187.

17 Alistair McCluskey, 'The Battle of Amiens and the Development of British Air-Land Battle, 1918–1945', in Gary Sheffield and Peter W. Gray (eds), *Changing War: The British Army, the Hundred Days Campaign and the Birth of the Royal Air Force, 1918*, Birmingham War Studies (London: Bloomsbury, 2013).

and 73 Squadrons RAF, mentioned earlier. Whereas all British army corps formations were allocated a 'Corps' ISR squadron, from 1 June 1918 No. 8 Squadron RAF, under the command of Major Trafford Leigh-Mallory, was allocated to the Tanks Corps to build on the lessons of the extensive air support during the Battle of Cambrai. No. 8 Squadron provided useful support to the tanks at the Battles of Hamel and Amiens, but the slow-moving Mark V tanks proved vulnerable to German artillery. To counter this No. 73 Squadron, flying Camels, was also allocated to the Tanks Corps to ground-strafe German guns or possible gun positions, providing as Vesey Holt argues a level of innovative British air-ground integration not seen elsewhere. The importance of strafing anti-tank guns was a point specifically identified in the *Field Service Regulations*, which set out that, in organising the use of aircraft in the offensive, 'whenever possible machines must be specially detailed to deal with anti-tank guns.' The RAF's *CD22 RAF Operations Manual* repeated the same advice.[18]

The inter-war period

This section comprises one chapter that provides a different perspective on the much-studied subject of air power thinking between the world wars, a period which saw air power transformed in technology, thinking and practice. Whereas, as previously highlighted, the main role of air power in the First World War was tactical reconnaissance, the great powers entered the Second World War with different doctrines, with none initially prioritising close air support. As the extensive literature highlights, broadly Britain's newly independent RAF, supported by the Government and public opinion, favoured independent air operations, whether strategic bombing, strategic air defence or substituting for the British Army in colonial control. In contrast, the conventional wisdom of the United States Army Air Corps is that it became dominated by strategic bombing. Whereas the French Air Force, independent from 1934, by 1940 was focused on battlefield control of the air and tactical reconnaissance. The chapter in this section adds to our understanding of close air support by examining the ideas of the relatively little-known US inter-war air power theorist, William Carrington Sherman, whose ideas included attack aviation on the battlefield.

Any inter-war developments, however, must be considered against those of Germany. Despite the 1919 Versailles Treaty prohibiting a German air service or aircraft, German concepts of air support, and the value of coordinating air and ground operations, advanced significantly during the inter-war period, starting with systemic lessons identified from the First World War codified in General Von Seeckt's 1921 tactical manual *Führung und Gefecht der verbundenen Waffen* (Command and Combat

18 *Field Service Regulations* (*Volume II, Operations*) (1920), p.187; *CD22 Royal Air Force Operations Manual*, p.106.

Employment of the Combined Arms).[19] Air power in support of ground operations was carefully studied, including close air support, interdiction and combined arms assault. Interdiction, both at the tactical level, immediately behind the frontline, and the operational level, designed to interfere with an adversary's mobilisation and movement of reserves, were important components of German air support doctrine.[20] The German Army's 1933 doctrinal regulations, *Truppenführung* (Unit Command), and subsequent *Luftwaffe* regulations, established that air support would typically be directed against targets beyond the range of friendly artillery.[21] Coordination between air and ground units was identified as a necessary condition for success, particularly for *Tiefangriff auf dem schlachtfeld* (low-level attacks on the battlefield), but the primacy of the *Luftwaffe's* air superiority mission was also established. Following the experience of providing air support in close proximity to ground forces in the Spanish Civil war, the *Luftwaffe* increased the number of units available to support the operation of army formations.[22] The August 1939 *Richtlinien für den einsatz der Fliegertruppe zur unmittelbaren unterstützung des heeres* (Directives for the deployment of the air force in direct support of the army) gave guidelines for air support directly in front of forward units and in such close proximity to friendly ground forces it required the closest coordination. Nonetheless, such support would only be used only in exceptional circumstances for decisive effect. Interdiction of the battlefield remained the *Luftwaffe's* priority where it was thought air power would have more effect than on the battlefield.[23]

Sebastian Lukasik's chapter examines the development of William C. Sherman's ideas about ground attack aviation through the prism of his three principal theoretical works: *Tentative Manual for the Employment of Air Service* (1919), *Training Regulation (TR) 440–15* (1921/1923), and *Air Warfare* (1927). Sherman, an officer in the US Army Air Service (the US Army Air Corps from 1926), has largely been overshadowed in historiography by his more famous contemporaries, such as Giulio Douhet, William L. (Billy) Mitchell, and Hugh Trenchard. As Lukasik highlights, this is surprising as Sherman's intellectual legacy marks him out as one of the most original and analytically rigorous airpower thinkers of the inter-war period. Historians normally associate

19 *German Truppenamt, D.V. Pl. Nr. 487., Führung und Gefecht der Verbundenen Waffen (F.u.G.)* (Charlottenburg, Germany: Verlag Offene Worte, 1921); Matthias Strohn, 'Hans von Seeckt and His Vision of a "Modern Army"', *War in History*, 12:3 (2005), pp.318–37 (pp.326–7).

20 James S. Corum, 'From Biplanes to Blitzkrieg: The Development of German Air Doctrine Between the Wars', *War in History*, 3:1 (1996), pp.85–101 (p.97).

21 Bruce Condell, James S. Corum, and David T. Zabecki (eds), *On the German Art of War: Truppenführung*, (Boulder: Lynne Rienner Publishers, 2022).

22 James S. Corum, *The Luftwaffe: Creating the Operational Air War, 1918–1940*, Modern War Studies (Lawrence: University Press of Kansas, 1997), p.248.

23 National Archives and Records Administration, Washington, DC: T321, R76: Hans Jeschonnek, *Oberbefehlshaber der Luftwaffe, Richtlinien Für Den Einsatz Der Fliegertruppe Zur Unmittelbarren Unterstussung Des Heeres*, 1 Aug. 1939.

Sherman, if at all, with the 'industrial web theory' approach to strategic bombing, an approach which dominates the inter-war US air power historiography. But as Lukasik emphasises, Sherman embraced the totality of air power roles, developing a sophisticated understanding of the relationship between air superiority, ground attack, and long-range interdiction embedded in an equally complex appreciation of the combat motivation and morale of fielded forces as the key determinant of victory and defeat. Ultimately, his greatest contribution is to be found in the nuanced way in which he approached the issue of cooperation between air and land forces as the basis for the effective use of airpower in support of the ground scheme of manoeuvre. Seen in this light, Sherman stands out as one of the first senior air officers to champion what today would be termed a 'joint' paradigm of airpower. Sherman is the only air power theorist Slessor cites in his *Air Power and Armies*.[24]

Close air support during the Second World War

Close air support was an important feature of the Second World War. The Spanish Civil War and the Second Sino-Japanese War both demonstrated the value that air support for ground forces could provide, lessons which were starkly illustrated during the Fall of Poland and France, in 1939 and 1940 respectively. As is well covered in the literature, as the war progressed, close support integrated with ground forces through innovations such as 'tentacles' and forward air controllers became an increasingly effective capability employed by the Allied air forces in every theatre. This section, however, provides three studies which consider close air support and its battlefield effect from a different perspective.

As Harry Raffal set outs, the Allies' use of close air support in the later part of the war are in sharp contrast to those encountered in the Battle for Malaya, 1941–42. Much as in the 1940 Battle of France, close air support was a capability applied in a relatively limited number of specific instances. Raffal highlights that assessments of the utility of close air support cannot be based solely on loss reports documenting the cost to both sides in men, material and equipment. The psychological and mental strain that close air support operations inflicted on the adversary's forward troops is highlighted in the Malaya campaign. Raffal also examines the priority afforded to close air support during the campaign. In doing so, Raffal identifies that neither side prioritised close air support at the outset of the campaign. Instead, the need for air support became a recurring request from the ground forces that, at critical points in the battle, the RAF and RAAF attempted to meet. Once the Hawker Hurricane arrived in theatre, the RAF attempted to renew aspects of its air-ground support, with operations which included strafing of Japanese army forces and a renewed attempt at interdiction. Conversely, the Japanese air forces,

24 Frederick M. Sallagar, *Operation STRANGLE (Italy, Spring 1944): A Case Study of Tactical Air Interdiction* (Santa Monica, CA: RAND Corporation, 1972), p.18.

having achieved air superiority, possessed sufficient resource to undertake a larger proportion of operations in direct support of ground forces. As Allied air opposition increased in theatre, however, with the arrival of reinforcements with more modern aircraft, the Japanese air forces returned their focus to achieving air superiority. Raffal's chapter starkly illustrates the extent to which the close air support capability in Malaya was dependant on air superiority.

John Alexander's chapter examines Bernard Law Montgomery's exceptionalism as the first British Army general to demonstrate an understanding of air support in the round. On taking command of Eighth Army on 13 August 1942, for example, Montgomery immediately moved Headquarters Eighth Army to collocate with Air Headquarters (HQ) Western Desert, recognising the importance of tactical air power. The historiography, perhaps distracted by Montgomery's personality and other controversies, largely ignores Montgomery's air-minded exceptionalism; at the same time his patron, Chief of the Imperial General Staff General Sir Alan Brooke, continued to argue for an army air arm or dedicated RAF command to provide 'flying artillery' and an 'air umbrella', and what Slessor called 'the subordination of the Air Force to the Army'. Yet this chapter shows how Montgomery advocated, before and after Alamein, in directives, lectures, conferences and pamphlets such as *Air Power in the Land Battle,* that all land operations were air-land operations which must be jointly planned and conducted by the army and air force commanders. Furthermore, he recognised the key utility of air power was its flexibility, its control must be centralised, and the interaction of close air support, interdiction and control of the air considered. In following RAF theory, Montgomery completely undermined Brooke's position. In seeking to explain Montgomery's exceptionalism, the chapter argues that his understanding of air power in the land battle evolved with his military philosophy based on J.F.C. Fuller's principles of war and through his experiences as a corps chief of staff in the First World War, teaching at Camberley and Quetta Staff Colleges alongside RAF instructors, in Palestine, in France in 1940, and in key home defence roles before taking over Eighth Army. Key to Montgomery's success with Eighth Army was his collaboration with the commander of Air HQ Western Desert, Air Vice-Marshal Arthur Coningham, which enabled Coningham to balance air superiority, interdiction, and close air support effort.

As the Allies in the Mediterranean increasingly gained air superiority, the question of air support became a balance of interdiction and close air support. Bill Pyke's chapter examines the effectiveness of this balance for Operation *Strangle* in Italy in 1944. The Allies' intent to advance rapidly northwards up the Italian peninsula foundered during the last two months of 1943. Italy was proving to be anything but what Winston Churchill had called 'the soft underbelly of Europe' with experienced and determined German troops holding a defensive line 75 miles south of Rome. It became known as the *Gustav Line*, and it extended across the peninsula from the Adriatic coast south-westwards to the Tyrrhenian Sea. The steep mountainous terrain gave the German defenders a distinct advantage in addition to the atrocious weather conditions during the winter of 1943/1944. By early March 1944, all attempts to break the German defences on the *Gustav Line* had failed. The stalemate became reminiscent of the static Western Front during the First World War. Set against this, the Allies had one distinct advantage: air superiority. The Mediterranean Allied Air Forces (MAAF) had a ten-fold dominance in air assets over the *Luftwaffe* in this theatre of operations. Plans were put in place to utilise tactical air power to break the deadlock on the *Gustav Line*.

On 19 March 1944 Operation *Strangle* commenced with the stated objective of 'reducing the enemy's flow of supplies to a level which will make it impossible for him to maintain and operate his [ground] forces in Central Italy.'[25] Over the following weeks tactical aircraft of the MAAF carried out operations primarily to destroy the German lines of communication up to 220 miles behind the *Gustav Line*. Although the original objective of *Strangle* was never achieved, the interdiction operations did succeed in paralyzing the movement of the defending German forces, thus enabling Allied ground forces to finally breach the *Gustav Line*. The follow-on operation, *Diadem*, continued with both air interdiction and close air support missions for Allied ground forces advancing towards Rome in early June. The chapter reveals the tensions that exists between air interdiction and air support. Pyke concludes by assessing the extent to which this first major Allied air interdiction and air support campaign lived up to prior expectations.

Close air support from 1945 to today

The four chapters which follow examine case studies of close air support (CAS) from the end of the Second World War until today. In the previous sections we have seen how air power, and the specific application of close air support, rapidly changed in and between the two World Wars. At the onset of the Cold War, however, tactical air power remained firmly seconded to strategic air power. Whilst lessons on the need for close air support had been clearly made, they were either purposely shelved or entirely forgotten. In the US, viewpoints diverged with USAF proponents arguing that strategic bombing should be the principal mission of air power as close air support wasted resources, whereas unsurprisingly, the Army viewed air power primarily to support ground campaigns.[26]

As John Schlight has explained, the formidable close air support capability developed by the US during the Second World War was blunted within five years of VJ-Day as a result of post-war budgetary savings.[27] This was exacerbated by the needs

25 Frederick M. Sallagar, *Operation STRANGLE (Italy, Spring 1944): A Case Study of Tactical Air Interdiction* (Santa Monica, CA: RAND Corporation, 1972), p.18.
26 Michael H. Johnson, *Cleared to Engage: Improving Joint Close Air Support Effectiveness* (Maxwell Air Force Base, Alabama: Air University Press, 2008), p.3.
27 John Schlight, *Help from Above: Air Force Close Air Support of the Army 1946–1973* (Washington, DC: Air Force History and Museums Program, 2003), p.53.

of demobilisation and national reorganisation, and the lack of a firm national security policy framework in which to place tactical air power. In this climate, strategic air power received the vast majority of available air power funding. Despite the American experience of the Korean War reiterating the utility of tactical air power, with an increasing fixation on the emerging Soviet nuclear threat, the Korean War came to be viewed as 'an aberration that would never be repeated'. Hence the US entered Vietnam with obsolete, slow, and vulnerable Douglas A-1 Skyraiders as its primary CAS aircraft.[28] The Vietnam War reinforced lessons learnt in Korea; hence the USAF procured the Fairchild Republic A-10 Thunderbolt II Warthog as the first aircraft specified precisely for CAS. The Warthog entered service towards the end of 1977, a few years too late to support American troops in Vietnam. However, it did reflect a change in the USAF's interest in CAS, with the emerging 'perception of tactical air needs on the NATO central front'.[29]

Clive Richards examines a more recent example of an army seeking to develop its own close air support in his chapter on the development and employment of Aerial Rocket Artillery helicopters by the US Army, 1963–1972. In a survey of American heavy artillery employment during the World Wars and the conflicts in Korea and Vietnam, published posthumously by US Army War College journal *Parameters* in 1978, military historian Brigadier General S.L.A. Marshal noted the appearance over the South Vietnamese battlefield of 'a new kind of flying artillery': Aerial Rocket Artillery (ARA), later redesignated Aerial Field Artillery (AFA). Its origin lies in the US Army experiments with the concept of air mobility in the early 1960s; it was intended that airmobile formations should include their own organic artillery support. However, the transport helicopters then in service proved incapable of lifting the Army's standard 155mm howitzer. An alternative general support weapon would therefore be needed.

The answer was not another artillery piece, but rather the rocket-firing ARA helicopter. The first ARA battalion to enter combat deployed to South Vietnam in 1965 as part of the 1st Cavalry Division (Airmobile). Later in the decade it would be joined in the theatre by a second battalion following the reconfiguration of 101st Airborne Division as an airmobile formation. As divisional artillery assets, the ARA/AFA battalions occupied the gap between conventional artillery and fixed-wing close air support aircraft. 'One of the major artillery innovations of the Vietnam War', according to a Department of the Army study released in 1974, 'was aerial rocket artillery'. Drawing upon a range of primary and secondary sources, Richards examines the origins of the rocket artillery helicopter, the ARA trials conducted by the US Army Artillery and Missile School prior to 1965, the activities of the ARA battalions in South Vietnam, and their success in the field, as well as the subsequent fate of the ARA/AFA helicopter concept in the immediate aftermath of the war.

28 Schlight, *Help from Above*, p.179.
29 Jeffrey G. Barlow, *Close Air Support and the Soviet Threat* (Washington, DC: Heritage Foundation, 1982), p.4.

The European theatre came to dominate America's focus, and this too was true for Britain. Air power would now be filtered through NATO's 'flexible response' strategy. Towards the end of the 1960s, after a sustained period of Soviet military build-up and France's withdrawal from NATO in 1966, the Alliance took stock and shifted away from its doctrine of massive nuclear retaliation, and towards a more moderate and modulated concept – flexible response.[30] Unlike massive retaliation, flexible response allowed for intermediate or transitional stages of conflict which would provide space for dialogue and de-escalation. The West understood that it was significantly outgunned conventionally, so its counterforce would rely on the use of tactical nuclear weapons, deployed either from ground units or aircraft. Strategic nuclear weapons would underwrite the entire engagement but would remain dormant until all intermediary stages had been passed. Under flexible response, 'It is the task of tactical air forces to achieve air superiority and to interdict enemy forces and lines of communication.'[31] Tactical air power was included within the responsibilities of NATO air forces to augment Western counterforces and offset the Warsaw Treaty's conventional superiority. In the 1980s air power became an essential element of the US Air-Land Battle.

John Alexander's chapter on British CAS in the Falkland's Conflict in 1982 reiterates the importance of operational-level command arrangements and cooperation to CAS. While British operations were successfully synchronised vertically from prime minister Margaret Thatcher's War Cabinet down to tactical actions in theatre, the absence of joint operational commander in theatre was particularly detrimental to what NATO at the time defined as offensive air support operations comprising battlefield air interdiction, tactical reconnaissance, and close air support and provided in the campaign by the 10 Hawker Siddeley Harrier GR3s of No. 1 Squadron RAF. While the GR3s were dedicated to and practiced offensive air support, including close air support, in NATO's Allied Command Europe, the Carrier Task Group's air operations were configured for air defence flown by Fleet Air Arm Hawker Siddeley Sea Harriers, and there was no centralised tactical air control or expert offensive air support advice and consequently no allotment of effort, planning facilities, or pre-planned ISR for the coordination of offensive air support to the Amphibious and Landing Force Task Groups. Hence, notwithstanding a decisive attack at Goose Green, many GR3 sorties resorted to armed reconnaissance which resulted in three GR3s lost re-attacking targets after failing to acquire them on the first pass. The six surviving GR3s (one was lost crash landing) were all damaged by small arms fire. The British lessons from the Falklands were addressed in the UK's 1997 Strategic Defence Review which established joint operations by a joint reaction force under a permanent joint commander underpinned by joint doctrine and joint professional military education. British close

30 Luca Ratti and Alessandro Leonardi, 'Reviving Flexible Response: An Assessment of NATO's Russian Strategy on the Alliance's 70th Anniversary', *Journal of Slavic Military Studies*, 31:2 (2019), pp.135–158 (p.135).

31 Gert Krell, 'The Controversy about "Flexible Response"', *Bulletin of Peace Proposals*, 17:2 (1986) pp.131–40 (p.131).

air support in operations since have been under the control of NATO or US Central Command, a joint combatant command set up under the Goldwater-Nichols Act.

Once such operation was in Afghanistan from 2006 to 2014. As Fergus MacDonald's chapter shows, RAF CAS operations in support of the International Security Assistance Force (ISAF) in Afghanistan highlight the episodic nature of the capability. Here, CAS became the priority role for air operations in support of hard-pressed ground forces. For the UK and its coalition partners, operations revealed the shortfall in aligned doctrine, which in turn produced 'on the hoof' adaptations at the operational and tactical levels. Cold War doctrine catered for close air support in the conventional European theatre of operations where Allied land formations required air support to allow manoeuvre and to target large enemy formations. This rapid transition left much US and NATO close air support doctrine behind, requiring innovation and constant development.

As MacDonald, writing from the perspective of an expert practitioner, demonstrates, the precision and last-second responsiveness of air munitions led to close air support being employed against targets that might otherwise have been targets for organic artillery. In Afghanistan, every released weapon possessed the power to save friendly forces, but also the ability to deliver highly undesirable consequences in the harming of civilians should anything go awry. With the stakes high politically, and the desire to keep civilian casualties to a minimum, the military were forced to alter their operational approach. At times elements of responsiveness had to be sacrificed to meet the larger operational imperatives. All of this was completed under constant media gaze, with international organisations and the Afghan government monitoring operations and outcomes. Close air support in Afghanistan therefore generated rapidly, evolving tactical doctrine for low-collateral weapons, the rediscovery of air-land integration using innovative technology and an incessant adherence to some of the tightest Rules of Engagement (ROE). The chapter covers the RAF Panavia Tornado GR4 deployment to Afghanistan from 2009 to 2014, covering the re-equipping of the aircraft and the varying issues in conducting dual Tornado Force operational deployments in Iraq and Afghanistan. It also addresses the levels of coordination required to deliver 'layers of air cover' in adjacent airspace and the difficulties of conducting close air support in urban areas. Finally, it assesses the lessons for subsequent operations.

Over more than a century of the history of air power and close air support for military operations, little attention has been given to the experiences and perspectives of many countries (small and medium/regional powers) in the Global South, especially those that do not pose direct threats to the dominant global powers. Drawing from the experiences of Nigeria, one of the leading military powers in Africa, Samuel Oyewole provides insights into close air support in the context of medium, regional, powers in the Global South. Nigeria has deployed and engaged its military in multiple internal and external conflicts since 1960, although its use of air support dates from 1967. This study examines close air support as an aspect of the Nigerian military capabilities, strategies and campaigns. Oyewole considers both internal and external operations, including the Biafran Secessionist War (1967–1970), the Liberian Civil War

(1989–1997), the Sierra Leonean Civil War (1991–2002), the Oil War in the Niger Delta and the anti-piracy campaigns in the Gulf of Guinea (from 2003), the war against Boko Haram and the Islamic State in West Africa (since 2010), and the anti-banditry campaigns (since 2018). In considering these operations, Oyewole assesses the tactical contribution and challenges the Nigerian military faced in the use of close air support between 1967 and 2022.

In the conclusion, we assess how the case studies reflect trends in close air support and the integration of air power on the battlefield. Close air support is often considered by ground forces to be the critical capability within the air power 'attack' role. As the case studies in this work demonstrate, however, it is only one aspect of how air power can affect the battlefield. This can create a tension with air forces who frequently identify that operations beyond the battlefield will have a greater critical influence. The conclusion also highlights the importance of close air support beyond the physical effect often demanded. As the case studies show, the psychological effect of close air support on the morale of an adversary's forces is of greater significance. Even with advances in precision guided munitions, ground forces should not believe that close air support will allow for more than the suppression and neutralisation of hostile forces. Close air support is nonetheless a capability which can dramatically influence both shaping operations, battles, and campaigns. Yet ground forces can become dependent on air power and fail to utilise their organic fire support to the fullest extent. The techniques, tactics and training needed to accomplish the balance of when close air support should be utilised, and how this can be done effectively, are discussed within the conclusion drawing out the lessons observed within the respective case studies.

The role of close air support in counterinsurgency is discussed and the conclusion also considers how the conflict in Ukraine, and the emergence of new variations of close air support, can inform our understanding. Throughout the collected case studies and the conclusion an enduring lesson emerges: control of the air remains critical. Effective close air support can only be consistently achieved once air forces have secured air superiority. The case studies in this work show that when an air force secures the necessary air superiority and is then able to draw on developed practices of cooperation and coordination, close air support can be decisive.

2

'Everything was Sheer Chance': No. 46 Squadron's Experiences with Close Air Support on the Western Front, 1917–1918

Mike Terry

From books to films to computer games, the representation of First World War aerial warfare in popular media is largely focused on depictions of aerial combat.[1] The identifying image of the first air war is that of the dashing fighter ace, an image that still has a powerful cultural resonance today. But in operational terms, aerial combat was only a secondary activity for the RFC (and, from 1 April 1918, the RAF) on the Western Front. As Gary Sheffield put it in his *Short History of the First World War*, fighter pilots were merely 'enablers', there to keep safe the slower and more vulnerable aeroplanes that were undertaking the primary role of the RFC/RAF in supporting the Army via tasks such as reconnaissance, artillery observation and early versions of close air support.[2]

At the heart of this issue is a difference that emerged during the war between the way aerial warfare was being represented by fighter pilots and the way it was described by those airmen performing the primary roles. An informative example of the latter can be seen in this 1918 depiction by an airman, using the name 'Night Hawk', of his experiences in providing bombing support for the infantry during the Battle of Cambrai in 1917:[3]

> It was dangerous flying weather, but we felt that the fellows in the trenches needed our help … the knowledge that on such occasions as these our work in

1 'Popular media' here is distinct from academic study and specialist magazines about First World War aviation, both of which have been more willing to discuss non-fighter roles.

2 Gary Sheffield, *A Short History of the First World War* (London: Oneword Publications, 2014), p.66.

3 Versions of Night Hawk's book sometimes identify him as W.J. Harvey of No. 22 Squadron RFC, but it is hard to be certain of this.

> the air was of *direct* and *immediate* advantage to our comrades in the trenches made the peril and the gamble of the game worthwhile.[4]

Night Hawk's enthusiasm for supporting the infantry is clear. His depiction of not just the 'peril' but also the 'gamble' of this 'game' is an acknowledgement that such work came with random risks. The benefit of aiding the infantry, however, justified these risks in Night Hawk's view. As we shall see later, this is a very different depiction of the idea of random chance in warfare to that portrayed by many fighter pilots. But also of significance is Night Hawk's use of italics with 'direct' and 'immediate'. He emphasises confidence that his actions have made a clear and tangible difference to the battle. This feeling of satisfaction in having an effect on the war was one often expressed by airmen writing about work done in cooperation with the army.

But fighter pilots very rarely expressed a sense of satisfaction in this manner. This is not because their role was unimportant. James Pugh, in *The Royal Flying Corps, the Western Front and the Control of the Air, 1914–1918*, has demonstrated how the RFC/RAF's efforts in maintaining 'control of the air' eventually grew into a sophisticated and effective operation.[5] But this form of success was only visible on a broad scale, not at the level of the individual. No fighter pilot wrote of having made a 'direct' and 'immediate' difference to the war. From their perspective, it was hard to tell if they were achieving anything of note. Generally, they repeated the same activity of going up and looking for enemy planes to engage, but no amount of success from a fighter squadron would perceptibly change their circumstances. The Germans never ran out of aeroplanes, and it was impossible for any fighter pilot to calculate what wider change was achieved by shooting an enemy aeroplane down. In *Aces Falling*, Peter Hart noted the difficulty of measuring the effect on the war of even the best-known aces: 'Who can discern any "real" effect of the death of even Richthofen, indubitably the greatest of them all?'[6] Ex-fighter pilot Stanley Walters put the issue more emotionally, decades after the war: 'We didn't do anything for the war, by two fellows fighting in the air … Nobody could say Great Britain was winning the war when one German went down in flames. That meant nothing.'[7]

As a result, instead of relating their efforts to the ground war, most fighter pilots embraced the concept of the 'score'. Shooting down enemy planes added to a pilot's personal tally. This eventually became an end in of itself, with no need for further justification. This approach won the approval of both military and public. Scoring got fighter pilots the respect of their peers, it got them mentions in official communiqués, it could lead to promotions and medals, and high scores were reported upon very

4 Night Hawk, *Rovers of the Night Sky* (Uckfield: Naval & Military Press, 2003), p.48, p.53.
5 James Pugh, *The Royal Flying Corps, the Western Front and the Control of the Air, 1914–1918* (Abingdon: Routledge, 2017), pp.164–8.
6 Peter Hart, *Aces Falling: War Above the Trenches, 1918*, Kindle Edition (London: Weidenfeld & Nicolson, 2008), p.195.
7 Joshua Levine, *On a Wing and a Prayer* (London: HarperCollins, 2008), p.124.

favourably in the press. This meant that in most fighter pilot accounts, the ground war is merely a background detail. This was a distorted view of the air war, but it was this vision that went on to have the most influence on popular representation.

But at many points during the war, fighter squadrons were ordered to provide close air support to the infantry, forcing them to consider the importance of the ground and placing them in a form of warfare where the idea of the 'score' had no power. In this chapter, I examine what effect this had on fighter pilots and how they attempted to represent it. The chapter focuses on the activities of No. 46 Squadron. This is partly because the Sopwith Camels of this fighter squadron were repeatedly ordered to support the infantry in several key battles during 1917 and 1918. The official RAF history of the war notes that, during the first month of the German spring offensive of 1918, No. 46 Squadron was 'the only fighting squadron on the Third Army front used solely for low-flying attacks'.[8] It is also because No. 46 Squadron was a particularly literary squadron, with several members providing both contemporary and retrospective accounts of their experiences. My analysis examines the official records of No. 46 Squadron held by the National Archives. It then compares and connects these records with the ways close air support was later represented in literature, focusing in particular on the experiences of four aces from the squadron. This analysis will demonstrate the contrast between the theory of fighter-based close air support and how it was actually experienced by the fighter pilots. It will show how the differing levels of prestige connected with support work and aerial fighting had a profound effect on how fighter pilots felt about ground-based objectives. Finally, it will show how the strong emotions fighter pilots felt about low-flying work only heightened their commitment to representing their war as one based around aerial combat. This helped lead to the public perception of early aerial warfare that still holds today.

The official history of No. 46 Squadron in the First World War was written by squadron member Second Lieutenant R.D. Gilpin-Brown and then given to the Air Historical Branch. The first version was written in January 1919, when the squadron was being reduced post-war to a cadre, and a second, more detailed version was written in December 1919 at the point when the squadron was disbanded.[9] The history was therefore written as a testament to the achievements of a squadron that had completed what were thought to be its final duties, although the squadron reformed in 1936. Gilpin-Brown displays clear pride in the 'important part' the squadron played at Cambrai in 1917 as well as in trying to halt the 'Enemy Advance in March 1918' and supporting the subsequent 'Allied Advance' later in the year, 'right up to the time of the Declaration of the Armistice.'[10] Gilpin-Brown offers little evidence of how

8 H.A. Jones, *The War in the Air*, (London: Clarendon Press, 1934), Volume IV, p.302.
9 The National Archives, Kew (TNA): AIR 1/173/15/170/11: 'History of No. 46 Squadron RAF, 20 Oct 1916–15 Jan 1919', 1919, p.10.
10 TNA: AIR 1/173/15/170/11: 'History of No. 46 Squadron RAF, 20 Oct 1916–15 Jan 1919', p.2.

Low-flying: Strafing machine gun battery. Sopwith Camels from an RAF handbook. (RAF Museum: X005-1442)

'important part' can be defined, so these statements are merely assertions. It is left unclear what No. 46 Squadron was expected to do in support of the infantry. As the Introduction to this book notes, the first air operations manual had little to say on the matter beyond the idea of simply attacking ground targets with machine guns.

The term 'close air support' was not yet in use. The only consistent term used in No. 46 Squadron's records is 'low-flying work'. The closest the history gets to a definition of this term is this depiction of the squadron's efforts at the Battle of Cambrai in late 1917: 'attacks with bombs and machine-gun fire on enemy troops in trenches and other ground targets were carried out … Nothing escaped the vigilance and determination of pilots', in their targeting of 'guns, troops, dumps, transport etc'.[11] Relating this to the modern-day definition of close air support given in the Introduction, this seems a reasonable match to the idea of 'air action against hostile targets which are in close proximity to friendly forces' as well as incorporating some elements of 'air interdiction' against more distant targets. As we shall later see, however, the concept of 'detailed integration of each air mission with the fire and movement of these forces' in close air support is an idea that was very underdeveloped at the time, and this was to give No. 46 Squadron considerable trouble. Such troubles are not visible in the history, however, which remains consistently upbeat about the squadron's work. For example,

11 TNA: AIR 1/692/21/20/46: 'History of 46 Squadron, RAF. April 1916–Dec 1919'.

writing of the battle to halt the German advance of 23 March 1918, it mentions how, despite 50 of No. 46 Squadron's 60 combined operation hours flown by pilots that day being directed to low-flying work rather than aerial fighting, 'seven [enemy aeroplanes] were totally destroyed, and ten others driven down out of control.'[12] The impression given by the history is that No. 46 Squadron could handle both aerial fighting and low-flying work, even simultaneously, with no issue.

Examining the records beyond the official history shows a more complex picture. There is much to support the idea that No. 46 Squadron was proud of its aerial fighting record. A message sent by its commanding officer Major R.H.S. Mealing to 13th Wing Headquarters RFC on 26 March 1918 asked what the record was for the number of enemy machines brought down by a squadron in one day, as his squadron was making a claim for the record. Mealing added, 'Can any squadron beat 30 in three days?' A report issued on 1 April showed that No. 46 Squadron's claimed score of 39 enemy machines in March beat any other in the Wing, even that of the renowned No. 56 Squadron.[13]

The records also show much evidence of No. 46 Squadron trying to get to grips with exactly what they were being expected to do with low-flying work and how best to carry it out. One clear problem was communication. There was no reliable way for aeroplanes to coordinate with ground forces. One document examines various ways in which communication could be managed with tanks. 'I suggested their carrying Very's [*sic*] lights with them which they could fire out of their top manholes. This they agreed was quite practicable,' read one report. A visual illustration, more practically, indicated how markings could be placed on the roofs of the tanks in order at least to be able to indicate which ones were friendly. In February 1918, the squadron was receiving orders that 'if employed on "Low Flying" duty the objective for the bombing must be the Tanks, and not the infantry with them,' an instruction considered so important that each member of the squadron was obliged to sign to indicate they had understood it. Trials were undertaken where bombs were dropped near tanks to see what effect bombs dropped from aeroplanes would actually have. The results were not greatly encouraging: 'If a 25lb bomb falls 6ft or further from a Tank, it is unlikely to do any serious damage … at 1ft … the bomb will blow holes through the armour plate and cause damage, though it will not necessarily stop the tank.' Though possible, such work was not going to be at all easy. In September 1918, by which point the German offensive was long spent and the Allies were advancing against an increasingly hard-pressed German army, these instructions shifted once more. A direction was received for a new priority target: 'without the [enemy] anti-Tank gun the advance of our line would be irresistible … the importance of offensive

12 TNA: AIR 1/692/21/20/46: 'History of 46 Squadron, RAF. April 1916–Dec 1919', p.7.
13 TNA: AIR 1/1430/204/31/25: 'No. 46 Squadron RFC & RAF. Confidential Reports on Officers from February 1918 to January 1919', 1919; TNA: AIR 1/1430/204/31/28: 'No. 46 Squadron, RFC Recommendations for Honours and Awards, Also Record of Enemy Aircraft Destroyed. Sept 1917 to January 1919', 1919.

No. 46 Squadron. An informal group photograph of unidentified officers relaxing outside the mess, probably at Droglandt, 1917. (RAF Museum: PC74/6/188)

action on the part of pilots against these guns becomes of paramount importance and no opportunity should be missed.'[14]

These records show that, despite the difficulties and shifting aims, the squadron was taking its commitment to low-flying work seriously. But there is nothing in the records that provides evidence that No. 46 Squadron felt a similar sense of pride or achievement in this work in the way that Mealing felt about their aerial successes. In order to examine this area more closely, my analysis considers the experiences of four of the squadron's aces that experienced low-flying duties: Arthur Gould Lee, later an Air Vice-Marshal; Donald MacLaren, the highest-scoring Camel ace of the war; Sydney Philip Smith, a low-flying enthusiast; and Victor Maslin Yeates, who wrote about many of No. 46 Squadron's ground attack missions in his 1934 novel *Winged Victory*.

Arthur Gould Lee

Arthur Gould Lee, born in 1894, is the most famous of these four pilots. He served in No. 46 Squadron from 22 May 1917 until 7 January 1918, ending his tenure there as a temporary captain.[15] Lee stayed in the RAF until 1946, reaching the rank of air vice-marshal. But much of his fame comes from two books he wrote about his experiences

14 TNA: AIR 1/1428/204/31/11: 'No. 46 Squadron, Co-operation: RAF and Other Arms. July 1917–Sept 1918', 1918.

15 Arthur Gould Lee, *No Parachute: A Classic Account of War in the Air in WWI*, Kindle Edition (London: Grub Street Publishing, 2013), p.25, p.248.

Arthur Gould Lee standing by a No. 46. Squadron RFC Sopwith Pup in 1917. (RAF Museum: X003-2602/14410)

in the RFC: *No Parachute* in 1968, heavily based on his contemporary wartime writings, and *Open Cockpit* in 1969, expanding on his thoughts from the previous book.[16] These books have become classics of First World War literature, and Lee's voice from these works remains an influential one.

Lee gained considerable experience in low-flying work in his time with No. 46 Squadron. He is one of the few pilots specifically named in the squadron history for an attack he made on enemy infantry at Fontaine.[17] Lee's infantry attack report for the incident makes exciting reading, covering his repeated attacks 'at Hun infantry attacking Fontane from North until street fighting began'. After flying away at low-level to clear his jammed guns, he was shot down by an artillery shell exploding directly beneath his plane, causing him to have to flee on foot to Allied forces.[18] This was the most dramatic of several times Lee was shot down performing low-flying duties. He was awarded the Military Cross for his 'gallantry and devotion to duty' in such work,[19] and so Lee can be considered a particular authority on commenting on the fighter pilot's perspective of close support.

The earliest comments by Lee on these experiences that can be definitively dated are from 1925, when Lee was invited to contribute material for the recently established RAF Staff College at Andover. Lee was one of dozens of veterans asked to help form a body of expert experiences for students to draw on during their studies. The Staff

16 Lee, *No Parachute*, p.9; Arthur Gould Lee, *Open Cockpit*, Kindle Edition (Grub Street Publishing, 2012).
17 TNA: AIR 1/692/21/20/46: 'History of 46 Squadron, R.A.F. April 1916–Dec 1919', p.5.
18 TNA: AIR 1/692/21/20/46: 'History of 46 Squadron, R.A.F. April 1916–Dec 1919'.
19 Recorded in The Gazette (Edinburgh Gazette), issue 13285, 8 July 1918, pp.2385–6.

College Notes issued to officer students in these early years discussed such matters as aerial fighting tactics, air superiority, strategic bombing and even the importance of contact patrols, but they had very little to say on close air support.[20] The testimonies of men like Lee were therefore one of the few sources on the topic available to students at the time. In these notes, Lee seems supportive of the idea of close air support. He tells of his experiences as part of an armoured car company in Iraq in 1925. One section of cars was on the verge of being wiped out by an ambush from the Syrian Shammar tribe until 'the situation was saved by a flight of Bristol Fighters from Mosul', whose support caused the enemy forces to flee 'in disorderly retreat'.[21] But this was against an enemy that presented little threat to aerial attackers, and it was also part of a conflict where there was no use for fighter pilots. Lee was significantly more critical about his own First World War experiences with such work. He emphasises the danger and casualties involved, informing the reader that 'I was shot down three times during the week by fire from the ground' at Cambrai. His conclusion was that 'It is doubtful whether these casualties could have been avoided except by use of armour. I held this view at the time, as did most of us.'[22] Lee's concerns here are practical. He felt that unarmoured fighter planes were inappropriate for close support work.

But in his 1960s books, Lee adopted a different perspective. Although these books are ostensibly based on his wartime diaries and letters, the originals cannot be located, and so it cannot be ruled out that Lee edited his writings to reflect his 1960s' rather than wartime views. By this time, Lee had seen considerable evolutions in the concept of close air support. During the Second World War, he was involved with training the Turkish Air Force, where he designed war games 'in light of the lessons' learned from the German use of close air support in their 'blitzkrieg techniques in Europe'. Later, in the Desert Air Force, he served under Air Vice-Marshal 'Mary' Coningham, a pioneer in close air support thinking, and was involved in providing air support for Long Range Desert Group.[23]

But his published thoughts in the 1960s on low-flying work in the First World War had little to do with practicalities or how effective such work was. Instead, Lee's thoughts were more conceptual, based not around the aeroplanes, but on the use of fighter pilots to do the work. He identified two such conceptual problems. The first was the issue of randomness. Lee described how 'the fighter pilot always had the feeling that in their duelling combats, their lives depended on their skill, wits, boldness and accurate shooting.' The emphasis on skill making a difference was one often expressed by fighter pilots. But Lee felt that low-flying work made this aspect

20 TNA: AIR 1/2386/228/9/1: 'Staff College Notes, RAF Staff College Andover', 1924.
21 TNA: AIR 1/2389/228/11/116: 'An Account by Course Students of War Experiences: S/L. A.S.G. Lee.', 1925, p.13.
22 TNA: AIR 1/2389/228/11/116: 'An Account by Course Students of War Experiences', pp.9–10.
23 Arthur Gould Lee, *Fly Past: Highlights from a Flyer's Life* (London: Jarrolds, 1974), pp.142–3, pp.170–1.

irrelevant: 'any bullet could hit you, and there was nothing you could do to avoid it. Skill, experience, boldness, none of these counted, everything was sheer chance.' Lee's second complaint was about the rewards from such work. In aerial combat 'if you were the victor, everyone knew of it, and you received proper credit.' But in low-flying work, 'nobody in the RFC knew whether you had done any real damage, and even if you had it did not count as a victory, in fact it counted for nothing.'[24]

The contrast between Lee's views and that of Night Hawk is striking. Both performed low-flying work at the Battle of Cambrai. But Night Hawk accepted the random risks associated with such work on the grounds that the benefit to the infantry made it worthwhile. Lee's account has nothing to say about the benefit to the infantry, only on the risk to himself. With no score on offer, Lee perceives no benefit in taking such a 'sheer chance'. This was a view widely held by fighter pilots at the time. Major B.E. Smithies, Officer Commanding No. 64 Squadron, wrote in 1918 of similar attitudes amongst his pilots. 'It may be petty, unmilitary and regrettable,' he commented, 'but it exists.'[25] Such opinions suggest a position of privilege, even arrogance, taken by fighter pilots. But the fighter pilot's commitment to the war of skill and scoring was an important part of their psychological coping mechanism for making sense of their conflict. Any challenge to this construction could cause resentment. In Lee's case, this resentment remained strong enough for him to feel the need to express it five decades after the war. Lee was making no broader comment on the nature of close air support and how it developed over time. According to him, it was simply conceptually unsuitable work for a First World War fighter pilot.

Donald MacLaren

Whilst Lee is the most well-known today of the people examined here, Canadian Donald MacLaren was the most well-known at the time. Born in 1893, he joined No. 46 Squadron in December 1917. He scored his first victory in March 1918 and stayed with the squadron almost until the end of hostilities, by which point he had become one of the greatest aces of the war.[26] His final tally of 54 victories made him the fifth highest-scoring ace of the RFC/RAF, the highest score of any pilot flying the Camel. He won the Military Cross (and Bar), the Distinguished Service Order, the Distinguished Flying Cross, the *Croix de Guerre* and the *Legion d'Honneur*, all for his aerial combat prowess. The squadron history proudly singles out MacLaren as 'an officer who greatly distinguished himself while serving in No. 46 Squadron.'[27]

24 Lee, *Open Cockpit*, p.198.
25 Hart, *Aces Falling*, pp.121–2.
26 Roger Gunn, *Masters of the Air: The Great War Pilots McLeod, McKeever, and MacLaren* (Toronto: Dundurn, 2019), pp.194, 209, 217.
27 TNA: AIR 1/692/21/20/46: 'History of 46 Squadron, R.A.F. April 1916–Dec 1919', p.6.

MacLaren did not write about low-flying work, but his presence in the records forms part of an interesting story. In January 1918, a complaint was made to the squadron that they had been targeting Allied rather than German positions. Mealing attempted to refute the accusations, but the Brigade Major for the RFC's 3rd Brigade wrote to say, 'It has been conclusively proved by reports from [anti-aircraft] observers that these bombs were dropped by Camels and the G.O.C. considers that the machines were undoubtedly those of No. 46.'[28] This was not a one-off incident. The records carry page after page of similar complaints. They had begun at a point where the front-lines were stable, but the rate of complaints increased after the Germans began their spring offensive in March 1918 and the state of the war became more chaotic. Many complaints were directed to the brigade, suggesting that the issue was widespread beyond just No. 46 Squadron, but many directly accused the squadron of further friendly fire incidents, despite repeated instructions from Mealing that pilots should be sure of their targets.

The accusations are often expressed with as much emotion as official language will allow. An official from 14th Wing, passing on a complaint in March 1918, noted that 'these are obviously Camels. Please point out again that pilots *must* know who they are shooting at.' One complaint in the same month described how an attack by No. 46 Squadron had knocked out the artillery wires connecting 15th Division Headquarters with their artillery. Lieutenant General Sir Charles Ferguson, commanding XVII Corps, noted that this strike had occurred 'more than 3,000 yards' inside the British lines. An exasperated Mealing, only a few weeks before he showed his great pride in his squadron's aerial combat record, wrote that his pilots' inability to resolve the friendly fire issue 'is a great disgrace to the whole squadron'.

The record of complaints only stopped in April 1918. This is the point where the initial German offensive was halted, but this does not appear to be the reason why the record stops. The last note in the file is a letter from Mealing to Lieutenant Colonel Maclean at 10th Wing Headquarters to say that 'I must admit that it has been stated by the infantry that bombs were dropped on our troops, but in a moving battle, that is extremely hard to prevent.' It seemed that complaining was not going to make any difference to an apparently insoluble problem. No further complaints were kept on file.

The relevance of MacLaren to these incidents becomes clear in a small and easily missed part of the records. Mealing, recognising MacLaren's clear talents, recommended him for command of a flight in May 1918. But the answer from Maclean hints at a story that seems to be largely unrecorded. Instead of accepting Mealing's recommendation, Maclean asks for a confidential report on MacLaren to consider whether 'this officer can be considered capable of leading patrols on Active Service.' He goes on to comment:

28 TNA: AIR 1/1431/204/31/35: 'Correspondence of Instructions on Bombing, Nov 1917–Oct 1918, No. 46 Squadron RFC RAF', 1918.

> I would point out that if a Flight Commander, through ignorance of our lines, or carelessness when the weather conditions are bad, causes casualties through firing into our Troops, severe disciplinary action should be taken. In all cases where our machines are fired on by British Troops action is taken by the Military Authorities.[29]

This is an oddly specific comment, and it takes on a particular meaning in the context of No. 46 Squadron's friendly fire issues. It suggests that MacLaren himself, the squadron's star pilot, had previously been involved with the friendly fire problems, and that Maclean was uneasy about a person with a record of friendly fire accusations being made a flight commander, where he would become considerably more accountable for such mistakes. The final sentence from Maclean is almost a threat. Mealing is reminded that troops that fire on planes will be dealt with. This implies that Mealing should consider whether, by the same logic, he really wants to risk one of his flight commanders being court martialled for firing on troops. Mealing offered no defence or mitigation for MacLaren. He simply replied that 'I consider this officer is quite capable of leading a patrol. I hold a very high opinion of his capabilities in this respect.' The appointment stood, and there is no evidence that any pilot from No. 46 Squadron was ever disciplined for these incidents.

The effectiveness of diverting fighter squadrons to low-flying work in 1918 is debateable. In *The Great War in the Air*, John Morrow argued that the work of such squadrons 'countered a new German offensive south of Ypres' in March 1918.[30] But Hart is more equivocal, feeling that 'what their efforts achieved in the context of wider battle it is difficult to say.'[31] The experiences of MacLaren and No. 46 Squadron suggest a darker side to such efforts. Trying to intervene in such a chaotic battlefield, with no practical means of coordinating with the infantry, fighter pilots clearly struggled to make helpful interventions. No. 46 Squadron was a competent squadron, and MacLaren was one of the greatest pilots of the war. If these people had such difficulty in avoiding friendly fire incidents, it raises a question mark over the wisdom of deploying fighter pilots for low-flying work. It was work they were untrained in and, as Lee depicted, work that they were psychologically averse to. The effect No. 46 Squadron had on the German advance, as well as the truth of what happened with MacLaren, can never be known. But the feeling of 'disgrace' it caused is on record, and this can only have contributed to a negative view of low-flying work from the squadron's veterans.

29 TNA: AIR 1/1430/204/31/25: 'No. 46 Sqn R.F.C. & R.A.F. Confidential Reports on Officers from February 1918 to January 1919'.

30 John Morrow, *The Great War in the Air: Military Aviation From 1909 to 1921* (Tuscaloosa: University of Alabama Press, 1993), p.311.

31 Hart, *Aces Falling*, p.129.

Sydney Philip Smith

However, the views of fighter pilots were not monolithic. For all of the issues that Arthur Gould Lee described, and for all the issues No. 46 Squadron had with low-flying work, it was possible for a fighter pilot to show enthusiasm for such tasks. One example is Sydney Philip Smith, born in 1896, previously of the Public Schools Battalion and the Army Service Corps. He joined the RFC in 1916 and was posted as a captain to No. 46 Squadron on 6 March 1918.[32] Exactly a month later, he was killed in action. In his short time with the squadron, he made an impression, partly for his bravery, but also for his dedication to low-flying work which he constantly pushed for his flight to perform.

The main source on Smith's tenure as a flight commander in No. 46 Squadron comes from Victor Maslin Yeates' 1934 book *Winged Victory*. Yeates, who served in flights under both MacLaren and Smith, wrote his book in part as a riposte to other 1930s aerial combat novels, such as the Biggles stories, that Yeates felt were fantastical and not telling the true story of aerial warfare. Although written as fiction, the book very closely follows Yeates' own career. One section of the book goes into detail about Yeates' relationship with Smith, named in the book as 'Beal'. Yeates provides several intense depictions of what following Beal/Smith into low-flying work was like, such as this one set during the German offensive of 1918:

> Beal flew straight down to Albert without crossing the lines. They could see the hell of a war on just in front of Albert and towards Beaumont Hamel. Then Beal went right down over the roofs of Albert, out of which all sorts of transport was pouring along the Amiens and Doullens roads. In a few seconds he was shooting up a wave of advancing Huns. [Yeates] followed him closely. Bursting shells bumped him about. The air must be thick with bullets. He saw holes in his planes. There were thousands and thousands of Huns; piles of dead and masses of living. He dropped bombs that could not miss, and dipped and fired, and pulled up and dipped again.[33]

Yeates makes no comment on the effectiveness of such work. He merely relays his experiences. However, he goes into detail about his thoughts concerning Beal/Smith. At first, Yeates is simply surprised to meet someone so enthusiastic about low-flying work: 'He was one of those people who liked fighting, even when it consisted in being shot at by unseen machine guns from the ground.' Then, he notes Beal's apparent obsession with such work: 'His methods were different from anyone else's. Whoever except him would take a flight along twenty miles of front at five hundred feet?' But increasingly, Yeates' thoughts on Beal turn to hatred for this man who is repeatedly

32 Gordon Atkin, *Winged Victor: A Biography of Victor M. Yeates, Author of Winged Victory* (Ramsbottom: Springwater Books, 2004), p.54.

33 Victor Maslin Yeates, *Winged Victory* (London: Jonathan Cape, 1961), p.109.

throwing Yeates into danger and getting his comrades killed. He starts to define Beal as a 'win-the-war-quick merchant' with 'an exaggerated sense of duty' to which 'heaven knew, he had sacrificed enough lives to'.[34] A more succinct summary of Smith came from Mealing in the letter he wrote to Smith's father after Smith died, where he described Smith as 'Wonderfully brave, perhaps too brave', a phrase which reads more harshly than Mealing likely intended.

But it is the manner of Smith's death on 6 April 1918 that is of most interest to my analysis. Smith was shot down during a low-flying mission. The cause was an enemy plane that got behind him, not ground fire. In fact, ground fire in 1918 was not the menace to No. 46 Squadron that some accounts make it out to be. April 1918 was the worst month of the war for British aerial casualties from ground fire, with 49 planes lost this way. But almost twice as many, 97, were lost to attacks from enemy aeroplanes.[35] Although No. 46 Squadron's casualty reports for March and April contain lots of incidents of planes damaged by ground fire, only one plane and pilot was recorded as lost in this way during low-flying work, whilst Smith was one of four pilots detailed to ground attack who was shot down by an enemy aeroplane.[36] This puts both Lee's 1920s and 1960s views in perspective. The armour he advocated at the Staff College may have offered some protection from ground fire, but it would also have slowed the plane and made it more vulnerable to aerial attack. The fear of the 'sheer chance' of ground fire that he wrote about later was probably genuine, but the larger threat was not based on chance at all – it was the skill of an enemy pilot mounting a surprise attack. But the psychological objections of fighter pilots to facing ground fire dominated later representations far more than the reality did, and Smith left no words of his own to counter this narrative.

Smith's legacy is another interesting issue. His killer is generally recognised as being *Hauptmann* Manfred von Richthofen, the German ace known after the war as the 'Red Baron'. Smith has received far more attention as the Richthofen's seventy-sixth victim than he ever did as a ground attack advocate.[37] If it was not for Yeates, there would be no record of Smith's thoughts at all. This aspect troubled Yeates. After writing about Smith/Beal's death, Yeates wrote of how he continued to ponder this figure that had obsessed him. Yeates' concerns can be seen in two contrasting passages. The first describes why MacLaren (named in the book as 'MacAndrews') became so famous, in part by doing what he could to avoid low-flying work:

> After all, you don't get much thanks for dropping bombs, and you don't often see anything to shoot at on the ground that makes a good story in Comic Cuts. But

34 Yeates, *Winged Victory,* p.95, p.107, p.156.

35 Trevor Henshaw, *The Sky Their Battlefield II* (High Barnet: Fetubi Books, 2014), p.347.

36 Henshaw, *The Sky*, pp.150–69.

37 For example, see Norman Franks and Hal Giblin and Nigel McCrery, *Under the Guns of the Red Baron: The Complete Record of Von Richthofen's Victories and Victims Fully Illustrated* (London: Grub Street Publishing, 2007), pp.193–5. Note there was some guesswork involved in identifying Smith as Richthofen's victim. Nonetheless, this is the place he holds in public memory.

> if you come back from nearly every job saying 'Lo, I have shot down a Hun' you are soon on the path of glory.[38]

The 'Comic Cuts' Yeates refers to were the official RFC/RAF communiqués, a curated selection of reports from frontline airmen that were only distributed internally. They evolved over time into a way for pilots to advertise their successes to other pilots, and here Yeates is describing how MacLaren was very aware that, by 1918, fighter combat was by far the best way to get your reports printed in them. In the wake of Beal/Smith's death, Yeates wrote this contrasting appraisal:

> Who would know [Smith] and honour his memory? He had gone out daily to confront incalculable death with risk-oblivious courage, without the stimulus of man-to-man combat; and there was no red triumph of broken or burning enemies reeling down the skies to be entombed in the perky officialese of Comic Cuts. He would be forgotten in a week.[39]

The only reason Yeates was wrong was because he underestimated how well Smith would be remembered as a victim. But Yeates' point is well made, and the record backs him up. There is no evidence that the communiqués were intentionally being pushed in a fighter-centric direction. The issue was more that the nature of the reports filled out for aerial combat gave far more space for pilots to write interesting narratives than the reports for other activities, which were more technically focused, and the communiqués naturally gravitated towards the more interesting reports. As Yeates said, you needed a 'good story'. The practical effect was that this record of the war was filled with aerial combat stories, whilst some activities were barely mentioned at all. As seen in the figure below, in April 1918, far more pilots were named for aerial combat narratives than for any other form of activity combined, with low-flying work barely mentioned at all, despite its prevalence in the period. During No. 46 Squadron's undivided low-flying duties in April 1918, it was not mentioned once in the 'Comic Cuts'. Over the entirety of the 1918 communiqués, MacLaren is mentioned 29 times, Yeates five times and Smith just three times. Not one of these mentions was for low-flying work. It was not, therefore, just the fighter pilot's sense of pride that put him at odds with the idea of low-flying work. By 1918, that work simply was not being valued or recognised by the system fighter pilots worked in, regardless of its importance. Smith became an example for others to learn from: there was nothing for a fighter pilot to gain by trying to dedicate himself to such work.

38 Yeates, *Winged Victory*, p.93.
39 Yeates, *Winged Victory*, p.174.

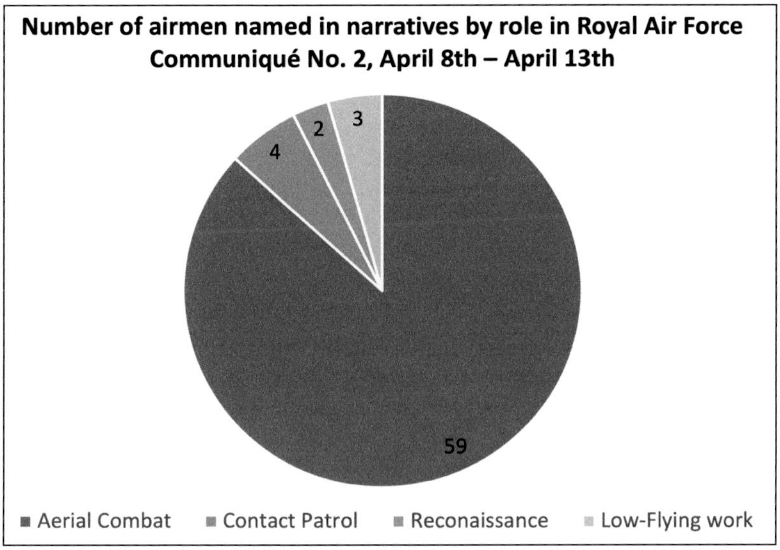

Figure 1: A breakdown of what activities airmen were named for in RAF communiqué No 2, issued at the height of No. 46 Squadron's low-flying efforts. Aerial combat reports overwhelmingly dominate. By this point, airmen were almost never named for bombing or artillery observation work, and aerial photography had ceased to be mentioned at all. *Compiled by the author from RFC and RAF Communiques.*[40]

Victor Maslin Yeates

Finally, this paper turns to the experiences of Victor Maslin Yeates himself. Born in 1897, Yeates volunteered to join the war just after his eighteenth birthday in November 1915, but an extended period of training meant that he did not actually arrive at No. 46 Squadron until February 1918.[41] Despite becoming an ace, Yeates had a difficult war. In mid-1918 he was hospitalised with a condition known as 'Pyrexia of Unknown Origin' which left him weakened. His mental health began to decline rapidly, and in September 1918 he was removed from the frontline.[42] His wartime sickness eventually developed into tuberculosis, and by the time he began writing *Winged Victory* in 1933, he was a dying man desperately trying to provide for his family. It was published in June 1934 to strong critical reviews but mediocre sales. Yeates died in December that year. Its critical reputation has remained strong ever since and its contrast to the likes of Biggles remains one of its most distinct features.

Yeates' book makes a detailed and brutally honest examination of what he felt was the reality of the experience of the fighter pilot. It has much to say about No. 46

40 TNA: AIR 1/2116/207/57: 'R.F.C. and R.A.F. Communiques', 1918, bk.1, pp.2–6.
41 Atkin, *Winged Victor*, p.1, p.15, p.40.
42 Atkin, *Winged Victor*, p.95, p.111.

Squadron's experiences with low-flying work, which Yeates often describes in detail. Much of his account resembles what Lee would later write, particularly on the distaste for its random dangers: 'You could do very little to avoid machine-gun fire from the ground. The most cunning and experienced pilot was liable to be brought down.'[43] Lee certainly read *Winged Victory*, which he described as an 'excellent book',[44] and it is possible that Lee's comments on low-flying work in the 1960s were influenced by Yeates' depiction. Yeates, however, added one aspect that Lee did not mention: he comments on the morality of such ground attack work. In doing so, Yeates provides a powerful alternative perspective on the relationship between the fighter pilot and the ground war. Yeates at one point gives this reason for his dislike of ground attack work: 'He hated it; he could see German soldiers crouching in shell holes, and he was supposed to go down on them in cold blood and kill as many as he could.'[45] This seems an odd objection for a fighter pilot, whose work involved killing people by design. But another recurring theme in fighter pilot accounts is an attempt to distance themselves from the act of killing. Canadian Billy Bishop, for example, the highest scoring RFC/RAF ace of the war, never once wrote a sentence in his 1918 memoir *Winged Warfare* explicitly saying he had killed a man, instead describing his war as one against machines: 'To bring down a machine did not seem to me to be killing a man; it was more as if I was just destroying a mechanical target, with no human being in it.'[46] Yeates depicts the same logic in *Winged Victory*, but the prospect of ground attack interferes with this justification. At one point, having just bombed enemy infantry, Yeates depicts an internal mind process bordering on the delusional as he 'hoped he'd distributed a few Blighties', as if his bombs could do favours for the Germans rather than killing them.[47]

But the climactic moment of *Winged Victory*, the point where Yeates describes the moment where his mental health was shattered, comes at the point where the illusion can no longer be maintained. Yeates describes how his analogue in the book becomes enraged when one of his comrades is downed by ground fire. In retaliation, he attacks a nearby machine gun pit and kills the crew, though he cannot be sure it is the same gun that shot down his friend. His reaction to this event is passionately expressed:

> He had killed those two Germans in rage and hatred; he had raised a devil that would not die. This was the frightful thing he had done for his own dead, whom nothing could benefit. This it was to fight for one's country.[48]

43 Yeates, *Winged Victory*, pp.31–2.
44 Royal Air Force Museum Archive, London: X002-9372: 'Arthur Stanley Gould Lee to Raymond Collishaw', 17 March 1966. Correspondence between Arthur Stanley Gould Lee and Raymond Collishaw,
45 Yeates, *Winged Victory*, p.100.
46 Billy Bishop, *Winged Warfare* (Toronto: McGraw-Hill Ryerson, 1990), p.141.
47 Yeates, *Winged Victory*, p.166.
48 Yeates, *Winged Victory*, p.455.

Throughout the book, Yeates is inviting the reader to recognise the absurdity in the fighter pilot mentality he describes. Obviously, the fighter pilots knew they were killing men, not just destroying machines, but they often tried to indulge in a fantasy where they could pretend they were not killers. For Yeates, the moment when he intentionally killed the gunners on the ground is depicted as breaking him because it made that illusion impossible to sustain. This is not to say that all fighter pilots were as badly affected by the issue as Yeates. But his depiction of how low-flying work destroyed the fantasy of the fighter pilot is, in my analysis, the single most convincing description of just why so many fighter pilots hated this work so much.

Conclusions

Close air support was not a priority for the RAF in the inter-war years. Wing Commander J.C. Slessor, later to become Marshal of the Royal Air Force, wrote in his 1936 book based on his lectures for the Army Staff College, Camberley that 'the aeroplane is not a battlefield weapon', and that it should only be used as one in 'occasions of great emergency'.[49] Shelford Bidwell and Dominick Graham, in their seminal book *Fire-Power*, first published in 1982, highlight given the apparent effectiveness of RAF battlefield support in 1918, the oddity of how 'Strategic bombing, ineffective in World War One, appealed more to the post-war RAF than ground attack which had proved itself.' They note the failure, unlike the *Luftwaffe*, of the RAF to create purpose-built ground attack aircraft between the wars.[50] Bidwell and Graham partly blame this on political interference, but they also note that 'pilots who proved again and again, in 1918, how effective low flying aircraft could be … heartily disliked the role.'[51] Could it be that this dislike was so strong that it actually affected the RAF's inter-war policy? Bidwell and Graham, however, have made one small but significant error in their analysis. As the example of Night Hawk shows, it was not 'pilots' who heartily disliked ground attack work. It was specifically fighter pilots who built a broad objection to being deployed in this way. Neither the records of No. 46 Squadron nor any of the writings of its pilots show any indication that their views had any long-term operational significance. Lee, for all his powerfully expressed distaste for his own low-flying work, seemed more positive about its application in other areas. The objection of fighter pilots to low-flying work was not about its value. It was a conceptual objection based on the specific image they had built for themselves as the aerial heroes of the First World War.

49 Wing Commander J.C. Slessor, *Air Power and Armies* (London: Oxford University Press, 1936), p.90.

50 Shelford Bidwell and Dominick Graham, *Fire-Power: The British Army Weapons & Theories of War, 1904–1945* (Barnsley: Pen & Sword Military Classics, 2004), p.199, pp.235–6.

51 Bidwell and Graham, *Fire-Power*, p.236.

This chapter has demonstrated the details of that objection. Low-flying work brought random dangers to pilots more used to a form of conflict where skill mattered, something they found objectionable even though they were much more likely to die in an aerial fight. No. 46 Squadron's issues with friendly fire show how chaotic and improvised much of their low-flying work was, a strong contrast to the apparent rationality of the scoring system of aerial fighting. Fighter pilots, used to adulation for their victories, resented being forced into work that neither their peers nor the wider world seemed to value. Finally, low-flying work undermined the carefully constructed fantasy of a bloodless war that many fighter pilots preferred to believe in.

But whilst there is no reason to feel fighter pilots' views had much operational influence, they certainly had an influence on the future representation of First World War aerial combat. Low-flying work was to become largely erased from the popular narrative of that air war. When the literary genre of aerial warfare become established in the 1930s, it was a market with little interest in ground attack depictions. *Winged Victory* was unusual in drawing attention to it. For a more mainstream example, take the Biggles books. There are 50 Biggles stories contained in the books *The Camels are Coming* (1932), *Biggles of the Camel Squadron* (1934) and *Biggles in France* (1935).[52] Of those 50 stories, only two of them depict Biggles, a Camel pilot just like those of No. 46 Squadron, attacking German infantry. Neither instance was any form of close air support. The association between First World War fighters and their fledgling efforts at close air support was lost, and it remains an activity still rarely associated with early fighter pilots in fiction to this day. The side effect of this is that the views of those such as Night Hawk were also largely silenced. This is a shame. The First World War fighter pilot's view of close air support work is fascinating and informative in showing how a mythology can evolve, but it is not an authoritative record of such work. It is fortunate that Yeates, at least, was willing to show that the fighter pilots' view of ground attack was deeply influenced by their psychological approach to the war. Hopefully, the thoughts of First World War airmen about the value of close air support will in future be seen as going far beyond Lee's fears of 'sheer chance'.

52 W.E. Johns, *Biggles in France*, Kindle Edition (London: RHCP Digital, 2008); *Biggles of the Fighter Squadron*, Kindle Edition (London: RHCP Digital, 2008); *The Camels Are Coming*, Kindle Edition (London: RHCP Digital, 2008).

3

Calling for Close Air Support: The Counter-Attack Patrol and the Central Information Bureau

Mike Meech

Introduction

Experience of the air support used on 8 August 1918, at the Battle of Amiens, led to a perceived need to make changes to the coordination procedures of air-ground operations then in use. A post battle report, called 'Counter Attack Patrol Work', observed that:

> Some means of co-ordinating the counter attack patrol work with the attack of ground targets by scouts and two-seaters appears to be very necessary. During the first few hours, targets in the area up to a few miles behind the lines were numerous and scouts had no difficulty in finding suitable objectives for their bombs and machine gun fire. Later on, when the infantry and tanks began to meet with more organised opposition, it would have been of great value if the efforts of our low flying machines could have been directed against the enemy's infantry, machine and field guns, that were giving our troops most trouble. Some attempts were made to do this by means of red Very lights. These fired from the ground were a signal that our troops wanted assistance from the air, while fired from the air they signified that the machine in question had discovered an important target which was holding up our advance, and called other machines to its assistance.[1]

1 The National Archives, Kew (TNA): AIR 1/725/97/2: 'Notes on Corps Squadron Work During the Somme Offensive August 1918', Artillery observation by RAF.

The counter attack patrol (CAP) work was undertaken by a CAP aeroplane, its duties being laid down in the April 1918 edition of Appendix 'B', 'Cooperation between Aircraft and Infantry' of SS 135.[2] These were:

1. To report on the enemy's dispositions and defences.
2. To locate the position of the enemy's frontline and watch for movements of reserves, massing of troops for counterattack, minenwerfer, machine guns and strong points holding up our advance and targets of such nature.
3. To call for concentrated fire (LL call) or barrage fire (SOS call) when required by the situation.[3]

The CAP aircraft, or machine as they were called at the time, would also warn the infantry on the ground by dropping a red parachute flare that trailed smoke (some other signals were also used) and would indicate the direction the German counterattack was coming from. The above post-battle report also mentioned that there was a connection between the CAP and other aircraft:

> The operations of the low flying scouts were also based on G.F. [Gun Fire or Fleeting Target] and N.F. [Guns firing in position at …] calls sent down by Corps machines. This requires careful pre-arrangement and rapid and reliable communication between Corps and Army Wings. Coordination might also be secured by having scouts available on an Advanced Landing Ground [ALG] at the call of counterattack patrol machines.[4]

The ALGs played an important role in speeding up response times in air operations. There is a reminder in the 'Somme Report' that they should be in the vicinity of army corps headquarters (HQ). This was so that squadron commanders could easily remain in personal touch with corps HQ despite any road congestion; the document also states that RAF 'Brigadiers and Corps Wing Commanders should impress this on their Army and Corps when operations are imminent and endeavour to ensure that this point is duly considered when selecting headquarters.'[5] Basically the need was to keep the relevant air and ground headquarters in close touch with each other. This document also mentions that:

> When an important target is discovered, the counterattack patrol machine, if assistance was required, could fly to the advanced landing ground and lead out

2 General Staff, S.S. 135: The Training and Employment of Divisions (France, GHQ, 1918).
3 General Staff, S.S. 135: Appendix 'B', p.7.
4 TNA: AIR 1/725/97/2: 'Notes on Corps Squadron Work During the Somme Offensive August 1918'.
5 TNA: AIR 1/725/97/2: 'Notes on Corps Squadron Work During the Somme Offensive August 1918'.

A staged photograph of the work of a Corps squadron staff. No. 12 Squadron, RAF at Boistrancourt, 1918. (RAF Museum: X006-5459)

> a patrol of scouts. Should the situation have changed on its return, the scouts could be notified by a 'wash out' signal by Very light, otherwise they would attack the target shown them. This was done on two occasions by machines of No. 9 Squadron on reports from a machine of No. 6, and resulted in one case in the capture of LE QUESNEL WOOD by the Cavalry, who had been previously held up.[6]

The report concluded by observing that, 'as operations tend more towards open warfare, this necessity for coordination will further increase and every means of securing it need to be developed.'[7] Before dealing with the means to improve the system some information on the CAP and air support during the period previous to August 1918 should be considered, although a fully detailed history is not possible here but some information may be helpful.

6 TNA: AIR 1/725/97/2: 'Notes on Corps Squadron Work During the Somme Offensive August 1918'.
7 TNA: AIR 1/725/97/2: 'Notes on Corps Squadron Work During the Somme Offensive August 1918'.

Air support development prior to August 1918

Air support for ground forces was in use from the start of the First World War, although confined initially to visual reconnaissance followed by photo reconnaissance and artillery spotting. The main problem in the use of the aeroplane in coordination with the ground was communication between the two which led to the use of pyrotechnic signals, plus signal lamps from both the ground and air, then wireless telegraphy from the aeroplane to artillery batteries, who would reply with fabric ground signals. To aid aeroplanes in finding the target for the artillery, the troops on the frontline would indicate the enemy position that was holding them up by laying out a white linen arrow about 15ft long and 3ft wide with an arrowhead at one end pointing towards the target. To indicate range to target further white strips, 6ft by 1ft six in could be laid at right angles to the arrow, each one indicating 100 yards, then:

> The aeroplane calling up a Battery for this work will use a prearranged prefix, and the Battery will only fire when 'G' is sent by the aeroplane. Immediately the signal is removed, the aeroplane ceases sending 'G', and the firing ceases.[8]

Although this may appear to be quite primitive, larger arrows were used to give directions to scouts so they could intercept enemy aircraft and it should be noted that a similar method was in use in North Africa by the RAF during 1941:[9]

> Leading troops will indicate a target to Support Aircraft by displaying ground strips in the form of a 'V' pointing to the target, with bars beneath to indicate distance. A 'V' will only be displayed on orders from the formation or units controlling the Tentacle from which the call for support has originated. Therefore only one 'V' will be displayed on any Brigade front at any one time.[10]

This was twenty-six years and a few days after the September 1915 document. During 1916, the role of what became the CAP aeroplane was part of the role of the Contact Patrol aeroplane. In operations, however, this became too much work for one aeroplane and another aeroplane would be allocated to the task of looking out for a counterattack. However, the term 'Counter-Attack Patrol aeroplane' only became standard by the end of 1917. Other terms used included 'Special Reconnaissance', 'Wireless

8 TNA: WO 95/592/3: I Corps General Staff War Diary p.044, dated 20 September 1915.

9 'Memorandum by Brigadier-General, General Staff for Lieutenant-General, Chief of the General Staff from Advanced G.H.Q., 22 June 1917: X Co-operation of Wireless Intelligence, A.A., R.F.C', in John Ferris (ed), *The British Army and Signals Intelligence in the Field during the First World War* (London: Frank Cass, 1989), pp.92–5.

10 AHB, *Air Publication 3235. The Second World War, 1939–1945, Royal Air Force, Air Support* (London: Air Ministry (AHB), 1955), Appendix 7, p.217.

aeroplane' and 'Infantry Protection machine', although the contact patrol aircraft could still use its wireless to call in an artillery response against a German counterattack if it spotted one. Indeed, at the Air-Tank Conference on 1 September 1918, Major Trafford Leigh-Mallory, Commanding No. 8 Squadron RAF, commented that, 'In small affairs it is best to combine the duties of contact and counterattack patrols in one machine but in a big battle it is essential to keep duties distinct.'[11] It appears allocation of aircraft for the task remained flexible to the end of the war.

An aeroplane would be dedicated to CAP duties throughout daylight hours, weather permitting, being replaced as they reached the end of their endurance or if they were damaged or shot down by enemy action. As well as calling for artillery support via wireless telegraphy, the CAP machine would use a pyrotechnic device to warn the infantry on the ground, generally a red parachute flare that trailed smoke in the direction the counterattack was coming from. However, there were variations in signals, including this example from May 1917:

> In event of a counterattack developing this machine will call on the artillery by the zone call, and will warn the infantry by flares; a red flare will signify that the attack is north of the canal and a green flare south of the canal.[12]

The CAP method of calling in artillery fire could be quite prompt as a report from Captain N.R.G. Lloyd, Commanding 'D' Company, 5th Shropshire Light Infantry, makes clear:

> On the evening of the 22nd August while in charge of the line in GLENCORRE WOOD I had reason to believe that a counter attack by the enemy on our position in the WOOD was imminent. I was preparing to use the S.O.S. should the occasion arise when I noticed a Contact Aeroplane of ours flying low over the wood. Within five minutes of this our guns opened a magnificent barrage on the enemy's positions which completely paralysed the threatened counter attack and it was unable to develop at all, although further to the right and opposite FITZOLARENCE FARM it did start to develop without success. As I never sent the S.O.S. up there can be no question that the alarm was given by the contact aeroplane above mentioned which remained flying low over one position for some time afterwards. There can be no question that the promptness of action of the contact patrol saved us from a counter attack in force.[13]

11 TNA: AIR 1/1074/5/1662: 'Covering letter of Brig.-Gen. P W Game BGGS, RAF to GOC RAF', 2 Sept. 1918. Notes on Conference held at Advanced Tank Corps H.Q. September 1st, 1918.
12 TNA: WO95/218/4: 'Second Army Offensive, 68th Brigade Instructions No. 4.' 23 May 1917, 68th Infantry Brigade War Diary.
13 TNA: WO 95/1871: 'Suggestions and Remarks for Future Engagements', 27 August 1917, 14th Division General Staff War Diary.

RFC armourer putting 20lb Cooper bombs onto bomb rack of a DH.9.
(RAF Museum: PC72/16/306)

Prompt actions such as the above should be borne in mind during any discussion considering the choice of calling in 'close air support' aircraft or using artillery support.

The CAP aeroplane could also use its own weapons to disrupt an enemy counterattack, usually machine guns but also 20lb Cooper bombs if they were being carried; they would also alert other aircraft to help by firing a red Very light to attract their attention. The RFC had used their aeroplane weapons against enemy ground troops from quite early in the war rather more opportunistically as opposed to planned. A rather interesting small scale action that combined air, tanks, artillery, and infantry against the enemy on 26 September 1916 was the attack on Grid Trench near the village of Gueudecourt by a bombing party of the 7th Leicesters as related in the Official History:

> Twenty-five minutes later an aeroplane of No. 3 Squadron (pilot, Second Lieutenant L.G. Wood, observer, Lieutenant H.J.L. Cappel) was sent out to see how the Leicesters were getting on. When the aeroplane got over the trench, the officers found that the bombers had already made some progress and that a tank

> was getting into position to help them. They saw this tank begin its crawl along the line in company with the bombers at a quarter-past seven [am]. Half an hour later the German infantry were compressed in great strength along about 500 yards of the trench between the oncoming bombers and the Guards [the British Guards Division who were operating south of the Leicesters], and the observer, giving the pin-points of their flanks, sent down an area call to the artillery for fire on them. Shells fell thickly at once. Within a few minutes the tank and its bombing party had got as far as the sector which was being bombarded, and a second call to the artillery to cease fire was tapped out. The shelling ceased, the pilot dropped to three hundred feet and flew along the trench raking the unhappy occupants with machine-gun fire. Their endurance snapped, and they waved their arms and white handkerchiefs in surrender to the airmen. This fact was transmitted to the infantry by message bag, and they advanced and accepted the surrender of eight officers and 362 men. The total of British casualties in this brilliant little action numbered five.[14]

This shows the rapid response of the artillery to a wireless telegraphy call from, in this case, a contact patrol machine, and also the requirement for the aeroplane to fly very low to identify and engage the enemy. However, there are also examples of an air attack alone appearing to make a difference despite not being planned to do so. This occurred on 13 September 1917 when the Germans put a complete box barrage down on the left portion of the Armentieres sub-sector of the XI Corps frontline system:

> At the time this occurred an artillery patrol aeroplane manned by Capt. R.N.G. Atkinson and A.M. Watson was flying overhead. As it was obvious that a raid was in preparation the aeroplane dived to 1,200–800 feet and opened fire on machine guns in strong points in the enemy's line. All the Lewis Gun ammunition was thus expended and nearly all the Vickers as well, but the Vickers Gun jammed when there was still half a belt unfired. The ammunition was unloaded by the observer from the Vickers belt and loaded into Lewis Gun drums. The aeroplane then fired into the enemy's trenches in the support and second line. During these manoeuvres the pilot fired five Very lights as dummy signals to mislead the enemy.[15]

The commander of XI Corps pencilled in a comment stating that, 'I am of the opinion that this action by Captain Atkinson prevented the enemy from carrying out a raid against our line.'[16] Both this and the 1916 action mentioned could be classed as 'close air support' using later terminology. They were, however, both not pre-planned actions

14 H.A. Jones, *The War in the Air* (London: Hamish Hamilton, 1969), Volume II, p.291.
15 TNA: WO 95/173/5: 'Letter from Commander XI Corps to Advanced First Army Headquarters', 14 September 1917. First Army General Staff War Diary, p.28.
16 TNA: WO 95/173/5: 'Letter from Commander XI Corps to Advanced First Army Headquarters', 14 September 1917. First Army General Staff War Diary, p.28.

although this was being developed during 1917. On 13 August 1917, a letter was issued by the 47th (London) Division General Staff reference RFC operations on 31 July:

> In connection with the work done by Fighting Squadrons of the R.F.C. in recent operations, the Commander-in-Chief desires the Commanders of all formations to explain to the troops under their command the tactics pursued in the air – results which the troops cannot otherwise be expected to realise. It should be carefully explained to the men that although they may not see our machines at work from their positions in the forward area, the work is going on all the time behind the enemy's lines.[17]

With the letter was a list of individual air attacks carried out by the army-level fighting machines, 48 listed, mainly by scouts using machine gun fire and some light bombs, plus 10 mainly two-seater bombers using heavier bombs. The fighting machines had a mixture of targets including trenches, artillery positions, transport and troops on the roads, encampments, and aerodromes. The letter commented on attacking trenches that the 'effect of firing ammunition from aeroplanes into front line trenches is chiefly moral; few casualties have been caused by this method of attack unless masses of troops are found on roads or in the open'.[18] This should come as no surprise as trenches were designed to protect troops from artillery, mortar and machine gun fire so machine gun fire and light bombs from aircraft would be more a nuisance in comparison. Attacks made on roads leading to the frontline could be more effective, for example on 13 August, aircraft:

> Attacked parties of troops on the YPRES-MENIN Road from 200 feet. On going further east he saw some machine gun emplacements with troops. He went down to 100 feet and fired 140 rounds into them. They were scattered.[19]

On the same day other aircraft fired '80 rounds from 500 feet into a column of horses and motor transport two miles long, on the Gheluwe-Menin Road. Great confusion was caused.'[20] Another report on the capture of Hill 70 on 15–16 August 1917 gives more operational detail:

> The machines of No. 43 Squadron, R.F.C. (two-seater Sopwith) were employed continuously during the 15th August watching a zone, from 1,500 to 2,500 yards from our original front line and about 7,000 yards wide, through which the German reserves must pass in order to counter-attack. The tasks of the Sopwiths were to engage aeroplanes operating over the area, to engage bodies

17 TNA: WO95/2703/3: '47th (London) Division General Staff War Diary', 13 August 1917.
18 TNA: WO95/2703/3: '47th (London) Division General Staff War Diary', 13 August 1917.
19 TNA: WO95/2703/3: '47th (London) Division General Staff War Diary', 13 August 1917.
20 TNA: WO95/2703/3: '47th (London) Division General Staff War Diary', 13 August 1917.

> of hostile infantry, particularly when passing through wire and other obstacles, where congestion must occur, to engage artillery in action or on the move, and to report indications of hostile counter-attacks. These tasks were most effectively carried out by the pilots and observers of No. 43 Squadron, who engaged a large number of targets of all descriptions with machine gun fire, and kept the Corps Headquarters and Corps Heavy Artillery constantly informed (by telephone from their Advanced Landing Ground at PETIT SAINS) of hostile concentrations and counter-attacks.[21]

It should be noted that in this case communication was undertaken on return to the ALG by telephone; presumably this would cause a delay in an artillery reaction to a counterattack compared with a CAP machine using wireless telegraphy direct to the battery for the same purpose. Even so, this was deemed a 'success' in the report. Contact Patrol aeroplanes had from 1916 taken part in exercises with infantry to practise the air-ground liaison procedures. By August 1917 aircraft were supporting troops on exercises in a more aggressive manner with instructions that the 'Contact Aeroplanes will demonstrate the method of assisting an Infantry advance by over-head fire from a low altitude.'[22] Note the use of plural for the aeroplanes as the contact mission over units was usually undertaken with a single machine so these were demonstrating 'close air support' in practice if not in name.

For actual operations, the role of the aviation assets would be laid down in orders and instructions. For Operation G/Y, better known as the Battle of Cambrai, the 3rd Brigade RFC had not only the reconnaissance, bombing and attacks on airfields, headquarters and train stations detailed but also a section on 'Low Flying machines'. This latter included four Airco DH.5s and eight Sopwith Camels dedicated to attack three groups of artillery batteries with bombs and machine guns at zero plus 15 minutes. Orders were also issued that:

> All available D.H.5s. and Sopwith Camels will attack troops, transport and other targets on the ground with bombs and machine gun fire from zero + 45 mins. onwards. These attacks will be distributed from FONTAINE-LES-CROISILLES to BELLICOURT between the hours of zero + 45 mins. and zero + 2 hours, with a view to deceiving the enemy as to the main point of attack. From zero + 2 hours onwards machines will be concentrated on the front of the main attack.[23]

21 TNA: WO95/173/2: 'Report on the Capture of Hill 70 and Operations of 15th-16th August, 1917', 17 August 1917, First Army General Staff War Diary.

22 TNA: WO 95/1661/4: 'Instruction No. 1, Issued with reference to 22nd Infantry Brigade Orders Nos. 003 & 004, for a Tactical Exercise', 21 August 1917, 22 Infantry Brigade: Headquarters.

23 TNA: WO 95/368/3: '3rd Brigade Royal Flying Corps. Special Operation Order No. 372', 16 November 1917, Third Army General Staff War Diary.

Deception operations of all types were common during the First World War and here aircraft played their part. At the start of the Cambrai battle, on 20 November, there were weather problems with low cloud and mist causing problems for air support, although it helped the infantry and tanks advance, and aided in causing relatively high casualties of around 30 percent for the low-flyers, much mentioned in the books of Arthur Gould Lee (see Chapter 2). He comments that:

> To me, and to every fighter pilot with whom I discussed this subject, then and later in 1918, low-flying attacks were, with few exceptions, were a wasteful employment of highly trained pilots and expensive aeroplanes. A 30 per cent rate of casualties meant a new squadron every fourth day and one rendered useless for normal air fighting duties.[24]

This may or may not be true amongst fighter pilots. It could, however, depend on the individual pilot. For example, Captain William Barker (later VC) of No. 28 Squadron flying Camels in Italy was rebuked for disobeying regulations on low-flying. Barker's justification was:

> ...2/Lt Hudson & I were up engaged in practice fighting after which we proceeded to enemy's lines to test our guns. We were engaged in doing this when I noticed two enemy balloons & column of enemy transport. I regret very much that for the moment I forgot the order against low flying.[25]

Barker appears not to have been worried about low-level attacks. He had been both an observer and pilot on Corps aeroplanes previously, undertaking not only artillery spotting missions but also contact and counterattack patrols at low level as a normal occupation. Something that Lee appears not to have considered was Corps pilots and observers were also highly trained and they had to undertake their missions at low-level for long periods of time in slow and unmanoeuvrable machines. It may be that an ex-Corps squadron airman like Barker saw low-level flying in a single-seat scout as being rather less risky than their previous occupation.

The Corps pilots and observers did have concerns some of which are illustrated by comments in December 1917 from Major L. Walker who commanded No. 15 Squadron RFC:

> It appears to me, that the type of machine we use for Contact Patrol work, is our main difficulty and that instead of using large two seater machines, which are always becoming heavier and therefore more difficult to manoeuvre quickly near the ground, we should use fairly fast single seater machines which should be light

24 Arthur Gould Lee, *Open Cockpit* (London: Grubb Street, 2012), p.169.
25 Wayne Ralph, *Barker VC: The Classic Story of a Legendary First World War Hero* (London: Grubb Street, 1999).

Major Barker's Sopwith Camel, B6313, No. 28 Squadron RAF, over an unidentified Italian airfield, September 1917. (RAF Museum: PC73/88/326)

> on the controls and capable of diving vertically, and rising quickly. Machines of this type should be lightly armoured in their vital parts such as the engine, petrol and oil tanks, pilot's cockpit, &c, in order to protect them from infantry M.G. and rifle fire.[26]

He wanted these machines to form one flight of a Corps squadron and during operations they could undertake Infantry Contact Patrols, CAP and engage hostile troops at low altitudes with machine gun fire and bombs. However, Walker did concede that there could be problems of a single pilot undertaking the practical tasks of observing and noting positions on maps while trying to fly at the same time, although believed this might be overcome by selective training for the pilot and special equipment. It should be noted here the request for light armour on the aeroplanes, and it may just be a coincidence that '...in January 1918 Sopwith were invited to design a

26 TNA: AIR 1/523/16/12/9: 'Comments from Major L. Walker, Commanding 15th Sqn. RFC. Generated in response to a GHQ request for ideas on the subject', c. 24 December 1917, Communication: Aeroplane and Ground.

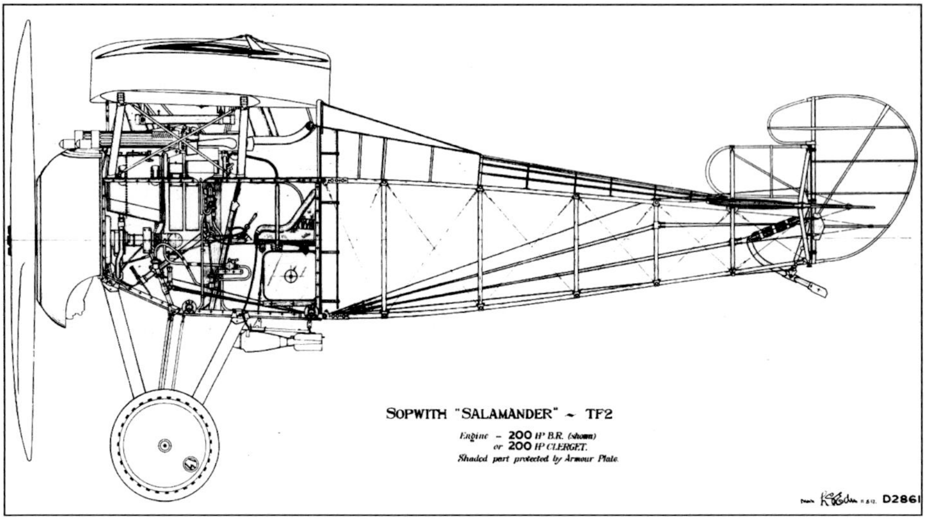

Sopwith Salamander. The British purpose-built ground attack fighter.
(RAF Museum: X003-2602/16495)

special armoured single-seater with a 230 hp Bentley B.R.2 engine, this aircraft later emerging as the Salamander.'[27]

Low flying to make attacks on troops, artillery and transport was necessary as it was the only way to make an air attack anywhere near accurate and even to identify a particular target. This was dangerous as it brought the flyers into the range of infantry machine guns and rifle fire, so could result in heavy casualties including Lee's 30 percent, although probably not as much as implied. For example, there follows a summary of No.19 Squadron's (Sopwith Dolphin) ground attack missions on 27 March 1918 against German troops during the Spring Offensive:

> The squadron put up three multi-aircraft patrols to undertake ground attack missions that day, the first, at 10am, dropped 34 x 20lb Cooper bombs and fired 2,450 rounds of machine gun ammunition at enemy troops and other targets. The second patrol, 1.45pm, dropped 27 bombs and fired 1,850 rounds, while the third patrol, at 5pm, dropped 11 bombs and fired 1,400 rounds. These attacks were all from under 1,000 feet, some being described as 'from very low altitude'.[28]

There does not appear to have been any loss of aircraft or pilots, although some must have been hit by ground fire and two aircraft had to return from the last patrol

27 H.F. King, *Sopwith Aircraft 1912–1920* (London: Putnam & Company Ltd, 1981), p.163.
28 Derek Palmer, *Fighter Squadron* (Upton-upon-Severn: The Self Publishing Association, 1991), pp.81–3.

with engine problems, not combat related. The squadron was also expected and did engage in air-to-air combat during these sorties. Another example is No. 4 Squadron, Australian Flying Corps (AFC) (Camels), which on 27 March undertook 38 sorties, dropping 75 Cooper bombs and firing their machine guns at enemy troops and motor transport from 2000 to 1000 feet altitude. They appear to have lost only one Camel (B7347) to enemy machine gun fire from the ground. However, the pilot, Second Lieutenant A.W. Adams, got back although wounded and sent to hospital.[29]

The problem of identifying friendly from enemy troops on the ground was problematic during the First World and later conflicts. From early in the war the RFC had undertaken experiments to identify what would be visible from various altitudes by an aeroplane observer. This included: 'From 1,500 feet. Dugout entrances. Comparative depth of trench. Men making signals, such as waving their helmets. From 1,000 feet or under our own troops can be distinguished from those of the enemy.'[30]

These trials were all undertaken without the use of additional visual aids being used by the troops. From the 1916 Battle of the Somme onwards various items of equipment were used to indicate the location of friendly infantry. These items included various coloured ground flares used alone or in conjunction with shiny discs of metal of different sizes, different pieces of cloth of various colours such as white, yellow, pink, and so on, on the back or hanging from the helmet or waved by the soldier, plus fans of different types.[31] It should be noted that 'shiny discs' were still in use during 1941 in North Africa to show the foremost line of friendly troops.[32] Also, tanks and armoured cars during the First World War had identification markings applied; this was mainly to differentiate the tanks serving the British from the captured British tanks being used by the Germans. Trials of different markings were part of the aeroplane and tank trials that took place at Fricourt on 28 February 1918, although they were all rejected by the RFC as appearing too small when viewed from 1,000 and 200 feet. Interestingly, one of these markings was the 'ordinary aeroplane marking' on the tank's cab.[33] This was a marking sometimes used on British vehicles to identify them

29 Australian War Memorial (AWM): RCDIG1006297: Australian Imperial Force War Diary (Squadron Record Book) 4th Squadron, Australian Flying Corps, March 1918; AWM: RCDIG1002362: RFC Communique No. 133; Trevor Henshaw, *The Sky Their Battlefield II* (High Barnet: Fetubi, 2014), p.157.

30 TNA: AIR 1/122/50/40/112: 'Provisional Instructions for Contact Patrol Work by Aeroplanes', 12 December 1916.

31 Mike Meech, 'Showing the Line on the Western Front in World War One', in Andrew Cormack (ed), *A Long, Long Trail a-Winding: Centenary Perspectives on the Great War, Commemorative Volume on the First World War*. Special Publication No. 18 (London: The Society for Army Historical Research, 2018), pp.132–59.

32 AHB, *Air Publication 3235. The Second World War, 1939–1945, Royal Air Force, Air Support* (London: Air Ministry (AHB), 1955), Appendix 7, 'Middle East (Army & R.A.F.); G.H.Q. M.E.F. and H.Q. R.A.F. M.E., Directive on Direct Air Support', 30 September 1941, 'Annexure "C" Recognition Signals', p.220.

33 TNA: AIR 1/1074/204/5/1665: 'Report on the Aeroplane and Tank Trials which took place West of FRICOURT on THURSDAY', 20th February 1918.

from the air during the Second World War. There were further trials and this led to the introduction of the famous White/Red/White marking used during 1918; again this and similar markings were used early on during the latter conflict.[34]

The Fricourt trials included demonstrations of air attack effectiveness against two field guns in the open using bombs and machine gun fire. It was considered that:

> In both cases the gun would have been damaged, and the team knocked out by the bombs. The machine gun fire was extremely accurate and undoubtedly would have driven the team from the gun, probably inflicting many casualties.[35]

In the case of using machine gun fire representing infantry following tanks, the results were that 'several of the targets were hit and the ground round the targets was cut up by Machine Gun bullets. The fire was extremely accurate and would have inflicted casualties to the infantry.'[36] Bombing attacks were also made on targets representing tanks and machine guns against real tanks, with the result:

> Although no bomb actually hit the Tank, they all fell close by. It is however very improbable that any damage would have been done to the Tanks. Two aeroplanes fired with Machine Guns at real Tanks to ascertain the effect of the bullets on the roof. No bullets penetrated any part of the Tank – The Tanks were hit in several places.[37]

From these trials it was considered that aircraft machine gun fire could be accurate and effective against infantry and guns, but not tanks. Bombs were less accurate but could still harm gun crews, but less so tanks. However, a related trial was undertaken with aeroplane bombs placed around a real tank, concluding:

> From recent experiments with hand bombs and grenades, it would appear better if an aeroplane could drop a shower of small bombs instead of a few large bombs. 1-lb of high explosive in a thin case will blow a large hole in any part of our present Tank. Possibly an aeroplane could drop, say, 12 2-lb. bombs with a slight cone of dispersion. The general conclusion from above is that aeroplane bombs (25-lb.) must either hit the Tank or fall within ½ yard to stop the Tank.[38]

The 12 small bombs with a 'slight cone of dispersion' appears rather like a cluster bomb used against tanks in later conflicts.

34 TNA: AIR 1/1074/204/5/1665: 'Letter from Capt. D. Wray Forshaw, No. 46 Squadron, R.F.C. to Headquarters 15th Wing, R.F.C.', 6 March 1918.
35 TNA: AIR 1/1074/204/5/1665: 'Report on the Aeroplane and Tank Trials'.
36 TNA: AIR 1/1074/204/5/1665: 'Report on the Aeroplane and Tank Trials'.
37 TNA: AIR 1/1074/204/5/1665: 'Report on the Aeroplane and Tank Trials'.
38 TNA: AIR 1/1074/204/5/1665: 'Trials with Aeroplane Bombs near Tanks'.

Royal Aircraft Factory RE.8, the most numerous type used for counterattack patrols. (RAF Museum: X003-2602/11421)

The CAP and Central Information Bureau (CIB)

In August 1918, an RAF document, relating to tank support, mentions:

> As is well known by now to all pilots and observers of Corps Squadrons, their wireless calls will largely control the action of the low flying scouts, subsequent to Zero hour. This system marks a large stride in the direction of close co-operation in the battle between the Wings of the R.A.F. Brigade. The result will also inevitably tend towards economy of energy and greater efficiency in applying force at the right point of attack. To be successful, however, and attain the desired aim, all such pilots and observers must be deeply imbued with their large responsibilities in the matter and neglect no opportunity of furthering the success of the scheme.[39]

Although this letter does not mention the CIB by name it appears to imply it is in use and that the pilots and observers of the Corps squadrons have a major responsibility in making it work successfully. A report dated 14 September 1918 mentions the CIB attack in use, stating that: '...in both armies the work of the artillery and counter

39 TNA: AIR 1/1074/204/5/1665: 'Letter to Officers Commanding 15th and 22nd Wings, RAF from Brigadier General L.E.O. Charlton commanding 5th Brigade, RAF', 14 August 1918.

patrols was co-ordinated with that of the scouts by the Central Information Bureau, usually established at the Central Wireless Stations.'[40]

The Central Wireless Station (CWS) was introduced into service around mid-1916 and was described as:

> An advanced squadron wireless unit, known as the 'Central Wireless Station', was established in each corps area, at or near the head-quarters of the Corps Heavy Artillery. The central wireless stations were equipped with several aerials and listened to the wireless progress of all shoots. If the communication between the aeroplane and battery broke down the observer could call up the central wireless station, which was well forward and therefore less subject to jamming, and learn, by ground signal, the cause of the trouble.[41]

The mention of the CWS at or near the HQ of the Corps Heavy Artillery is continued with the location of the CIB, as confirmed in the following:

> A C.W. [Continuous Wave] net is being established at the C.I.B. at Corps H.A. [heavy artillery] Headquarters. The call of the station is C.I.B. and its wave length 1220 metres. This station is intended for the reception of messages from aeroplanes; those messages are collated, and sent out as CQ [all stations] messages to all Squadrons and Wings.The Corps C.W. Control Station will arrange that, when possible, any information received likely to be of use to the R.A.F. is transmitted to the C.I.B. on the 1220 metres wave length.[42]

The Corps Heavy Artillery Headquarters was where the Counter Battery Staff Officer (CBSO) was located. This post was introduced at the time of the battle of the Somme during 1916 and by the end of 1916 all Corps had a CBSO. The CBSO became integrated increasingly with ground attack missions, and this is described in a September 1918 RAF HQ report on Corps squadrons with the First and Third Armies, under 'Counter Attack Patrol Work'. It comments:

> This was combined on the First Army front with artillery patrol work, and both armies the work of artillery and counter attack patrols was co-ordinated with that of the scouts by the Central Information Bureau, usually established at the Central Wireless Stations. In the First Army all GF and LL calls were passed direct to the C.B.S.O. who was also responsible for long range harassing fire. The C.B.S.O. transmitted such targets as he did not deal with by artillery fire

40 TNA: AIR 1/725/97/2: 'Notes on Corps Squadrons' Work on the First and Third Army Fronts During Recent Operations.' 14 September 1918.

41 H.A. Jones, *War in the Air Vol. III* (Oxford: Clarendon Press, 1931), pp.311–2.

42 TNA: WO 95/845/4: 'A.D. Signals, IX Corps. Technical Instruction Series IV. No. 6', Para. 4, 'Liaison with R.A.F.' IX Corps Signal Company War Diary, 26 September 1918.

> by Wireless to the Army Wing in the ordinary S.S. 131 [S.S. 131 Cooperation of Aircraft with Artillery] Code. These calls were translated by an officer of the Corps Wing and the Army Wing Commander took action as necessary. If the C.B.S.O. received information concerning hostile movement from sources other than the air, he himself initiated a message to the Army Wing.[43]

The report considered scouts attacking ground targets could be costly and should be directed with discretion and that:

> Except for the first few hours after a successful surprise attack when targets will be numerous, low flying patrols should not as a general rule be sent out unless good targets have been reported from one source or another.[44]

That included the CAP machine calling in air support by wireless via the CIB system. The report continued:

> In the Third Army the first Scout patrol each day consisted of two formations each of three flights at three, five and seven thousand feet. The lowest flight carried bombs and was made responsible for reconnoitring the area for ground targets and dropping their bombs on the best target seen. They then returned to the lines, the upper flights continuing the patrol. Except for those two early morning patrols no scouts were sent out low flying except on receipt of definite information.[45]

An example of use of this 'definite information' can be found in an operation order in which No. 201 Squadron (Camels) were required after their early morning operation, that:

> For the remainder of the day the Squadron will be employed in attacking suitable ground targets from low altitude under the orders of Officer Commanding 13th Wing, who will receive targets sent down by wireless from Corps machines, and will telephone them through to Officer Commanding 201 Squadron at the Advanced Landing Ground.[46]

43 TNA: AIR 1/725/97/2: 'Notes on Corps Squadrons Work on the First and Third Army Fronts During Recent Operations.' H.Q. R.A.F., 14 September 1918.
44 TNA: AIR 1/725/97/2: 'Notes on Corps Squadrons Work on the First and Third Army Fronts During Recent Operations.' H.Q. R.A.F., 14 September 1918.
45 TNA: AIR 1/725/97/2: 'Notes on Corps Squadrons Work on the First and Third Army Fronts During Recent Operations.' H.Q. R.A.F., 14 September 1918.
46 TNA: AIR 1/1512/204/58/28: '13th Wing Special Operation Order No. 12', 24 September 1918.

Note the use of both telephone and wireless. There were concerns over keeping up communications during 'open warfare' situations; for example, a Fifth Army Instruction expressed concerns relating to telephone lines:

> During a rapid advance it will not be possible to provide long direct lines, and in order to obtain the best communications, units must group themselves close to Communication Centres; thus R.A.F. Brigade Headquarters should be at Army Headquarters; Army Wing and squadrons should be grouped together; Corps Wing, Balloon Wing, Anti-Aircraft Defence Commander and Advanced Maps should be at Centre Corps Headquarters; R.A.F. Corps Squadrons should be near respective Corps Headquarters; Balloon Companies should be with Corps Heavy Artillery Headquarters;[...] [47]

As in later wars, joint coordination of operations between all branches needed good communications and, in many situations, the relevant headquarters needed to be close to each other.

As has been mentioned, it was not just scouts undertaking ground attacks. The two-seater Corps machines were also very active. A No. 3 Squadron AFC Instruction comments that the 'C.I.B. will be used as before, as the role of the Army Wing will be largely dependent on news transmitted by these means.'[48] It continues with squadron tasks:

> Two machines will be detailed to stand by during the following hours by Flights as shown to answer CIB Bombing Calls – 0630–0830 'C' Flight, 0830–1030 'C' Flight, 1030–1230 'C' Flight, 1230–1430 'B' Flight, 1430–1630 'B' Flight. In the event of no target being obtained at the end of each period, machines will be sent up to bomb targets which will be communicated to Flight Commanders.[49]

Throughout the daylight hours No. 3 Squadron AFC had machines ready to respond to CIB calls for 'close air support' in addition to any scouts. In addition, every aeroplane sent up, except for those on photographic missions, would carry six bombs, therefore being able to attack targets of opportunity.

47 TNA: WO 95/522/5: 'Special Instruction No. 10', 15 October 1918. Fifth Army General Staff War Diary.

48 AWM: 4-8-6-22: '3rd Squadron Australian Flying Corps Battle Instructions' pt.1, 22 October 1918.

49 AWM: 4-8-6-22: '3rd Squadron Australian Flying Corps Battle Instructions' pt.1, 22 October 1918.

Tanks and the CIB

Although air and tank cooperation is dealt with elsewhere in this volume, a brief mention should be made of the integration with the CIB system. This integration was agreed at an RAF and Tank Corps conference held at Advanced Tank Corps HQ on 1 September 1918 as the quickest way to pass information. The Tank Corps used different wavelengths to the RAF so they would have another receiving set for CIB work using Continuous Wave (CW) wireless. This method was used in the final months of the war and was also incorporated into the November 1918 edition of SS 135, where it states:

> Wireless messages take the form of zone calls. In addition of being received at the Battery station, these are taken in at the central information bureau established by the R.A.F. at Corps central wireless stations or elsewhere. A tank wireless transmitting station (C.W.) should be established at the central information bureau working on the R.A.F. wavelength. Messages of interest to tanks received at the central information bureau can then be passed on to tank battalions and companies over the tank wireless system.[50]

It was difficult to use artillery against anti-tank guns due to them being used very close to the tanks and it became important to use aeroplanes. Both Corps and scouts No. 8 Squadron (Armstrong Whitworth FK.8) and No. 73 Squadron (Camel) were both being used together by the end of August 1918, so were pioneers in this respect. It was recommended that the squadrons used for this purpose should be based on the same aerodrome to aid communication. SS 135 also mentions:

> This offensive action will be undertaken by the counter-attack patrols when their other duties permit, but, whenever possible, special machines should be detailed for the work. It is essential that the pilots of these machines should be thoroughly acquainted in detail with the ground on which they are to operate. The actual methods of carrying out the work must depend upon circumstances; it may be advisable to detail a few machines to reconnoitre the area and fire a percussion smoke bomb as a signal when they discover a target, while the remaining machines fly just behind the advancing tanks ready to attack immediately whenever any target has been signalled.[51]

The last sentence on aircraft in the air ready to attack targets immediately appears to be rather similar to the 'cab rank' system used during the Second World War.

50 General Staff, SS 135: Cooperation Between Aircraft and Tanks (France: GHQ, 1918), p.58.
51 General Staff, SS 135: Cooperation Between Aircraft and Tanks (France: GHQ, 1918), p.58.

Was the CAP/CIB system a success?

The CAP/CIB system was certainly an improvement in measures to speed up the response time in engaging enemy targets and it appears to have been available to the majority, possibly all, Corps on the Western Front. The CAP machine sent messages via the CIB, where the CBSO could either use artillery fire or contact the Army Wing by wireless or telephone to request bombed up scouts to make attacks instead. The scouts were being used in the 'fighter-bomber' role and being used for – what would be called in a later war – close air support, armed reconnaissance, or even interdiction operating from advanced landing grounds fully armed and awaiting a call. The system connected the CAP machine of the RAF with the artillery, infantry and tanks, therefore speeding up the process of the 'on call' air support. It was criticised, however. For example, in the Official History:

> About noon on the 8th October a message from an observer of No. 35 Squadron was received in the Central Information Bureau telling of German columns converging upon Clery. A Sopwith 'Camel' Squadron, No. 208, which had been allotted for attacks upon such targets, was sent out in the afternoon and the pilots bombed and shot at the enemy columns. The corps squadron aeroplanes also took a hand in this work... [52]

Apparently a successful use of the system, however, it continues '...but there was no attempt to make a concentration of aeroplanes against the reported columns'.[53]

What the author considered as a 'concentration' is not defined. The Camels and FK.8s of Nos. 208 and 35 Squadrons respectively did engage, and earlier in the war this would have been considered a 'concentration'. Of course, it may just have been no other squadrons were available at the time, but No. 35 Squadron was part of 15th (Corps) Wing (5th Brigade), which was commanded by Lieutenant Colonel J.A. Chamier, whose views on the CIB system in use are recorded eleven days after the above incident. These are in a letter to Lieutenant Colonel T.W.C. Carthew who commanded 81st (Corps) Wing in 10th Brigade. In this letter, Chamier mentions:

> There is a tendency among Squadrons to overdo the C.I.B. call and send to C.I.B. information which is the legitimate property of the gunners. This will at once arouse antagonism in their bosoms and will make them hostile to the system.[54]

It appears that Chamier was concerned that the RAF was 'poaching' targets from the artillery and thereby 'upsetting' them. This is a different complaint to that made in the

52 H.A. Jones, *The War in the Air* (Oxford: The Clarendon Press, 1937), Volume VI, p.536.
53 Jones, *The War in the Air*, p.536.
54 TNA: AIR 1/919/204/5/882: 'Letter Chamier to Carthew', 19 October 1918.

Second World War when it was alleged that the Army overused air support comparatively to their own artillery. Chamier goes on to give examples:

> The pilot sees a road in the enemy back areas crowded with troops – he is personally convinced that these are out of range of our guns and sends a C.I.B. call. If he is right no harm is done; the information goes to those it concerns (e.g. Corps, R.A.F. as a bombing target etc.). Take it however that he is wrong and that the guns can reach the target – the R.A. stations with the batteries, etc. do not take the call and the gunners will at once say that we are trying to win the war on our own and will curse the day that the C.I.B. was born. But let us disabuse the pilot of all responsibility for range and see what happens? He sends an LL call, the R.A. take it and gnash their teeth because they cannot reach it. BUT the C.I.B. also intercepts it and the R.A.F. dash out and bomb and shoot up the target.[55]

He summarises the system:

> Thus there can be no possible doubt in the pilot's mind as to 'what form the message should take.' Here is the enemy in sufficient numbers to warrant artillery fire – it may be out of range, but that does not matter 2 damns. I will send a 'purely artillery' call on it and the R.A. will engage it if possible; the R.A.F. will supplement in any case with bombs and machine gun fire.[56]

Emphasising the decision needed to be made by the Royal Artillery, Chamier then gives another example:

> [...]a road is being constantly used by single motor vehicles at long intervals. This cannot be by any stretch of the imagination be construed into a GF target and no other call is applicable. I will C.I.B. the information. The R.A.F. will phone the information if possible to the heavies so that they may harass the road with 6 in Mk VII's – the Corps will be informed of this unceasing road movement, the R.A.F. will keep an eye on the road and bomb and shoot it up.[57]

On the wireless calls taken and transmitted by the CIB, Chamier lists them as:

1. All SOS, LL and GF 'normal artillery', sent by any old machine.
2. All calls prefixed by 'C.I.B.' these comprise:-
   EA activity, e.g. 7 EA 200.
   i) Protractor references of the position of our own troops.

55 TNA: AIR 1/919/204/5/882: 'Letter Chamier to Carthew', 19 October 1918.
56 TNA: AIR 1/919/204/5/882: 'Letter Chamier to Carthew', 19 October 1918.
57 TNA: AIR 1/919/204/5/882: 'Letter Chamier to Carthew', 19 October 1918.

ii) Anything else that the pilot considers to be of interest or value which it is not possible to notify as a target for the artillery.[58]

The CIB was part of an integrated system where the air support and artillery worked in conjunction, using both wireless and telephone for communications to support infantry and tanks during their advances in 1918. It was not perfect but did improve the response time of the RAF in their support of the frontline using methods that would be recognisable to armed forces in later wars. Problems arose which had to be solved, including with the communication equipment used and the methods to recognise friendly from enemy troops on the ground. These problems reoccurred in later conflicts.

58 TNA: AIR 1/919/204/5/882: 'Letter Chamier to Carthew', 19 October 1918.

4

Close Air Support to the Tank Corps in the First World War: A Developing Success

Geoffrey Vesey Holt

Introduction and background

Just after the end of the Great War, Brevet-Colonel J.F.C. Fuller DSO, who after his initial visit as the Tank Corps GSO1 to the first four tank battalions in January 1917 had described them as 'a band of brigand',[1] wrote in his 1920 *History of the Tanks in the First World War*:

> Major T. L. Leigh-Mallory, D.S.O., O.C. 8th Squadron, R.A.F., whose energy resulted not only in the cementing of a close comradeship between the two supreme mechanical weapons of the age but of a close co-operation which saved many lives in battle.[2]

Fuller later acknowledged that Leigh-Mallory contributed most of the chapter 'Aeroplane Cooperation' to his book. This chapter will examine the close and unique links between the Tank Corps and No. 8 Squadron RAF, and later No. 73 Squadron, forged in combat in the First World War, and the support that these squadrons provided to the Tank Corps in the Hundred Days Campaign. It does not look at the wider RAF ground support in 1918 or in any detail at casualties because of limited data and sample size.[3] This chapter is based on the extensive Tank Corps and RAF

1 Major-General J.F.C. Fuller CB, CBE, DSO, *Memoirs of An Unconventional Soldier* (London: Ivor Nicholson and Watson, 1936), p.89.
2 Brevet-Colonel J.F.C. Fuller DSO, *Tanks in the Great War, 1914–1918* (New York: E.P. Dutton and Company, 1920), p.xiii.
3 For an excellent analysis of this see Alistair McClusky, 'The Battle of Amiens and the Development of British Air-Land Battle, 1918–45', in Gary Sheffield and Peter Grey (eds), *Changing War: The British Army, the Hundred Days Campaign and the Birth of the Royal Air Force, 1918* (London: Bloomsbury, 2013), pp.231–47.

First World War records including war diaries and histories, Fuller's accounts, more recent works and the official histories.[4] The more detailed coverage of No. 8 Squadron reflects the available material.[5] Given that I served for 37 years in the Royal Tank Regiment (the Tank Corps in its current title) this chapter will have a Tank Corps slant but in my defence my grandfather was Air Vice-Marshal Felton Vesey Holt, CMG, DSO, who served in the RFC and RAF throughout the First World War.

Background: up to and including Cambrai

The RFC (from 1 April 1918, the RAF) and Tank Corps were both new corps in 1918 trying to harness, exploit and overcome the limitations of new technologies. The tank, however, was an even more immature technology than the aircraft. It should be remembered that the first tank did not move until January 1916. It was slow (3.7mph), difficult to manoeuvre, and only provided protection against small arms. These vehicles also suffered from terrible ergonomics and had no means of communications. The first tanks went into action on 15 September 1916. Their success was limited due to lack of crew training, coherent doctrine and tactics. Nevertheless, BEF GHQ saw the potential and a few days later asked for 15 tank battalions (about 540 tanks) in five brigades as soon as practicable. This was achieved for the Battle of Amiens in August 1918, arguably the most important First World War Allied victory.

The year of 1917 was one of formation, training, consolidation, and experimentation culminating in what the historian Cyril Falls called 'The Great Experiment'.[6] The new Mark V tank was about to enter service. It was a significant improvement over the Mark IV tank used at Cambrai. It had a more powerful engine and was significantly more manoeuvrable. However, it could do no more than 4.7 miles an hour and it retained the two significant weaknesses of all First World War tanks: a lack of effective communications between tanks and their HQs, and as a result, of command and control, and protection limited to small arms and not against German field guns in the anti-tank role.[7] Air power was to play a developing and key role in mitigating these two weaknesses in 1918. Aircraft dropping messages to Tank Corps' HQs were a vital means of rapid and informed collection and passage of information and, as will be highlighted, aircraft were used to suppress anti-tank guns.

Initial aircraft-tank communication experiments in early 1917 were unsuccessful. Nevertheless, aircraft reported with considerable accuracy the progress of tanks in the 1917 battles.[8] There was extensive air support during the Battle of Cambrai despite the

4 Each tank brigade, battalion and organisation produced war histories just after the Armistice. RAF Wings and Squadrons did likewise.

5 For example, the No. 8 Squadron history is 34 pages long and No. 73 Squadron's one page.

6 Cyril Falls, *The First World War* (London: Longmans, 1960), p.294.

7 See David Fletcher, *Mark V Tank* (Oxford: Osprey, 2011) for details.

8 Fuller, *Tanks in the Great War*, p.242

mist, although low-flying aircraft proved more effective against infantry than against guns.[9] Nevertheless, on 23 November an Airco DH.5 temporarily silenced two guns which had brought three tanks to a halt. The tanks' success at Cambrai led to a flurry of activity including confirmation of the expansion of the Tank Corps to 18, later 26, battalions and amongst other measures the Tank Corps pressed to regularise aircraft-tank cooperation, but it took until 1 June 1918 for No. 8 Squadron RAF to be allocated to the Tank Corps. In the interim, on 28 February, a trial was run by 1st Tank Brigade which concluded that:

1. Anti-tank guns and infantry in the open could be effectively dealt with by aircrafts using machine gun fire and bombs.
2. Aircrafts could not 'seriously endanger tanks.' [10]

A white square with a black centre could be seen and distinguished by an aircraft at 1,000ft. In April 1918, all British tanks were painted with white and red marking stripes to distinguish them from recovered Mark IV British tanks in German use which had large Maltese and Latin (straight edged) crosses, sometimes in a white box.[11]

On 1 June 1918 No. 8 Squadron, RAF was allocated to the Tank Corps. Prior to this, from 21 March to 5 April, the Squadron had done 'a considerable amount of low bombing and shooting up' (347 bombs and over 36,000 SAA rounds) in addition to its normal corps role. In May and June its prime role was day bombing. From early April its establishment was for 18 Armstrong Whitworth F.K.8 two-seater biplanes and 20 pilots.[12]

From 1 June to the Battle of Amiens on 8 August, the 25-year-old Leigh-Mallory drove forward trials, training and the development of links between the Tank Corps and his squadron.[13] Leigh-Mallory wrote that 'it was a great pity that there was no longer than a month to prepare for the battles', but this was more time than most infantry units got to train with tanks and build up person to person links.[14] The three No. 8 Squadron RAF Flights worked with 1st, 3rd and 5th Tank Brigades and carried out experiments with signalling. In practice, visual signalling was difficult to use effectively. Although wireless was already in extensive and successful use, the

9 H.A Jones, *The War in the Air Being the Story of the Part Played in the Great War by the Royal Air Force* (Oxford: Clarendon Press, 1937), Volume VI, p.238.
10 The National Archives (TNA): WO 95/93: 'HQ Tank Corps G1241/5 Letter by Fuller', 6 Mar 1918, HQ Tank Corps War Diary February 1918, Appendix 17.
11 Maxwell Hundleby and Rainer Strasheim (eds), *The German A7V Tank and the Captured British Mk IV Tanks of World War I* (Sparkford: Haynes, 1990), pp.98–216.
12 TNA: AIR 1/688/21/20/8: 'History of 8 Squadron, R.A.F', pp.18–20; TNA: AIR 1/2388/228/11/80: 'An account by course students of war experiences: W/C. T. Leigh-Mallory', p.11.
13 Fuller, *Tanks in the Great War*, p.243.
14 TNA: AIR: 1/1671/204/109/26: 'History of tank and aeroplane co-operation', p.1.

combined limitation and immaturity of wireless and tanks hampered this promising means of communication.[15]

As this training and experimentation was taking place, No. 8 Squadron took part in its first battle in cooperation with the Tank Corps, the Battle of Hamel on 4 July 1918. This successful action by a reinforced Australian division with 60 Mark V tanks in support also had extensive air support that would also be seen in the Hundred Days. Its C Flight, reinforced with senior A and B Flight pilots, flew over the tanks to cover their approach, dropped useful information on tank progress to their HQs and Captain Frederick West, who would win a VC on 12 August, and Lieutenant J.A.G Haslam's aircraft went through the smoke screen to silence 'very active' guns.[16]

The Battle of Amiens (8 to 11 August)

The Battle of Amiens was the first offensive of the Hundred Days. The plan was for a surprise advance of five to seven miles to the old Amiens Defence Line led by tanks and, initially, a rolling barrage. Eight infantry divisions in two echelons were supported by 2,070 artillery pieces, 800 British Empire aircraft and 414 fighting tanks.[17] In contrast to Cambrai, where the advance of just under four miles was just within field artillery range, at Amiens the subsequent advance from the first objective was beyond field artillery range and was therefore dependant on tanks, a limited heavy artillery barrage and aircraft to support the infantry's advance.

Prior to the attack, RAF night bombers drowned the noise of assembling British tanks, offensive air patrols denied German air reconnaissance while RAF reconnaissance aircraft took 37,825 whole plate photographs on Fourth Army front in the first week of August, which combined with sound ranging and flash spotting meant ninety-five percent of German guns were detected.[18] RAF day bombers attacked German airfields at daybreak and later railway stations. The advance was also directly supported by seven fighter squadrons including five for low-level attacks, eight observation balloons and five Corps squadrons, including No. 8 Squadron. One flight was

15 TNA: WO 95/94: 'Notes on Conference Held at Advanced Tank Corps HQ, 1 Sept. 1918', HQ Tank Corps War Diary 1918 June – Sept Appendices; TNA: AIR 1/1671/204/109/26: 'History of tank and aeroplane co-operation', pp.1–2; Fuller, *Tanks in the Great War*, pp.244–5; Jones, *The War in the Air*, Vol IV, pp.464–5.

16 TNA: AIR 1/688/21/20/8: 'History of 8 Squadron, R.A.F', p.22; Fuller, *Tanks in the Great War*, p.244; Jones, *The War in the Air*, Vol IV, pp.416–7.

17 Brigadier General Sir James E. Edmonds (ed), *History of the Great War Military Operations, France and Belgium 191, Volume IV, 8th August–26th September. The Franco-British Offensive* (London: HMSO, 1947), pp.21–5, pp.30–1.

18 Archibald Armar Montgomery-Massingberd, *The Story of the Fourth Army in the Battles of the Hundred Days, August 8th to November 11th, 1918* (London: Hodder and Stoughton ltd, 1920), p.x.

allocated each to 3rd, 4th and 5th Tank Brigades. No. 8 Squadron was tasked to cover the last hour of the tanks' final approach march, keeping the tank unit 'constantly informed … as to the progress of the battle' by dropping messages, and to 'help tanks whenever possible'.[19] These tasks under the headings of contact and counterattack patrols and offensive action were later included in SS.135.[20]

There was also a continuing need for aerial photography. For example, in preparation for the attack on Drocourt Quéant Line (see below for details), 3rd Tank Brigade asked urgently for vertical photographs of part of this system, and three Armstrong Whitworth FK.8 were sent on this task with a Sopwith Camel fighter escort. However, the latter were so heavily engaged that the FK.8s had to continue on their own, fight off seven German scouts and although they took the photos, they came back riddled with bullets. No. 8 Squadron in 1918 took 7,424 negatives.[21]

The first task was from 0250 hours, achieved by three aircraft covering the final move of the tanks and dropping bombs. The second task was delayed by heavy mist until 0830 when the first No. 8 Squadron RAF intelligence report was dropped to Advanced HQ Tank Corps and other reports followed to it and to tank brigade HQs.[22] Heavy mist hampered air support during the first phase but also covered the advance. The third task, 'To help tanks whenever possible', would prove more difficult. The initial advance to the first objective, the Green Line, had been covered by a rolling barrage and thick mist. However, the subsequent advance from 0820 was beyond field artillery range and would be dependent on a combination of guns brought forward, aircraft and a limited heavy artillery barrage. Unfortunately, the mist was so thick, until it started to clear between 0800 and 0900, that after dropping a message informing 4th Tank Brigade HQ about the advance of its tanks, West could only land at the third attempt despite rockets to guide him in, and he hit a hanger in doing so.[23]

Although the continued attack was in general a decisive success, the following incident illustrates the problems facing the tanks when both artillery and air support were unavailable due to, in the case of the aircraft, the mist not clearing enough to fly until about 0900. At 0820, as the mist was clearing at ground level, 11 tanks of A Company 13th Tank Battalion and two Australian infantry battalions came up a slope to cross the Green Line and move east on the open plain. One thousand yards east of them, the two surviving German *6th Battery 58th Regiment* 77mm field guns were pushed out from their concealed gun positions, opened direct fire and in the ten minutes or so that it would have taken the Mark V tanks to cover the 1000 yards,

19 TNA: AIR 1/688/21/20/8: 'History of 8 Squadron, R.A.F', p.24.
20 General Staff, *S.S. 135 The Division in the Attack* (France: GHQ, 1919), Appendix C Co-operation between Aircraft and Tanks.
21 TNA: AIR 1/1671/204/109/26: 'History of tank and aeroplane co-operation,' p.13; TNA: AIR 1/688/21/20/8: 'History of 8 Squadron, R.A.F', p.35.
22 Fuller, *Tanks in the Great War,* p.246.
23 TNA: AIR 1/688/21/20/8: 'History of 8 Squadron, R.A.F', p.25.

Armstrong Whitworth FK.8 C8594 in which Captain F.M.F. West of No. 8 Squadron RAF fought the action at the Battle of Amiens and was awarded the VC. (RAF Museum: PC72/115/8)

knocked six of them out. Despite this, the surviving tanks and Australian infantry eventually overran the guns and continued to success and the second objective.[24] Once the mist had cleared, four aircraft of No. 8 Squadron took off and delivered many messages. The squadron aircraft also used 81 × 25lb bombs and 6,570 SAA rounds against German infantry and batteries.[25]

The lessons of Amiens and the advance to the Hindenburg Line (21 August to 26 September)

No. 8 Squadron had fulfilled its prime role, the passage of information, with success but the Battle of Amiens had confirmed the urgent need to deal with the main threat to tanks: German field artillery, usually 77mm guns, acting as anti-tank guns

24 Geoffrey Vesey Holt and David Pearson FSA, 'Duel of the Roman Road – a micro-analysis of an artillery-tank action at the Battle of Amiens, Part 1', *The Western Front Association Stand To!,* 125 (2022), pp.13–21; Geoffrey Vesey Holt and David Pearson FSA, 'Duel of the Roman Road – a micro-analysis of an artillery-tank action at the Battle of Amiens, Part 2', *The Western Front Association Stand To!* 126 (2022), pp.2–10.
25 TNA: AIR 1/688/21/20/8: 'History of 8 Squadron, R.A.F', p.27.

particularly once the advance went beyond field artillery range. As Leigh-Mallory subsequently reflected:

> The German army clearly perceived the tank menace and expended considerable energy on anti-tank tactics. Since these anti-tank guns were well concealed and did not generally open fire until the tanks were within 400 to 1,000 metres, there was not time for indirect fire artillery to respond even if it had been available and ground attack aircraft were 'the only really feasible means to assist.'[26]

As a result, directly after Amiens, Major General Hugh Elles CB, General Officer Commanding (GOC) Tank Corps in France, asked Major General John Salmond CMG, DSO and Bar, GOC the RAF in the Field 'if the RAF could assist in silencing these guns.'[27] In response, No. 73 Squadron, a fighter squadron with single-seater Camels, was attached to the Tank Corps in this role. It was probably selected because it had extensive recent experience of 'low-level strafing' and bombing during the March Retreat 'to the exclusion of all other work', in support of the French in June and July and at Amiens.[28] Also it was commanded by the 22-year-old Major C W Le Blanc-Smith DFC, who would have seven victories by the end of the war.[29]

There was also a requirement to develop associated tactical doctrine and procedures to deal with the anti-tank guns. Colonel Henry Karslake, Fuller's successor as the Tank Corps Chief of Staff and a gunner,[30] and Leigh-Mallory, 'went over the Amiens battlefield thoroughly and examined the positions of German anti-tank guns during the various stages of the fighting.' This reconnaissance, combined with a detailed study of maps and air photographs and, from 2 September, a captured German order which detailed 'their policy for the disposition of these guns' enabled the creation of maps showing with red markings likely anti-tank gun areas. Each No. 73 Squadron Camel pilot had allocated danger areas to watch and 'only about 2,000 yards of front to watch' rather than, as in the past, roving freely. This system worked well. To achieve this, No. 73 Squadron had to be specially trained in low-flying and 'accustoming themselves on the appearance of the trench area from 3,000 feet and below.'[31] A Tank and Air coordination paragraph was included in most Tank Brigade operations orders.[32] Tank

26 TNA: AIR 1/2388/228/11/80: 'Account of war experiences: Leigh-Mallory', p.15; TNA: AIR 1/1671/204/109/26: 'History of tank and aeroplane co-operation', p.9.
27 TNA: AIR 1/2388/228/11/80: 'Account of war experiences: Leigh-Mallory', p.15.
28 TNA: AIR 1/694/21/20/73: 'History of 73 Squadron', R.A.F.
29 Maurice Le Blanc-Smith, <https://www.theaerodrome.com/aces/england/le_blanc-smith.php> accessed 27 Oct. 2023.
30 Nicholas Smart, *Biographical Dictionary of British Generals of the Second World War*, (Barnsley: Leo Cooper Ltd, 2005), p.175.
31 TNA: AIR 1/2388/228/11/80: 'Account of war experiences: Leigh-Mallory', pp.15–7; Fuller, *Tanks in the Great War*, pp.247–8.
32 TNA: WO 95/99/4: '1st Brigade Tank Corps HQ Mar to Aug 1918 Mar, p.99, addendum to 1st Tank Brigade Order No 37', 19 Aug. 1918.

Brigade report on operations commented on aeroplane cooperation. For example, 5th Tank Brigade's report on operations between 18 to 24 August commented that No. 8 Squadron provided several very valuable messages and both Squadrons engaged and silenced several batteries firing on tanks. It went on: 'There is no doubt the aeroplane protection afforded the tanks assisted very largely in the success of the operations.'[33]

The two squadrons moved on 18 August and collocated at an airfield behind the front between Albert and Arras in preparation for a Third Army offensive on 21 August. This offensive was organised in haste under pressure from Marshal Ferdinand Foch, the Supreme Allied Commander since 26 March 1918, to maintain pressure on the Germans.[34] It had a different concept of operations to Amiens: the advance on the first day, 21 August, was limited to 4,400 yards, well within field artillery range. A pause the next day allowed the field artillery to be brought forward, to be able to hit the Germans' main defensive position during the advance the next day, 23 August.[35] The attack on 21 August was by seven frontline divisions supported by 1,294 artillery pieces, ten fighter squadrons and 156 tanks.[36] The shortage of Mark V and medium tanks helps explain why the six tank battalions in the offensive were not only under-strength but that two battalions had to be equipped with obsolescent Mark IV tanks. The establishment strength was 240, comprising two medium and four 36 heavy tank battalions.[37]

The thick mist helped the advance to near the objective. However, as it lifted around 1100 hours, many tanks were hit by German anti-tank guns. For example, 3rd Tank Battalion Whippets were hit by isolated German anti-tank guns in the railway embankment near Achiet le Grand (four miles north-west of Bapaume). The possible locations of these guns had been selected for special attention and no doubt marked as red blobs on the special maps. The mist made it 'quite impossible for aircraft to leave the ground until 1100 am'. This, and the inexperience of No. 73 Squadron, reduced the effectiveness of the air support to the tanks on 21 August. One report gives a total of 103 tanks engaged but this includes three battalions in Fourth Army's area. The six battalions in Third Army's area should have had 240 tanks.[38]

33 TNA: WO 95/112/2: '5th Tank Brigade – Report on Operations of 18th September 1918 by 2nd Tank Battalion with IIIrd, Australian and IXth Corps', p.103.
34 Edmonds (ed), *History of the Great War, Vol. V*, pp.166–71.
35 J.P. Harris and Niall Barr (eds), *From Amiens to the Armistice: The BEF in the Hundred Days' Campaign, 8 August–11 November 1918* (London: Brassey's, 1998), p.125 and p.132.
36 Edmonds (ed), *History of the Great War, Vol. V, pp.180–1.* A Third Army source gave 1,478 artillery pieces (p.180, Note 4).
37 Tank Museum, Bovington (hereafter TM): E2007.2249: 'Summary of Tank Corps Operation between 15th September 1916 and 7th October 1918', Weekly Tank Notes [Published Version] No 17 to 21.
38 TNA: AIR 1/1671/204/109/26: 'History of tank and aeroplane co-operation,' p.11; TNA: AIR 1/688/21/20/8: 'History of 8 Squadron, R.A.F', p.29; Number of tanks based on TM: E2007.2249: 'Summary of Tank Corps Operation between 15th September 1916 and 7th October 1918'.

Sopwith F.1 Camel, the British aircraft most used for ground strafing, including by No. 46 Squadron and No. 73 Squadron. (RAF Museum: X003-2602/15216)

The 23 August proved a much better day for the Squadrons. By 0500 hours, there was just enough light for the first aircraft to take off. By 0650, tanks had reached the Arras to Bapaume road and came under fire from anti-guns just south and south-east of Boyelles (seven miles north of Bapaume on the road to Arras). Aircraft from the squadrons were able to locate 'many anti-tank guns' and several were destroyed. No. 8 Squadron dropped 111 bombs and fired 18,000 SAA rounds and No. 73 Squadron 114 bombs and 13,200 rounds. For example, No. 73 Squadron's Camels silenced with 1,500 rounds a firing battery a mile south south-east of Boyelles. Comparison of ammunition consumption with the Tank Corps is difficult because of the patchy Tank Corps records. A Mark V tank carried 207 6-pounder shells and 5,700 SAA rounds or 14,100 rounds.[39] However, the aircraft had a flexibility of movement and observation that allowed them to attack targets with relative precision and enabling them to use their munitions effectively. The advance continued in the afternoon. The Camels saw German batteries coming into action near Béhagnies (three miles north of Bapaume on the Arras road). They dropped 24 bombs and fired nearly 2,000 rounds at them, '…causing the greatest confusion. Several limbers were overturned, and horses stampeded, and the personnel scattered in all directions.' The No. 8 Squadron aircraft kept brigade and battalion HQs informed of the progress of their tanks.[40] As a result of this support, the British Official History subsequently

39 Fletcher, *Mark V Tank,* p.27.
40 TNA: AIR 1/1671/204/109/26: 'History of tank and aeroplane co-operation', pp.11–2; TNA: AIR: 1/688/21/20/8: 'History of 8 Squadron', RAF, p.30.

recorded that 'Third Army had had a very successful day … and had taken over 5,000 prisoners.'[41]

It is worth noting that from 23 August onwards, the element of surprise was lost. The advance continued with Third Army advancing towards the Hindenburg Line and its north; the Canadian Corps, now in First Army, advancing from 26 August east from near Arras towards an extension of the Hindenburg Line, the Drocourt Quéant Line. It took the Canadian Corps, in hard fighting, until 1 September to reach it. 3rd Tank Brigade, and Nos. 8 and 73 Squadrons were transferred to support it. On 2 September three divisions, supported by 20 field artillery brigades, 11 heavy artillery brigades, 59 Mark V tanks (against a minimum establishment strength of 108) and 11 RAF squadrons, breached the Drocourt Quéant Line against determined German resistance. Nos. 8 and 73 Squadron aircraft were unable to silence German guns that were firing because of the strength of their emplacements. However, during a pause in the fighting an aircraft called for and successful adjusted artillery fire on these guns and No. 73 Squadron attacked numerous targets, dropping 136 bombs and firing 19,050 SAA rounds.[42]

The second breaching of the Hindenburg Line (27 September to 8 October)

A pause in fighting followed as the Germans fell back to the Hindenburg Line which allowed for recovery. No. 8 Squadron had between 21 August and 2 September lost 14 aircraft, or assuming 18 aircraft on strength, a 77 percent casualty rate compared to 20 percent casualties of the 558 tanks that went into action over the same period.[43] The lull also allowed the two squadrons to visit the battlefield, confirm their knowledge of the tanks and visit the tank battalions 'to find out to what extent they had benefitted from the messages we had dropped'. From then on, messages were dropped on battalion dropping zones. It was also agreed that tanks would fire a coloured flare to indicate a possible or actual threat, and this would cue aircraft to suppress it.[44]

The next major BEF battle was the second breaching of the Hindenburg Line by First, Third and Fourth Armies from 27 September to 8 October. This was a gruelling but decisive battle; it was the last major battle of the Tank Corps and it presented particular problems for the Tank Corps. The 14 tank battalions in action had about 240 tanks only (against an establishment strength of 600) to support three armies. To

41 Edmonds (ed), *History of the Great War, Volume V*, p.233.

42 Edmonds (ed), *History of the Great War, Volume V*, pp.397–398; TNA: AIR 1/1671/204/109/26: 'History of tank and aeroplane co-operation', pp.14–5; Number of tanks: TNA: WO 95/104/5: p.5, p.9 and p.11.

43 TNA: AIR 1/1671/204/109/26: 'History of tank and aeroplane co-operation', p.15; TM: E2007.2249: 'Appendix A: Summary of Casualties in Tanks and Personnel 8 Aug to 24 Oct', Weekly Tank Notes No 21, 4 Jan 1918

44 TNA: AIR 1/1671/204/109/26: 'History of tank and aeroplane co-operation', p.15.

cover the wide front, No. 8 Squadron concentrated on Fourth Army's front, and the main axis of advance, with an advanced landing ground on Third Army's front. This allowed the Squadron to drop 'a great many messages' on 27 September, but on 29 September mist initially and low cloud all day hampered air operations. The weather would do likewise in October and November. Nevertheless, No. 8 Squadron managed to drop messages and one FK.8 dropped a message on some tanks telling them that the village of Bony (18 miles south-east of Cambrai) was still in German hands and watched as a few minutes later several tanks moved towards Bony. Both squadrons attacked anti-tank guns, with No. 73 Squadron dropping 88 bombs and firing 14,000 rounds of SAA.[45]

From the Hindenburg Line to the Armistice (9 October to 11 November)

The next major action was on 8 October when Third and Fourth Armies finally broke into open ground against strong German rear guards. The two squadrons supported 82 tanks and the following action illustrates their contribution in this battle. In its first action the newly reconstituted 66th Division advanced north-east towards its final objective, Serain (12 miles south south-east of Cambrai). No. 35 Squadron (FK.8) covered this attack from 0600 to 0800 hours with an effective smokescreen west of Serain made up of 40lb phosphorous bombs dropped about 220 yards apart at intervals of about 20 minutes.[46] Just after 0800 hours, and the capture of the first objective, 11 Whippet medium tanks of 3rd Tank Battalion raced (they could do 8mph) either side and into Serain followed by 5th Connaught Rangers, 9th Manchester and a company of 18th King's.[47]

A No. 8 Squadron pilot, Lieutenant Trites, observed the tanks attacking Serain:

> As the tanks were approaching, we dropped bombs on various parties of Germans who were in the village. The tanks were then surrounding the village, one going right into the centre of it; a second attacked the orchard to the south, mopping up parties of Germans; whilst a third came round the north of the village and was approaching a small valley in which were 200 to 300 Germans covered by a stretch of dead ground. On seeing the tank approaching the Germans fled eastwards, whereupon we flew towards them firing our machine guns, doing great execution.[48]

45 TNA: AIR 1/688/21/20/8: 'History of 8 Squadron, R.A.F', pp.32–3; TNA: AIR 1/1671/204/109/26: 'History of tank and aeroplane co-operation', pp.16–20 cover in some detail actions 29 September to 9 October.

46 Jones, *The War in the Air*, Vol IV, p.230 and Vol VI, p.536.

47 Edmonds (ed), *History of the Great War, Volume V*, p.195; TNA: WO 95/104/6: 3rd Tank Battalion War History, p.95.

48 Fuller, *Tanks in the Great War*, p.249. Fuller does not name the pilot whereas TNA: AIR 1/1671/204/109/26: 'History of tank and aeroplane co-operation', p.20 does, with almost the same description of the action as Fuller.

To complete this example of the versatility of the support given, Trites then dropped an update message to HQ 3rd Tank Battalion. Five out of 33 Whippet crewman were casualties. Seven Whippets rallied. Serain was cleared by 1900 hours.[49]

The Germans then withdrew to a hastily, but effectively, improvised defensive line on the River Selle which runs roughly north-south through Le Cateau. The Battle of the Selle was the last major Tank Corps battle with 48 and 37 tanks in action on 17 and 23 October. Despite adverse weather, the squadrons continued to provide useful support. On 13 October, a No. 8 Squadron aircraft conducted, at the request of the Tank Corps, a detailed and successful reconnaissance of possible crossing points.[50] On 17 October, despite mist followed by very low cloud and finally rain, No. 73 Squadron dropped 48 bombs and fired 5,000 rounds of SAA on anti-tank guns and an No. 8 Squadron pilot and observer were awarded DFCs for managing, despite darkness and torrential rain, to bring back:

> [...]most valuable information; shoot down a German two seater aircraft over Le Cateau and the land in conditions that were so bad that the aerodrome guiding lights were fired up to guide them because it was assumed that no aircraft could possibly be up.[51]

Despite the very bad weather the two squadrons continued to support the Tank Corps until its last tank action on 6 November.

During this period No. 8 Squadron suffered 44 casualties, including 10 killed and nine injured between 8 August and 11 November or 122 percent of the 36 aircrew in 18 squadron aircraft. This compares to about 60 percent of Tank Corps fighting personnel over same period. Fuller stated that:

> Such actions as these [the one at Serain] were of daily occurrence and they only went to prove what the headquarters of the Tank Corps had long held –namely, that the cooperation of aeroplanes with tanks is of incalculable importance, the aeroplanes protecting the tanks and the tanks protecting the infantry. In the future, no doubt, not only will messages be dropped and hostile guns silenced, but the commanders of tank battalions will be carried in the air, these officers communicating with their machines by means of wireless telephony, and supplies of petrol will be transported by means of aeroplane for the replenishment of the tanks.[52]

49 TNA: WO 95/106/3/2: '3rd (Light) Tank Battalion Report on Attack on Serain on 8th October 1918, in Co-Operation with 66th Division, VIII Corps', pp.1–5.

50 See TNA: AIR 1/1671/204/109/26: 'History of tank and aeroplane co-operation', p.21, for a detailed description of the reconnaissance and its results.

51 TNA: AIR 1/1671/204/109/26: 'History of tank and aeroplane co-operation', p.21.

52 Fuller, *Tanks in the Great War*, p.249.

Fuller's comments about the importance of air support are endorsed by Tank Brigade and Battalion reports. For example, 8th Battalion commented on the 'Many instances of aircraft spotting and knocking out anti-tank and field guns'.[53]

Conclusion

The experience of air support for the Tank Corps in 1918 demonstrated the importance of air-land cooperation. Where air-land cooperation was effective in 1918, the Tank Corps greatly benefited as demonstrated after the Battle of Amiens during the battles from 21 August to 8 October that led to the second breaching of the Hindenburg Lines. The development of this cooperation is also an object lesson in how to build cooperation between two organisations at the cutting edge of technology. The Battle of Cambrai had demonstrated the vulnerability of the tank due to its slow speed and lack of protection against anti-tank artillery, the lack of intra-Tank Corps effective communications systems and the need for closer cooperation between air support and the tanks.

In response to the Tank Corps' request after Cambrai, No. 8 Squadron RAF was attached to the Tank Corps in June 1918. Its squadron leader, Leigh-Mallory, drove forward cooperation with the Tank Corps through trials, training, and close cooperation. The roles for aircraft were confirmed before Amiens: covering the approach of tanks before battle through overhead flights, passage of information from frontline to HQs and help to tanks particularly in defeating the growing German anti-tank guns. No. 8 Squadron fulfilled the first two roles at the Battle of Amiens but the heavy tank losses to German anti-tank guns remained a capability gap. The allocation of a fighter squadron, No. 73 Squadron, and the development of tactical doctrine filled this gap. There were clear lessons for those who wished to absorb them: air-land cooperation combined with the mobility of the tank could transform the battlefield.

In 1940, the Germans demonstrated that they had learnt the importance of air-land cooperation. *Generalleutnant* Heinz Guderian, commanding XIX *Panzerkorps*, was 'personally in touch with the leader of the close support planes … and with the air group.' A joint air-land plan for the Meuse crossing was agreed with timed attacks against French batteries 'to force the enemy gunners to take cover.' The Meuse was crossed and his three armoured divisions reached the sea, cutting the Allied armies in two.[54]

53 WO 95/112/5 1917: 5th Brigade Tank Corps. 8th Battalion. War Experiences, Chapter IV. Section 5.

54 General Heinz Guderian, *Panzer Leader* (London: Michael Joseph, 1952), pp.97–8, p.102, p.104.

5

'New Vistas of Usefulness': William C. Sherman and the Development of Ground Attack Aviation in the United States, 1919–1927

Sebastian H. Lukasik

A veteran of the Great War who spent much of the 1920s as an instructor at the fledgling US Air Service Tactical School, Lieutenant Colonel William Carrington Sherman (1888–1927) has long occupied a peripheral place in the historiography of early air power development in the United States. It is not for nothing that historian Tami Davis Biddle refers to him as America's 'unsung air theorist'.[1] When historians remember him at all, it is usually as a member of the professional and intellectual circle of strategic bombing enthusiasts who surrounded the much more famous and notorious Brigadier General William 'Billy' Mitchell. Viewed in this light, Sherman emerges as a little more than a bit player in the story of the development of ideas concerning strategic attack that Mitchell and so many of his acolytes championed in the inter-war period.

Sherman's contribution to this process is usually depicted as resting on two pillars. From a socio-cultural perspective, historical literature presents him as an integral member of the 'bomber mafia' whose advocacy of the strategic attack mission at the expense of all other missions allegedly came to dominate American air power thought well into the second half of the twentieth century. More to the point, several historians rightly credit Sherman with the authorship of the first coherent articulation of what would subsequently become known as the industrial fabric or key-node theory of targeting, one that stressed striking from the air sensitive elements of an enemy nation's industrial and logistical system far behind the frontlines.[2]

1 Tami Davis Biddle, *Air Power and Warfare: A Century of Theory and History* (Carlisle, Pennsylvania: U.S. Army War College Press, 2019), p.23.

2 Phillip S. Meilinger, *Airmen and Airpower Theory: A Review of the Sources* (Maxwell AFB, Alabama: Air University Press, 2001), p.111; Tami Davis Biddle, *Rhetoric and Reality in Air Warfare: The Evolution of British and American Ideas about Strategic Bombing, 1914–1945*

Lieutenant Thomas DeWitt Milling and Lieutenant Sherman in airplane at Texas City after breaking the American duration and distance record, 28 March 1913. (Library of Congress: 2002698465)

Sherman's authorship of the 'industrial web theory' is beyond dispute, but the tendency to boil down his historical importance to little more than one of Billy Mitchell's intellectual satellites and an uncritical advocate of strategic bombing does little justice to the complexity of his ideas or the value of his contribution to air power thought. Sherman's air power vision transcended a simple advocacy of strategic bombing. In fact, it was his ideas concerning ground attack aviation that may be said to have represented the conceptual and functional centrepiece

(Princeton, New Jersey: Princeton University Press, 2002), p.140; Stephen L. McFarland, *America's Pursuit of Precision Bombing, 1910–1945* (Washington, DC: Smithsonian Institute Press, 1995); Michael S. Sherry, *The Rise of American Air Power: The Creation of Armageddon* (New Haven Connecticut: Yale University Press, 1987), pp.51–8; Peter R. Faber, 'Interwar U.S. Army Aviation and the Air Corps Tactical School: Incubators of American Airpower', in Philip S. Meilinger, (ed), *The Paths of Heaven: The Evolution of Airpower Theory* (Maxwell AFB, Alabama: Air University Press, 1997), pp.183–238; David E. Johnson, *Fast Tanks and Heavy Bombers: Innovation in the U.S. Army, 1917–1945* (Ithaca, New York: Cornell University Press, 1998), pp.153–66; James P. Tate, *The Army and Its Air Corps: Army Policy toward Aviation, 1919–1941* (Maxwell AFB, Alabama: Air University Press, 1998), pp.157–70; Biddle, *Rhetoric and Reality*, pp.153–70.

Martin MB-2. The MB-2 was the US Army Air Service's primary heavy bomber when William C. Sherman was writing, n.d. (RAF Museum: X003-2602/18532)

of his air power thought. Anchored firmly in his experiences of the Great War, Sherman's ideas about ground attack found expression in three major publications he authored between 1919 and 1927. Written in 1919, the *Tentative Manual for the Employment of Air Service* sought to harness the historical experiences of the Great War for the purpose of distilling general principles and 'best practices' underpinning the employment of air power in wartime and represented the first attempt in American history at formulating a coherent air power doctrine.[3] *Training Regulation 440-15*, which Sherman wrote in 1921 and revised in 1923, built on the foundations he set down in his *Tentative Manual* and addressed the employment of air forces across the broad spectrum of missions, from observation, through attack, bombardment, and pursuit.[4] The document sealed Sherman's reputation as a foundational figure of American air power thought when, in 1923, the US Army Air Service sanctioned it as an expression of its official doctrine. Finally, in 1926, Sherman published *Air Warfare*, a book that introduced his air power ideas to a non-specialist national audience.[5]

Although they reflect a nearly decade-long process of intellectual gestation, the three works exhibit a remarkable degree of conceptual and thematic continuity, with only minor details subject to modification over time. One of the most important patterns emerging from all three is the primacy of ground attack in Sherman's air power thought. The ground attack mission encapsulated in microcosm Sherman's

3 Reproduced in Maurer Maurer (ed), *The U.S. Air Service in World War I: Volume 2, Early Concepts of Military Aviation* (Maxwell AFB, Ala.: Albert F. Simpson Historical Research Center; Washington: Office of Air Force History, Headquarters USAF, 1978), pp.313–410.
4 Training Regulation No. 440-15, *Fundamental Principles for the Employment of the Air Service* (Washington DC: Department of the Army, 26 January 1926).
5 William Carrington Sherman, *Air Warfare* (New York, NY: The Ronald Press, 1926).

understanding of the relationship between air power and surface forces, opening up, as he put it, 'new vistas of usefulness' for air and ground forces alike.[6]

Unusually for an air power thinker associated with independent, long-range strategic attack, Sherman argued that 'in the future, as in the past, the final decision in war must be made by [the] man on the ground, willing to come hand to hand with the enemy.' In consequence, it was 'the role of the Air Service ... to aid the chief combatant, the infantry.' But this did not in any way diminish Sherman's corollary argument, namely his insistence that air units function as a distinct combat arm. This imperative placed a premium on the ability of soldiers and airmen to develop a mutual understanding of each other's respective warfighting domains and domain-based perspectives. Thus, on the one hand, 'the Air Service must know infantry and its assistants.' On the other hand, Sherman asserted that the 'general officers and their staffs cannot hope to produce the most efficient knowledge, tactical combinations [*sic*], unless they have a thorough knowledge not alone of infantry, but of its assistant arms, which include the Air Service.'[7] Sherman's insistence on this point represented an early manifestation of what would become two defining attributes of his mature air power thought. The first was an emphasis on the need to distinguish between 'air service' and 'air force' – the former a supporting, the latter an independent arm – that would recur again and again in his writings. The second consisted of the corollary emphasis on the need to conceptualise air power in terms of all-arms integration as the key to maximising the battlefield effectiveness of the air weapon, rather than solely with reference to strategic attack.

Proceeding from the premise that war was, above all, a contest of combatants' morale and opposing wills, Sherman argued that 'in the future, as in the past, the final decision in war must be made by man on the ground, willing to come hand to hand with the enemy. When the infantry loses, the Army loses. It is, therefore, the role of the Air Service, as well as that of the other arms, to aid the chief combatant: the Infantry.'[8] Sherman's wartime service at division and corps-level headquarters provided him not only with valuable staff experience, but also attuned him to the challenges of land warfare, as well as the difficulties inherent in generating conceptual and cognitive alignment between soldiers and the airmen tasked with supporting them. Writing shortly after the Great War, he underscored the need for the development of effective frameworks of air-ground cooperation as key to air power's ability to contribute to the land battle.

In Sherman's mind, ground attack aviation functioned as the connective tissue between 'auxiliary' aviation on the one hand, and independent, long-range strategic attack on the other. On the one hand, Sherman insisted that 'the primary duty of attack aviation is still determined by the demands of the infantry.'[9] Ground attack

6 Sherman, *Air Warfare*, p.154.
7 Sherman, *Tentative Manual*, p.I.I.2.
8 Sherman, *Tentative Manual*, p.I.I.2.
9 Sherman, *Air Warfare*, p.154.

assets represented the ultimate form of a battlefield 'force multiplier', affording ground commanders a set of capabilities endowed with remarkable mobility, responsiveness, firepower, and capacity for effecting surprise. Collectively, these characteristics rendered attack aviation 'the arm, *par excellence*, of opportunity' on the battlefield.[10] For this reason, ground attack units, Sherman argued, were 'peculiarly adapted to form a mobile reserve', an asset whose commitment to battle should take place at the discretion of the higher command 'for the purpose of meeting unforeseen contingencies, or of exploiting unexpected opportunities.'[11]

On the other hand, Sherman made it clear that attack aviation's mandate to work *with* and in *support of* ground forces did not imply a subordination *to* ground forces, either functionally or organisationally. There was no denying, Sherman acknowledged, that the 'primary objectives' of attack aviation 'are determined by the direct or indirect needs of ground troops.' But he objected to the tendency to view attack aviation as 'merely a special form of artillery' or as nothing other than 'a machine gun organization of rather unusual mobility.'[12] Conceptualising attack aviation in such terms marginalised its unique properties – especially speed, surprise, and superior view of the battlefield – while reinforcing the 'widespread tendency', which Sherman emphatically deplored, 'to parcel out attack aviation among the infantry units, down to include the division and even the brigade.' Not only did such a tendency violate the principle of mass, it also detracted from attack aviation's stature as the ultimate form of a flexible, centrally controlled reserve. Unlike a reserve consisting of ground units, which could be committed to combat only once during an engagement, a central reserve consisting of attack aviation assets could be thrown into the scales of battle again and again. After carrying out its initial mission, 'the attack unit returns to its aerodrome, and in a short time after landing – twenty minutes to an hour – may be given another task, its organization intact and its power undiminished, except for the airplanes actually destroyed in the first sortie.'[13] To break up attack aviation assets and distribute them along lower command echelons would have cancelled out this inherent flexibility and responsiveness.

The same principle held true for the selection of optimal targets for attack aviation units. Though its ultimate purpose was to support the ground scheme of manoeuvre, Sherman argued, attack aviation's highest utility did not consist in providing 'immediate and close support to the leading waves of infantry.'[14] To do so would conspire to dilute and diminish its flexibility as a reserve force and, by implication, as 'a force of opportunity'. In what he posited as yet another argument in favour of centralising the control of ground attack assets under a higher command echelon, Sherman asserted that as far as attack aviation was concerned, its optimal targets were to be found

10 Sherman, *Air Warfare*, p.157.
11 Sherman, *Air Warfare*, pp.171–2.
12 Sherman, *Air Warfare*, p.156.
13 Sherman, *Air Warfare*, p.159.
14 Sherman, *Air Warfare*, pp.171–2.

behind rather than directly over the frontline; in other words, not 'in that part of the combat zone for which the smaller units are responsible, but farther in rear of the area, where decisions for counter measures come within the sphere of responsibility of higher commanders.'[15] These targets included columns of troops on the march, troop assembly areas, concentrations of artillery, and railroads. Sherman also envisioned using ground attack aviation in what today would be called the suppression of enemy defences (SEAD) and anti-shipping missions, although he conceded that the latter fell more properly within the purview of bombardment aviation.[16]

Sherman's ideas about targeting in the context of attack aviation reflected the intellectual debt that he and other American air power thinkers owed to French air power doctrine and application during the Great War. Unlike their British and German counterparts, both of whom used attack aviation to directly target the enemy's frontline troops, French airmen prioritised the use of attack aviation in what today would be called the air interdiction (AI) mission – leveraging air ground attack assets to strike targets behind the front in an effort to sever the flow of supplies and reinforcements from the enemy's rear areas to its frontline units.[17] In practice, this implied prioritising much the same target set that Sherman emphasised as the ideal focal point for attack aviation: troop concentrations, key road and rail junctions, supply dumps, and command and control nodes located behind the firing line. While French airmen have been criticised for their tendency to neglect CAS at the expense of AI, their approach made a lot of sense in light of how flexible, responsive, and accurate artillery had become by the end of the conflict; ground-based fires proved much more effective in supporting frontline infantry than air power, with its limited CAS capabilities at the time. At the same time, targets located behind the frontline were less heavily defended and easier to locate than those at the front. Interdiction targets could also be located and identified more easily given that they were not as well concealed as those in the combat zone proper. Finally, attacking targets far behind the front significantly reduced the possibility of fratricide.[18]

Regardless of the choice of targets, Sherman remained firmly convinced that whatever kinetic impact attack aviation might be capable of effecting against the enemy's troops and materiel, its greatest advantage consisted of the extent to which it affected the opposing side's morale. Reiterating his central theme and applying it to the issue of ground attack, Sherman restated that 'war is essentially a conflict of morale', and that, consequently, 'a study of the moral effect of any weapon is certainly not secondary in practical importance to an investigation of its physical powers.'[19] This was especially

15 Sherman, *Air Warfare*, p.172.
16 Sherman, *Air Warfare*, pp.163–71.
17 Richard Hallion, *Strike from the Sky: The History of Battlefield Air Attack, 1911–1945* (Washington, DC: Smithsonian Institution Press, 1989), pp.19–20; Lee Kennett, 'Developments to 1939', in Benjamin Franklin Cooling (ed), *Case Studies in the Development of Close Air Support* (Washington, DC: Office of Air Force History, 1990), pp.16–8.
18 Kennett, 'Developments to 1939', p.53.
19 Sherman, *Air Warfare*, p.160.

the case, he claimed, with attack aviation. 'In estimating the value of such attacks,' he claimed as early as 1919, 'we must again bear in mind that an army is defeated not by destroying it, but by destroying its morale.'[20] He advanced this argument on both empirical and theoretical grounds. The Great War, he pointed out, offered such extensive testimony 'on the moral effect of attacks from the air ... that no attempt can be made, in the limits of this work, to embrace more than a very small part of it.' Troops subjected to aerial attack in that conflict, he claimed, invariably gave in to 'a complete surrender to the desire to escape.'[21] In keeping with his insistence on analytical rigor and the 'scientific spirit', Sherman acknowledged that the limited historical examples he provided to support his claims could not 'be accepted as an invariable index of future results' without further analysis. He admitted that 'some of the moral effect was due to the very novelty of this method of attack', a condition that might not carry over into 'the next war' which 'will assuredly see all ground troops well trained to withstand this new form of attack', a reality that could undoubtedly dull some of the moral effects of attack aviation.[22]

All the same, Sherman remained confident that attack aviation would retain its power to undermine the morale of ground troops, no matter how well trained. 'Much of the effect,' he predicted, 'will still remain: for the element of surprise will frequently enter into the situation.' Again, proper training might help diminish the effects of a surprise air attack, and assist troops in recovering quickly, 'but it is doubtful if even the best of training can rob surprise of its full demoralizing effect during the actual time of its duration.'[23] Sherman marshalled two items of theoretical evidence that, no matter how tenuous in retrospect, served as the principal pillars sustaining this claim. First, he argued that attack aviation exploited the atavistic human fear of being assaulted by an opponent who enjoyed the advantages inherent in holding the high ground. Though he conceded that this point amounted to little more than 'an unproved hypothesis', he nonetheless asserted that 'there is indeed an abundance of evidence in support of the believe [*sic*] that man has an inherent feeling of inadequacy in the face of an enemy whose physical location is the higher.'[24]

What was true of individual soldiers facing air attack was equally true of armies at the organisational level. Here, Sherman resorted to the organic analogies so popular with early twentieth century military thinkers such as J.F.C. Fuller and Basil H. Liddell-Hart, who frequently drew analogies between military organisations and living organisms. Though there is no evidence that Sherman was familiar with Fuller's concept of the 'brain of an army', first articulated in the context of Fuller's famous 'Plan 1919', he used a similar analogy to underscore his arguments concerning the moral effects of attack aviation on enemy ground forces. 'The morale of an army may be compared to the human body,' he echoed Fuller; 'to destroy it, it is necessary to

20 Sherman, *Tentative Manual*, p.I.I.10.
21 Sherman, *Air Warfare*, p.160.
22 Sherman, *Air Warfare*, p.161, p.162.
23 Sherman, *Air Warfare*, 162.
24 Sherman, *Air Warfare*, 163.

destroy only one of several of its component parts. The battle then resolves itself into an attempt, by a crushing blow, to destroy but a limited portion of an enemy's army, while holding over the remainder the threat of impending destruction.'[25] Subsequent historical experience showed Sherman's conclusion about the moral effects of ground attack to be ambivalent at best. But his depiction of military organisations as organic entities anticipated the work of such theorists as John Warden and John Boyd, both of whom visualised enemy forces and societies as systems, and who posited that their defeat could best be affected by means of paralysis rather than physical destruction.[26]

Given his interest in 'tactical' aviation, the inter-war air power thinker Sherman resembled most was neither Douhet nor Mitchell, but Amadeo Mecozzi, the Italian theorist who was Douhet's greatest intellectual antagonist. Like Sherman, Mecozzi emphatically rejected the vision of air power as a tool of total war wielded against civilians. Instead, he articulated a paradigm that privileged 'assault aviation' – an 'inherently joint' concept that stressed the primacy of ground attack and aerial interdiction in support of the ground scheme of manoeuvre and underscored the synergy between air and surface forces.[27]

The resemblance between Sherman and Mecozzi's ideas was likely coincidental – there is no evidence the former was familiar with the latter. But the similarity suggests two important points. First, it shows that just as there existed in the inter-war period a transnational, trans-Atlantic conversation about strategic air power, so, too, there existed a parallel intellectual community dedicated to ideas about tactical air power – a community no less vibrant than its strategic bombing counterpart. Second, the care with which Sherman crafted and developed his ideas concerning 'auxiliary' aviation indicates that the time has come for historians to revise the established interpretation of American air power thought in the inter-war period as consisting almost exclusively of strategic bombing concepts. To be sure, bomber advocates unduly dominated the US Army Air Service/Corps professional military education at the ACTS and helped stifle the development and refinement of the attack mission.[28] This does not

25 Sherman, *Tentative Manual*, p.I.I.4.

26 David S. Fadok, 'John Boyd and John Warden: Airpower's Quest for Strategic Paralysis', in Phillip S. Meilinger (ed), *Paths of Heaven*, pp.357–98; Frans P.B. Osinga, 'The Enemy as a Complex Adaptive System,' in John Andreas Olsen (ed), *Airpower Reborn: John Boyd and Airpower in the Postmodern Era* (Annapolis, Maryland: Naval Institute Press, 2015), pp.93–127.

27 On Mecozzi, see James S. Corum, 'Airpower Thought in Continental Europe between the Wars', in Phillip S. Meilinger, (ed), *Paths of Heaven,* pp.160–1; John Gooch, *Mussolini and His Generals: The Armed Forces and Fascist Foreign Policy, 1922–1940* (New York: Cambridge University Press, 2007); Thomas Hippler, *Bombing the People: Giulio Douhet and the Foundations of Air-Power Strategy, 1884–1939*, First Edition (Cambridge: Cambridge University Press, 2013), pp.217–48.

28 Richard R. Muller, 'Close Air Support: The German, British, and American Experiences, 1918–1941', in Williamson Murray and Allan R. Millett (eds), *Military Innovation in the Interwar Period* (New York: Cambridge University Press, 1996), pp.172–80; Richard P. Hallion, *Strike from the Sky,* pp.46–54; Kennett, 'Developments to 1939', pp.59–60.

mean, however, that attack aviation did not have its intellectual champions – most notably Sherman. After his death, the cause of attack aviation at ACTS was carried on by George C. Kenney, who served as an ACTS instructor in the late 1920s, and who sought to keep alive a professional interest in this vital mission.[29] Enough of it remained vibrant to allow Kenney to successfully implement attack methods in the south-west Pacific theatre of the Second World War. As commander of the US Fifth Air Force, Kenney used attack aviation in keeping with Sherman's ideas on the subject: not in direct support of ground troops, but in deep aerial interdiction and anti-shipping roles.[30]

As this survey of Sherman's principal ideas has shown, his air power thought amounted to much more than a mere reflection or an echo of his more famous contemporaries' advocacy of strategic bombing. This is not to deny his authorship of the concept of 'vital centers' or his contribution to the development of what would eventually become, after his death, the so-called 'industrial web theory'. Nor is there any doubt about his enthusiasm about the latent potential of the long-range, multi-engine bomber as a strategic instrument. At the same time, however, the historiographical tendency to depict Sherman as, at best an acolyte and at worst a mere clone of Billy Mitchell's represents a distortion of Sherman's ideas and significantly downplays their richness and complexity. During his short life, Sherman produced a corpus of thought characterised by the sort of intellectual rigor and analytical nuance that was largely missing from the writings of his more notorious contemporaries. In particular, he envisioned air power as something other than an instrument of total war. He did so by championing a paradigm of air power that focused on maximising the usefulness of what thinkers such as Mitchell and Douhet contemptuously referred to as 'auxiliary' air power, particularly observation and attack aviation: forms of air power that derived their value from their ability to support and enhance the effectiveness of surface forces within a joint operational framework.

To conclude, Sherman's contribution to air power thought transcends his role in developing the twin concepts of vital centres and the industrial web for which he is best known – that is, when his name is mentioned at all in the historiography. And it goes beyond even his advocacy of tactical aviation in support of surface forces. Sherman also demonstrated a set of remarkably prescient insights about the future of air power. He predicted such technological and organisational developments as airborne command-and-control centres and mobile expeditionary basing facilities akin to the USAF's modern Agile Combat Employment (ACE) concept.[31] Practically alone among inter-war air power thinkers, he subjected to systematic analysis the concept of air logistics and base security.[32] Above all, Sherman stands out as the thinker whose ideas, more

29 Thomas E. Griffith, Jr., *MacArthur's Airman: General George C. Kenny and the War in the Southwest Pacific* (Lawrence, Kansas: University Press of Kansas, 1998), pp.25–9.

30 Griffith, *MacArthur's Airman*, pp.92–3.

31 Sherman, *Air Warfare*, pp.32–3, 234.

32 Sherman, *Air Warfare*, pp.232-40.

than Mitchell's, reflect the broader patterns of American air power at the beginning of the twenty-first century. While America's air capabilities continue to rest, ultimately, on strategic attack and deterrence, they also emphasise 'full-spectrum' air dominance anchored in the concept of jointness and a synergistic relationship between all the services and warfighting domains. One has only to survey how American air power has functioned in the last two decades to discern the continued relevance of Sherman's vision for contemporary airmen.

6

Malaya, 1941–42

Harry Raffal

Introduction

The Malayan Campaign began on 8 December 1941, when the Japanese seized ports in south Thailand, to sustain an overland advance into north-west Malaya, and launched an amphibious assault on Kota Bharu, on its east coast. The Japanese 25th Army then advanced rapidly down the main road arteries of the west and east coasts, with the two fronts of advance largely separated by the mountainous centre of Malaya. On 31 January, British forces withdrew from Malaya into Singapore, which subsequently surrendered on 15 February 1942. The historiography of the Malayan Campaign largely focuses on the failure of the British defence, the subsequent fall of Singapore, and the consequences for the British Empire.[1] Air power has rightly been identified as a vital aspect of the campaign. Studies of air power in the Malaya campaign are, however, largely restricted to the initial Japanese counter-air operations and the resulting heavy initial losses on the Royal Air Force (RAF) and Royal Australian Air Force (RAAF) squadrons in north-west Malaya. The long-range bombing of Singapore has also received attention as has the sinking of the Royal Navy battleship HMS *Prince of Wales* and battlecruiser HMS *Repulse* (Force Z) by the Imperial Japanese Naval Air Service (IJNAS). The air operations both sides undertook in support of the ground campaign, and why these operations were not always prioritised, is relatively understudied. Air power in the Malaya campaign is, therefore,

1 Louis Allen, *Singapore 1941–1942* (London: Davis-Poynter, 1977); Brian Farrell, *The Defence and Fall of Singapore* (Singapore: Monsoon, 2015); Karl Hack and Kevin Blackburn, *Did Singapore Have to Fall: Churchill and the Impregnable Fortress* (London: Routledge, 2004); Stanley Woodburn Kirby, et al., *The War Against Japan, Volume I, The Loss of Singapore* (London: HMSO, 1957); Ronald McCrum, *The Men Who Lost Singapore, 1938–1942* (Singapore: NUS Press, 2017); Colin Smith, *Singapore Burning: Heroism and Surrender in World War II* (London: Penguin, 2006); Peter Thompson, *The Battle for Singapore: The True Story of the Greatest Catastrophe of World War II* (London: Portrait, 2005).

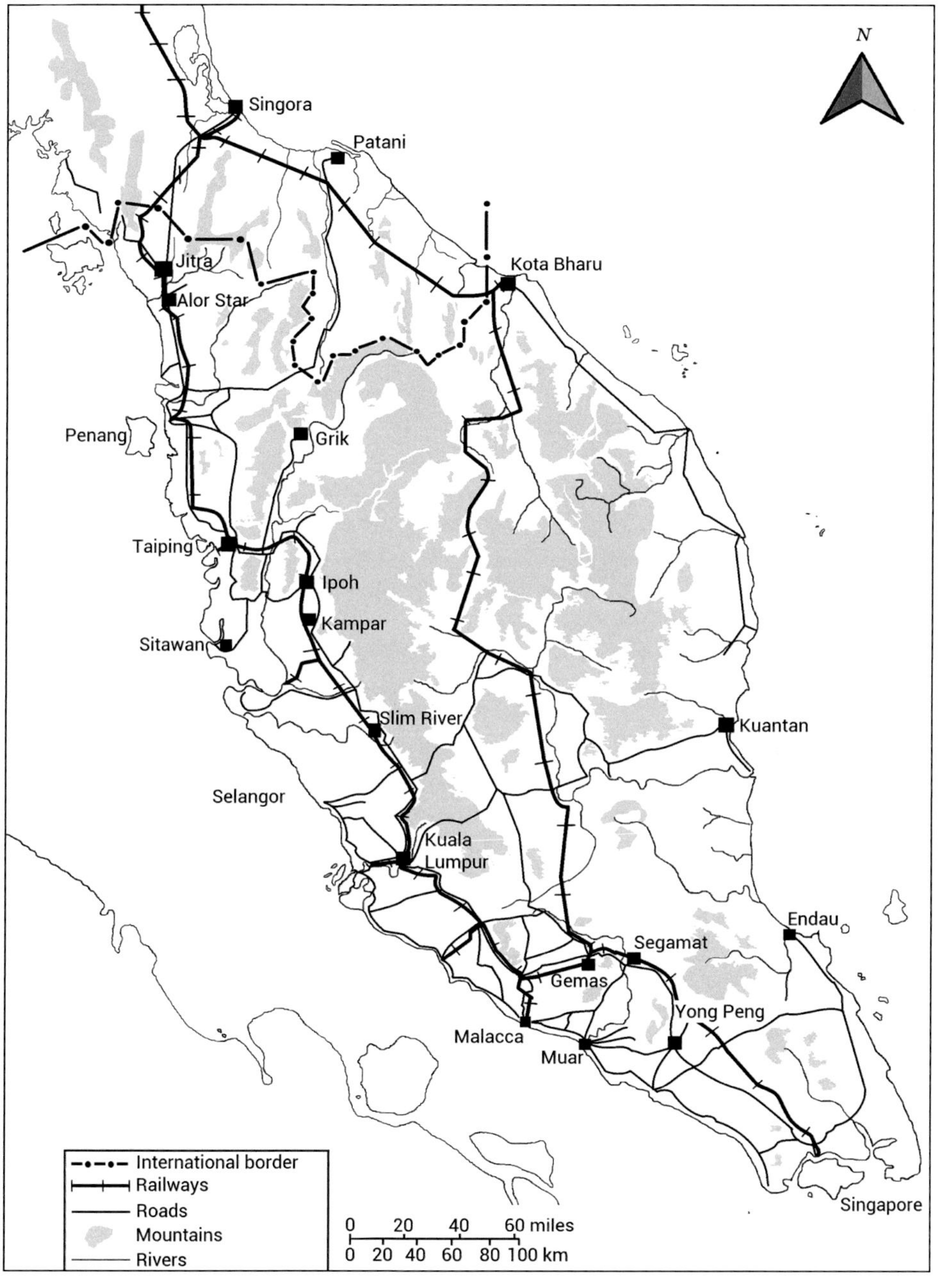

Map of Malaya, 1941. Author's Illustration.

only partially understood.[2] As this chapter shows through its examination of the air support operations of the RAF, RAAF, and Imperial Japanese Army Air Service (IJAAS), the Malayan Campaign can only be fully understood by examining the air operations of both sides and connecting their work to the ground campaign. Air support for ground forces was a significant aspect of the air operations connected to the Battle of Malaya with the resourcing and demands for this capability changing in balance with the ground battle and wider air campaign.

Japanese forces

The Malayan Campaign was fought by the Japanese 25th Army, with a strength of 70,000 men commanded by Lieutenant General Tomoyuki Yamashita. For the British Empire, Malaya was essential for the defence of the naval base at Singapore, the capture of which was Yamashita's ultimate objective. The Japanese Army's landings in Malaya received support from both the IJAAS and IJNAS. Following this initial phase of operations, however, the IJNAS undertook longer range operations against Singapore and against British shipping.[3] The air support for ground forces was, therefore, principally the responsibility of the 450 aircraft of the IJAAS and discussion of Japanese air support in this chapter relates to IJAAS forces unless stated otherwise.

Pre-war Japanese Army doctrine placed significant emphasis on the destruction of the enemy air force and direct support of ground operations. Although forces would be assigned to achieve both tasks, at the outset the battle for air superiority was given primacy. After gaining air superiority, IJAAS doctrine set out that it would increasingly engage in the ground battle. When the infantry became decisively engaged, the battle would then receive direct support from the full strength of the air forces available.[4] This emphasis on direct support of ground operations reflected the view within the Japanese Army that air power should closely support ground operations.

2 Peter Dye, *The Man Who Took the Rap: Sir Robert Brooke-Popham and the Fall of Singapore* (Annapolis, MA: Naval Institute Press, 2018), p.200; Lim Choo Hoon, 'Joint Operations in the Malayan Campaign', *Pointer: Journal of the Singapore Armed Forces*, Monograph No. 6, (2008), pp.30–45; Martin Middlebrook and Patrick Mahoney, *Battleship: The Loss of the Prince of Wales and the Repulse* (London: Allen Lane, 1977); Henry Probert, *The Forgotten Air Force: The Royal Air Force in the War Against Japan 1941–1945* (London: Brassey's, 1995); Kaushik Roy, *Battle for Malaya: The Indian Army in Defeat, 1941–42* (Bloomington, IN: Indiana University Press, 2019), p.82; Christopher Shores, Brian Cull and Yasuho Izawa, *Bloody Shambles, Vol. I, The Drift to War to the Fall of Singapore* (London: Grub Street, 1992); Hisayuki Yokoyame, 'Air Operational Leadership: Imperial Army Aviation's Trial to be an "Air Force" in the Malaya Air Offensive' in Brian Bond, Kyoichi Tachikawa, (eds), *British and Japanese Military Leadership in the Far Eastern War, 1941–1945* (Frank Cass: London, 2004), p.138.

3 Shores, *Bloody Shambles*, p.205, p.334.

4 The National Archives, Kew (TNA): WO 208/958: '*Oyo Senjutsu No Sanko*', Revised 1938, Translation by U.S. Military Intelligence Division, Pacific Unit (1943), p.34.

From 1937 onwards the IJAAS acquired experience in supporting the Army during the fighting in China. At the outset, IJAAS support was undertaken in 'direct co-operation' with ground operations and intended to supplement the ground forces in short-range operations against tactical targets.[5] Direct cooperation involved attacks on battlefield targets, that were directly related to ground combat, with the objective of destroying critical enemy ground forces through physical attack. Although falling short of the detailed integration between air and ground forces involved in close air support, direct cooperation involved elements of coordination between air and ground forces. Increasingly, however, the strategic value of air interdiction of rear areas was established, and such attacks began to be conducted alongside tactical strafing and bombing.[6] By the time of the Malaya campaign IJAAS doctrine had evolved and greater emphasis was placed on the value that could be gained behind the battlefield as well as counter-air opportunities. The targets that were emphasised in the rear of the battlefield were headquarters, mechanised units and supply organisations. Direct cooperation remained an important element, but doctrine warned it should not come at the expense of support for the wider ground battle.[7] To support air cooperation, air communication sections had also been established in army headquarters. The signal service's air-ground liaison extended to the level of the regiment. In addition, both infantry and artillery liaison officers were posted to IJAAS units to ensure close coordination during planned air action in support of ground forces.[8] It was, however, explicitly recognised within instructions accompanying direct support that when air superiority had not been achieved, the IJAAS would maintain its aim of destroying its adversaries' air power.[9]

The IJAAS doctrinal emphasis on air superiority was reinforced in 1939 by its experience against the Soviet air force in the Soviet-Japanese Mongolian border conflict. During the Battles of Khalkhin Gol the Soviets gained air superiority through an attritional air battle which eventually wore down the outnumbered Japanese pilots.[10] The IJAAS incorporated the importance of air superiority with traditional spiritual martial valour and pilots were indoctrinated and 'taught under

5 TNA: WO 106/5542: 'One Year of the China Incident: Japanese War Office publication (with English translation)'; Edward J. Drea, *Japan's Imperial Army: Its Rise and Fall, 1853–1945* (Lawrence, KS: University Press of Kansas, 2009), p.214.

6 Central Archive of the Ministry of Defence of the Russian Federation (TsAMO RF): Ф.500 оп.12451 д.213: OKH-Abteilung Fremde Heere, Referat III: *Studie – Erfahrungen und Betrachtungen aus dem japanisch-chinesischen Feldzug* 1937–1938, 1938, p.25.

7 Masao Matsuda and Makoto Ikuta, *Senshi Sōsho*, kanno 078, 'Armament and Operations of the Army Air Service (2), 1934 to the Beginning of 1942' (Tokyo: Asagumo Shimbunsha, 1974), pp.222–223.

8 U.S. War Department, 'Japanese Signal Services' *Tactical and Technical Trends*, No. 46 (May 1944), pp.38–51 (pp.41–5); Hoon, 'Joint Operations', p.38.

9 TNA: WO 208/958: 'Oyo Senjutsu No Sanko', p.34.

10 Edward J. Drea, *Nomonhan: Japanese-Soviet Tactical Combat, 1939* (Fort Leavenworth, KS: Combat Studies Institute, 1981), p.200.

severe training to paint the clouds crimson with their blood.'[11] The doctrinal importance on securing air superiority was incorporated into the IJAAS planning for invasion of Malaya. The IJAAS operational plans for the 3rd *Hikō Shudan* (Air Corps) in Malaya were endorsed by Yamashita, under whose operational command the IJAAS units in Malaya were placed, as part of the overall campaign strategy. Yamashita, formerly the Chief of Army Aeronautical Headquarters, had led the 1940–41 Japanese military mission to Germany. Having studied *Luftwaffe* operations in the 1940 Battle of France, Yamashita's report noted that 'direct co-operation on the ground is only desirable after air superiority is obtained.'[12] The operations in Malaya followed the IJAAS doctrine in support of offensive operations which prioritised neutralising the enemy air force.[13]

British forces

The British forces in Malaya comprised forces from the British Empire and Commonwealth Dominions. Grouped within Malaya Command, unusually for the time a joint Army and RAF command, under Air Chief Marshal Sir Robert Brooke-Popham, the Army force had a strength of nearly 90,000 to resist the Japanese invasion. This formation came under the command of Lieutenant General Arthur Percival, General Officer Commanding Malaya, and included the Indian Army III Corps and the Australian 8th Division. Following the Japanese invasion, Malaya Command received reinforcements; amongst these were infantry from the 44th and 45th Indian Brigades, and the British 18th Division. The air forces in Malaya were comprised of 158 operationally serviceable aircraft, from RAF and RAAF squadrons, under Air Vice-Marshal Conway Pulford, Air Officer Commanding (AOC), Air Headquarters Far East, RAF (hereafter the local forces in theatre are referred to simply as RAF except where a distinction will usefully aid the reader).[14] As well as being outnumbered, these squadrons were equipped with obsolete or inferior types such as the twin-engined Bristol Blenheim bomber, and the Brewster Buffalo, a relatively underpowered single-engine fighter. This inadequacy was compounded by the difference in training and experience between the two sides, with the RAF aircrew,

11 TNA: WO 208/2548: Ryuichi Yokoyama, with Colonel Nago Yahagi (Fwd), Chief of Army Information Section, 'Malaya Campaign', 8 Oct. 1942, p.273; TNA: AIR 40/2173: Chief Intelligence Officer, Air Headquarters India, Report on 'Japanese Army Air Service Training 1937–1943', 26 Apr. 1943.

12 Centre for Asian Historical Research, National Archives of Japan: C15120145100: *Bōeishō Bōeikenkyūsho*, Yamashita shisatsudan hōkoku [Yamashita Inspection Group Report], p.21.

13 TNA: AIR 20/5326: Wing Commander J. Biggar, 'Brief Summary of Japanese Air Tactics as Experienced in the S.W. Pacific Area, December 1941 – April 1943', 30 Sept. 1943.

14 Air Chief Marshal Sir Robert Brooke-Popham, Despatch on 'Operations in the Far East, 17 October 1940 – 27 December 1941', *London Gazette* (20 Jan. 1948), p.574.

Bristol Blenheim Mk I in flight over Brewster Buffalo aircraft, Sembawang 1941. (RAF Museum: X004-7598/042/019)

many of whom were posted direct from their having completed training, being at a distinct disadvantage.[15]

The RAF was not well equipped, or well prepared, to provide close support to the ground forces in Malaya. Although RAF doctrine laid out the importance of direct cooperation between the services, what the RAF termed direct support for ground forces was seen as, other than in exceptional circumstances, being an inappropriate use of air power. Direct support encompassed those attacks which would have an immediate effect on ground operations. It included what might now be termed battlefield air interdiction and close support, which was provided 'in close proximity to our forward troops' and could include both bombing and strafing.[16] The RAF believed that direct attacks were seen as liable to incur heavy casualties whilst being of limited value against unshaken troops. Instead, support was to be

15 TNA: AIR 20/5326: Biggar, 'Brief Summary of Japanese Air Tactics'; TNA: WO 172/9: War Diary GHQ Far East, 2 Jun. 1941; Denis Richards and Hilary Saunders, *The Royal Air Force 1939–1945, Vol. II: The Fight Avails*, (London: HMSO, 1954), p.10; Farrell, *Defence and Fall*, p.148.

16 TNA: AIR 10/5547: Air Historical Branch (AHB), 'Second World War 1939–1945: Air Support', 1955, p.7.

provided beyond the immediate frontline and not as a substitute for artillery.[17] The RAF War Manual warned that 'only a desperate situation, when every possible means to avoid imminent disaster must be used, will justify the diversion of aircraft from their proper task.'[18] In Malaya, where the RAF's primary objective in the event of a Japanese invasion was to prevent a successful landing, the RAF's doctrine compounded already difficult service relationships to ensure that training between the RAF and Army lacked practical and sustained cooperation.[19] The British Army, concerned owing to a shortage of artillery held by forces in Malaya in Spring, 1941, and its lack of range, considered 'close support bombing' to be a necessary part of any defence of Malaya.[20] Prior to September 1941, however, Air Headquarters Far East, RAF produced no operational instructions for the close support of the Army, or for tactical reconnaissance. Percival was therefore instructed, despite the presence of Army Cooperation squadrons in Malaya, to assume that aircraft for these roles would be limited.[21]

In autumn 1941, Air Headquarters Far East, RAF published on the operations of bombers in support of troops and sought to provide its squadrons with experience of these operations. Every squadron was affiliated to an Army formation, and they were allotted flying hours for combined training. Frequently unrealised due to low serviceability rates and basic service training needs in many of the RAF's squadrons, and commencing in October 1941, only two months before the Japanese invasion, these changes had limited effect on operational readiness. Training for the ground attack role was reduced by a lack of appropriate ranges, whilst general proficiency in the use of machine-guns was limited by a lack of sufficient ammunition reserves for firing practice. The forces of the British Army Malaya Command also lacked the training or experience to effectively collaborate with the RAF as part of their defensive campaign. There was also a general lack of anti-aircraft guns to allow the ground units a realistic measure of self-protection if the Japanese gained air supremacy.[22] Although Indian Army formations were in theatre, opportunities to draw on lessons from the North-West Frontier of India on how to integrate air support and ground operations were left unrealised. This failing rested on a shortage of printed manuals and the relative inexperience of the officers and men in these

17 Royal Air Force Museum (RAFM): 017706: AP 1300, Air Ministry, RAF War Manual, Part One, Operations, Feb. 1940, Ch.XI-n.38; TNA: CAB 21/903: 'Bomber Support for the Army', p.2.
18 RAFM: 017706: AP 1300, 1940, Ch.XI-n.48–49.
19 Farrell, *Defence and Fall*, p.149; A.D. Harvey, 'The Royal Air Force and Close Support, 1918–1940', *War in History*, 15:4 (Nov. 2008), pp.426–486 (p.480).
20 TNA: Air 20/2114: Telegram from War Office to GOC Malaya, 'Defence of Malaya Policy', 31 May 1941.
21 TNA: AIR 20/2114: Telegram from War Office to GOC Malaya, 'Defence of Malaya Policy', 4 Jun. 1941; RAFM: AC73/15/3/5: Group Captain A.G. Bishop, 'Pre-War Notes', p.1.
22 RAFM: AIR 41/63: AHB, Campaigns in the Far East, Vol II, Malaya, Netherlands East Indies and Burma, app III, p.ii.

units – few of whom could therefore draw from first-hand experience of air-ground cooperation outside of Malaya.[23] The lack of signal equipment further reduced the extent these changes improved the readiness of either the air or ground units prior to the Japanese invasion.[24]

North Malaya

The Japanese invasion of Malaya commenced on 8 December 1941, with landings at Kota Bharu, in the north-east of Malaysia, and Singora, Thailand. The airfields and harbour facilities in Thailand were essential to sustaining the Japanese invasion. Having seized Singora, the Japanese were able to provide air cover and logistics for their invasion into north-west Malaya. On the other side of the Malay Peninsula, the landing at Kota Bharu drew in almost all the immediately available resources that were available to the RAF in north Malaya. The squadrons despatched to Kota Bharu suffered heavy losses, with nine aircraft destroyed, but did sink one of the three landing ships. Despite significant losses, some 850 casualties, the Japanese succeeded in securing a landing.[25] More significantly, however, the IJAAS directed most of its resources to an 'air annihilation' counter-air offensive that within 48 hours effectively destroyed RAF forces in north Malaya. Inter-war airfields, such as Alor Star, were vulnerable to air attack as they had been constructed with their buildings closely grouped, but even recently constructed airfields were ill-equipped to disperse and conceal aircraft.[26] By the end of the 8 December, the IJAAS had destroyed or damaged 60 aircraft, and only 50 RAF aircraft in north Malaya remained serviceable. Most of the RAF losses occurred on the ground, although nine aircraft were destroyed during the anti-invasion operations at Kota Bharu. The Air Historical Branch narrative of the campaign records that 'so well timed were their initial blows that after the first day the RAF virtually ceased to exist as a means of defence.'[27]

The IJAAS counter-air focus has led to criticism of its overall operations in the Malayan Campaign, with it being suggested the IJAAS neglected the ground campaign and left the Japanese Army's ground forces to fight with little direct assistance.[28] Although neutralising the RAF was identified as the first priority, the IJAAS also directed that as well as establishing and maintaining air supremacy,

23 Roy, *Battle for Malaya*, pp.33–38.
24 RAFM: 73/15/4/12: Air Vice-Marshal Paul Maltby, 'Air Operations During the Campaigns in Malaya and North East Indies from 8 Dec. 1941–12 Mar. 1942', 26 Feb. 1948.
25 Colonel Masanobu Tsuji, *Japan's Greatest Victory, Britain's Greatest Defeat* (Staplehurst: Spellmount, 1997), pp.75–79.
26 TNA: AIR 28/1: RAF Station Alor Star to Headquarters, Royal Air Force, Far East, 'Dispersal and Concealment of Aircraft', Oct. 1940.
27 RAFM: AIR 41/63: AHB, Malaya, p.16, app. IV, p.iii.
28 Dye, *Man Who Took the Rap*, p.200; Yokoyame, 'Air Operational Leadership', p.137.

Singora airfield under Japanese occupation, 1941. (RAF Museum: X004-7598/042/014)

resources were to be available to 'directly co-operate with [the] ground operation of advance units.'[29] Ground support was therefore established as a key objective for 3 *Hikō Shudan* which, following the initial landings, was to rapidly deploy its main force to Malaya and Thailand and cooperate directly with the ground operations while continuing to destroy the air power of the enemy. The extent of the IJAAS's direct cooperation was not pre-defined, and it was recognised that such decisions could only be based on the operational situation that developed. Nonetheless, direct support for ground forces was a key aspect of the IJAAS operations in Malaya.[30] The

29 Colonel Minoru Miyako, *Japanese Monograph 55: Southeast Area Air Operations Record, Phase I, November 1941–February 1942* (Washington, DC: Office of the Chief of Military History, Department of the Army, 1962), p.22.
30 Miyako, *Japanese Monograph 55*, p.26.

Alor Star airfield, Kedah Province, Malaya 1940. (RAF Museum: X004-7598/042/013)

army cooperation squadron and the IJAAS Chief of Intelligence enjoyed positive relationships with the staff officers of 25th Army, and overall, the air and ground forces cooperated effectively.[31] At the outset of the campaign, however, tensions did arise between the respective Staffs of 25th Army and 3 *Hikō Shudan*. This tension was particularly acute during what the Army perceived as a lack of air cover during the initial landings at Kota Bharu. [32] The success of ground operations eased anxiety, but the overall balance of operations continued to cause tensions throughout the advance in northern Malaya.

It is, however, important not to overstate these differences, or to assume that support for ground forces was not provided because of 25th Army frustrations that the IJAAS did not prevent all RAF attacks in north-east Malaya. IJAAS interdiction attacks on the forces withdrawing from Kota Bharu were, with several limited exceptions, noticeably absent.[33] The limited interdiction operations in the east of Malaya in

31 Tsuji, *Japan's Greatest Victory*, p.45, p.161.

32 Foreign Histories Division, General Headquarters Far East Command, *Japanese Monograph 31: Air Operations in the Southern Area, 1941–1945* (Washington, DC: Office of the Chief of Military History, Department of the Army, 1960), p.11.

33 Imperial War Museum (IWM): Documents/3396: Brigadier EW Goodman, Diary of Malaya Campaign; Lionel Wigmore, *Australia in the War of 1939–1945*, Series 1 (Army)

the first 20 days of operations was a consequence of the IJAAS prioritising support for the decisive point of operations, the advance on the west coast. In the north-west of Malaya, behind the British frontline at Jitra and the subsequent retreat to Kampar, the IJAAS did attack lines of communication. These were principally directed at supply routes a relatively short distance behind the frontlines and road movements leading up to forward positions.[34]

As the Japanese advanced further into northern Malaya effective attacks began to be made on locomotives and rail lines running up to, and through, Ipoh. Direct hits on the rail lines produced delays of up to eight hours before repairs could be effected.[35] These attacks, a number of which did considerable damage, were made immediately behind the next major defensive position available to British forces, Slim River.[36] Towards the end of December, as the British forces were making their final withdrawals from northern Malaya, the IJAAS also made repeated attacks on Allied troops crossing Perak River.[37] On 26 December, the war diary of the British General Headquarters, Far East, recorded that IJAAS aircraft which had been 'most active in attacking railway communications' had successfully cut them in areas where they crossed the Perak river.[38] Having achieved air superiority, the IJAAS was able to undertake interdiction attacks which, designed to stymie the flow of reinforcements, were in direct response to the needs of the Japanese ground campaign.

The IJAAS also undertook attacks in direct support of the battlefield as the Japanese army advanced in north Malaya. On 16 December, fighting developed on the Grik Road during which the Japanese forward units were brought under artillery fire. Artillery, rather than bomber aircraft, was established in Japanese army doctrine as the best form of fire support in close proximity to the frontline.[39] Despite this, during the Malaya campaign, and in particular during encounters such as those on the Grik Road, air power was used to offset 25th Army's comparative shortage in artillery, as well as the difficulty and delays experienced in advancing artillery behind the rapidly moving frontline. During the fighting on the Grik Road, the IJAAS made numerous attacks on forward positions. Suffering casualties from repeated bombing, whilst making continuous withdrawals, had a definite psychological effect on the defending British forces.[40] The IJAAS also

Vol. 4, *The Japanese Thrust* (Adelaide, Aus: Griffin, 1957), p.155.

34 IWM: Audio/16276: Charles Wylie, Reel 4, 00:10:45; IWM: Audio/13095: Michael Tice, Reel 3, 00:10:30.

35 TNA: WO 172/15: War Diary, GHQ Far East with Appendix, 18 Dec 1941.

36 IWM: Documents/3396: Goodman, Diary; TNA: WO 172/18: 'ALO 3 Corps to G.III', 31 Dec. 1941.

37 IWM: Documents/3396: Goodman, Diary.

38 TNA: WO 172/15: War Diary, GHQ Far East. 'Appendix, 353 27/12 Intelligence Summary', 26 Dec. 0800–27 Dec. 0800.

39 Drea, *Japan's Imperial Army*, p.153.

40 Roy, *Battle for Malaya*, p.120.

effectively dive-bombed field artillery batteries supporting the frontline.[41] These attacks were indictive of the ground support that the IJAAS provided – frequent operations, in relatively low strength, which harassed both forward defensive positions and movements immediately behind the frontline. This trend continued during the remainder of December. The air and ground units involved in the fighting were able to liaise with one another, and air superiority allowed the IJAAS to develop a comprehensive air reconnaissance picture. As the Japanese Army approached Ipoh, and fighting developed in the area on 25 December, small formations of IJAAS aircraft were constantly active over the British forces' positions.[42]

Having captured Ipoh, 25th Army advanced towards Kampar. Well-concealed defensive positions had been established by the British forces which, combined with fire support from artillery batteries, offset the lack of close air support for the defensive force. During the fighting at Kampar, the IJAAS continued its direct cooperation attacks in support of 25th Army. Having gained air superiority, the IJAAS was able to undertake low-level bombing and strafing attacks without interference. Such attacks were undertaken during the fighting at Kampar to interdict movements towards the frontline. Reconnaissance and artillery spotting for the ground forces was also undertaken and Japanese air power was employed to help offset the British force's advantage in artillery fire power with the IJAAS actively targeting artillery batteries.[43] The IJAAS, although continuing to ensure a focus on air superiority, was increasingly active at low level over the battlefield. John Wyatt, an NCO with 2nd Battalion East Surrey Regiment, recalled that starting at Kampar, and continuing for the remainder of the campaign, 'Every time you went into a counter-attack or were withdrawing you were machine gunned.'[44] By the end of December, however, air support operations on the west coast were, for a period, not the IJAAS's operational priority. Instead, the IJAAS continued to ensure the reduction of the RAF and was required to support operations on the east coast. A surprise landing to capture Kuantan was planned for 28 December. Yamashita postponed the landing on 23 December, however, because he was not satisfied that the remaining RAF forces had been sufficiently reduced to prevent them interfering with the landings. Yamashita decided to instead take advantage of 56th Infantry Regiment's rapid advance to make an overland attack on Kuantan, which was defended by the 22nd Indian Brigade. On 30 December, at the same time fighting was commencing at Kampar, on the west coast, the IJAAS was being tasked to provide air support at Kuantan to pin the 22nd Brigade and enable the 56th Regiment to concentrate against it. The IJAAS made a mixture of attacks in support of ground forces,

41 TNA: WO 172/155: 137 Army Field Regiment, Royal Artillery, War Diary, 23 December 1941.

42 IWM: Documents/3396: Goodman, Diary.

43 TNA: WO 172/155: 137 Army Field Regiment, Royal Artillery, War Diary, pp.29–31 December.

44 IWM: Audio/4814: John Augustine Wyatt, Reel 1, 00:25:12.

both direct air support and interdiction attacks, including repeated, and partially successful, attempts to put the ferry at Kuantan out of action. Nonetheless, 22nd Brigade was able to cross at night, when the IJAAS was not operating, with all their guns and transports. [45]

In understanding the balance of IJAAS close air support operations during the fighting at Kampar and Kuantan, it is necessary to recall that a force of 450 aircraft – less some 100 which were unserviceable – was meeting the dual demands of two lines of advance whilst simultaneously being required to maintain the suppression of RAF.[46] In doing so, the IJAAS for much of the fighting in north-west Malaya was not operating from well-prepared air fields. Instead, its units were situated at congested airfields in Singora where service facilities were generally lacking.

Despite the limitations it faced throughout December, the IJAAS effectively coordinated with 25th Army units, providing both air support for advances and fighter patrols to guard troop movements in northern Malaya. In common with other air forces, direct communication with forward troops in combat was difficult. Air to ground communication was achieved through airplane panels, but such communication was difficult in the rainforests and rubber plantations of Malaya. Radio communication extended down to company headquarters but, outside of the more powerful transmitters, difficulties were frequently encountered by both sides in employing radio equipment in Malaya.[47] Possessing air superiority ensured that, despite these communication difficulties, the IJAAS were able to maintain intercommunication. The IJAAS was also aware of the Army's plan of operations in Malaya and liaison between unit headquarters had established how those air units tasked with close cooperation of ground forces could most effectively support the advance. The combination of communication and operational planning allowed a high degree of cooperation between the IJAAS and ground forces during the latter's advances.

The Japanese bombers maintained a regular tempo of attacks on British forces during their withdrawal from northern Malaya.[48] Having secured air superiority, Japanese fighter sorties which encountered no air opposition were often employed in strafing against ground targets.[49] The primary feature of their air support battle

45 Kirby, *Loss of Singapore*, p.372; Wigmore, *Japanese Thrust*, p.92.

46 TNA: AIR 20/12343: 'Japanese Air Force', c. Oct. 1942; TNA: AIR 23/4720: Norgroup, 'Japanese Aircraft Operating in Various Areas', 23 Jan. 1942.

47 TNA: AIR 20/5576: Wing Commander Cave, 'Report by Command Signals Officer, Far East Command, RAF, on Malayan Operations, 1941–42', Dec. 1945, p.3; US War Department, 'Communications', *Intelligence Bulletin*, I:7 (Mar. 1943), pp.17–22, (pp.17–8); US War Department, Technical Manual TM-E 30-480, (Washington, DC: United States Government Printing Office, 1942), pp.272–3.

48 WO 172/18: Malaya: Headquarters, 'Situation Report from 22 Indian Infantry Brigade', 31 Dec. 1941.

49 TNA: AIR 20/5326: Air Tactics, Air Ministry, 'Japanese Air Tactics since the Commencement of Hostilities in the Pacific, up to the end of 1941', 5 Jan. 1942.

tactics was observed to be 'high level and intensive bombing of key ground objectives and positions, under fighter cover, followed by persistent and well maintained ground strafing tactics.'[50] Troops who had been in continuous contact with the enemy were now becoming fatigued. Japanese air attacks made movement at night the safest course of action, and when this was not taking place, the troops were working on defensive positions. During the day troops were harassed by seemingly constant air attacks which prevented them from obtaining any sleep.[51] Phillip Dixon, an NCO with 1st Battalion, Leicestershire Regiment, described how the nature of the retreat, and the lack of sleep, left the troops like zombies.[52] Douglas Finlayson, commanding 1/8th Battalion, Punjab Regiment, recalled that 'there was no British air power and morale was pretty low when you were constantly being battered by enemy aircraft … the whole thing was a morale problem.'[53] Although not overly significant in physical effect these attacks deprived the troops of rest, eroded their morale and the psychological effect was a contributory factor behind their failure to hold positions. The rapid Japanese success was directly facilitated by the IJAAS attacks.[54]

The IJAAS did not focus solely on close air support for the ground forces. It continued to ensure the suppression of the RAF and maintain air superiority – which ensured that the attacks it did conduct could be made at low level and without interference. Despite requests from the 25th Army, when defending forces attempted to make a stand, many of the targets in the frontline were more effectively dealt with artillery and mortars.[55] Able to generate organic fire support on the frontline, the primary air power need of the 25th Army was not close air support. The IJAAS ensured the army's own advance could not be interdicted. Continuing its counter air campaign, as well as striking targets on and immediate behind the frontline with the aim of making the defending forces vulnerable to shock and envelopment, the IJAAS effectively enabled the rapid Japanese advance. On 12 December, Major-General H. Gordon Bennett, Commanding 8th Australian Division, wrote to Australian Army Headquarters that the army was unable 'to carry out its role without molestation from the enemy's air force. I fear a repetition of Crete.'[56] The demoralisation of the opposing force through constant harassment in close coordination with the ground campaign was in keeping with the IJAAS doctrine which had identified the 'great psychological effect' that bombs had in

50 TNA: AIR 20/12343: Squadron Leader Loman, RAF Interrogation Officer, Delhi, 'Memorandum the Japanese Navy and Army Air Service', Jul. 1942.
51 Kirby, *Loss of Singapore*, p.337.
52 IWM: Audio/11356: Philip Frederick Dixon, Reel 1, 00:27:26
53 IWM: Audio/9206: Douglas Finlayson, Reel 1, 00:02:55.
54 IWM: Audio/10813: Ian Wethey, Reel 3, 00:17:22; Australian War Memorial (AWM): 54-81/4/140: W.R. Lyster, First Narrative of RAAF Participation in the Campaign of 1941–42 in Malaya, Sumatra and Java, Jun–Sep 1946, p.58.
55 TNA: WO 172/18: Adv H.Q.M.C. to G.H.Q.F.E., 'Situation Report No. 21', 30 Dec. 1941.
56 H. Gordon Bennett, *Why Singapore Fell* (London: Angus & Robertson, 1944), p.58, citing letter to Australian Army HQ.

addition to their physical effect.[57] The deleterious moral effect on Allied troops caused by the Japanese air support was cumulative and had been appreciable by 12 December.[58]

By contrast, by the time the British forces had retired beyond and taken up their positions on the next major defensive line, at Slim River, they had received little effective air support.[59] Following the initial Japanese invasion, a low-level attack had been made on the rail bridge over the Golok River. If successful, the attack would have denied supplies or reinforcements from Thailand reaching the Japanese thrust on the east coast – which would have meant a reliance on the limited quantity of men and material that could be brought ashore via the beaches at Kota Bharu.[60] As with all the RAF operations in December, however, the forces committed to the attack were limited. Throughout December, the RAF did not concentrate its forces against one objective it considered of primary importance. The Air Staff at Air Headquarters Far East favoured moving to a campaign of interdiction strikes on the limited routes sustaining the Japanese frontline positions. Instead, Pulford, the AOC, adopted a counter-air strategy targeting Japanese occupied airfields. The airfields attacks were of limited value given the RAF's strength. Percival had, however, requested strikes that would have an immediate effect on the battle by limiting IJAAS attacks on forward positions.[61] The attacks by Blenheim bombers, made without adequate fighter cover, suffered loss without meaningful results and led to the suspension of further daylight bombing raids.

Targets of opportunity, reported by ground units or aerial reconnaissance, were often unmet during the fighting in northern Malaya or attacked after such delay that the air support provided was no longer of value.[62] On 13 December, two Buffalo fighters attempted isolated low-level strafing attacks against Japanese troops on the road leading to Jitra.[63] These attacks were made in response to requests received during 12 December, and subsequent instructions from GHQ Far East to Air Headquarters Far East, RAF that every effort was to be made to stop and repel the Japanese advance in Kedah and that 'for the present assistance to 11 Ind. Div is to take precedence of other RAF offensive tasks.'[64] The need for effective control of resources increased as the morale of the Army declined which led to increasing calls for direct air support, often against unprofitable targets.[65] There was, however, no effective coordination

57 TNA: WO 208/958: '*Oyo Senjutsu No Sanko*', p.202.
58 RAFM: 73/15/4/12: Maltby, 'Air Operations'.
59 AWM: 54-81/4/140: Lyster, First Narrative, p.58.
60 RAFM: AIR 41/63: AHB, Malaya, p.19.
61 RAFM: 73/15/4/12: Maltby, 'Air Operations'.
62 TNA: WO 172/18, War Diary 'Appendix H.18', 31 Dec. 1941.
63 RAFM: AIR 41/63: AHB, Malaya, pp.53–4.
64 TNA: WO 172/15: 'Instruction No. 1, General Headquarters Far East to Air Officer Commanding, Far East', 12 Dec. 1941, War Diary GHQ Far East.
65 TNA: AIR 10/5547: AHB, Air Support, p.103.

with the ground forces.[66] Towards the end of December, the Japanese army crossed the Perak River and, as discussed below, despite their vulnerability were not subjected to air attack. Equally, however, without a solidified defence on the ground there was little the air force could do through tactical air attacks to alter the campaign's progress.

At the outset of the fighting in northern Malaya requests for air to ground support were received by headquarters, No. 223 Group (Norgroup). Formed in the summer of 1941, Norgroup established a small operational headquarters to act in conjunction with III Indian Corps.[67] On 8 December, however, operations in coordinated support of ground forces were prevented by a breakdown in communications between Norgroup Headquarters, at Kuala Lumpur, and stations in north-west Malaya. Norgroup relocated its headquarters adjacent to advanced headquarters III Corps. Although located in position to closely coordinate with the defending British forces, the Group's support was limited both because of heavy initial losses and the RAF's prioritisation of counter-air attacks.[68] Requests for air support were therefore made to the RAF staff in the combined operations room.

The combined operations room was a large space, constructed following a combined operations exercise in 1941, which adjoined the RAF headquarters at Sime Road. Alongside were built offices for the Army operational staff which aimed to provide a space for collocation.[69] Percival would note that, although excellent in theory, in practice the combined centre had many faults. Notably there was too little space for the efficient working of the combined staff, but the centre was too far from Headquarters to allow work to be done elsewhere. Percival would later reflect that the space had an extremely negative influence on the higher direction of the campaign because of the 'very great influence on their [headquarter staff] efficiency and, in consequence, on the efficiency of the fighting formations.'[70] This lack of efficiency was of serious consequence for the RAF given it had limited resources remaining. Most of the requests for support which reached the combined operations room were considerably delayed, and many could not be met because of an absence of resource, but where they were actioned, further delay ensued. The communication between Air Headquarters and Squadrons at stations in central and northern Malaya relied on a limited number of cables subject to extensive delay both ways – air observation reports could be the subject of delays of four hours before they were received by the operations room at Air Headquarters.[71] The effect of delays in the communication network was worsened by the over-prescriptive orders issued by Air Headquarters. Sorties made on outdated information therefore lacked the flexibility to best adapt their task to the

66 AWM: 54-81/4/140: Lyster, First Narrative, p.13.
67 RAFM: AC73/15/3/1: Air Vice-Marshal Paul Maltby, 'Notes on Norgroup', 1948.
68 Brooke-Popham, Despatch, p.556; RAFM: AIR 41/63: AHB, Malaya, p.25.
69 RAFM: AC73/15/3/5: Air Commodore B.J. Silly, Senior Air Staff Officer Air Headquarters, Air Headquarters Far East, RAF, 'note on RAF in Malaya pre-war', p.4.
70 Lieutenant General A.E. Percival, *The War in Malaya* (London: Eyre & Spottiswoode, 1949), pp.185–6.
71 AWM: 54-81/4/140: Lyster, First Narrative, p.83.

situation they encountered during their air operation. The limitations of the communication between the air and ground forces prevented close coordination between air and ground operations. It also reduced the effectiveness of air support for the ground forces at a time when, having suffered extensive early losses, a dissipation of effort could not be afforded.

Slim River

Having advanced more than 300 kilometres in a little over 20 days, the 25th Army now threatened central Malaya. If Central Malaya was rapidly captured the British had little prospect of successfully defending Singapore. The defences that had started to solidify at Kampar, now reached the line of Slim River. The 12th and 28th Brigades, Indian 11th Division, adopted a position which, supported by artillery, had the potential to halt 25th Army's 'driving charge'. Early on 4 January 12th Brigade moved into its sector of defence and began preparing ground positions. Slim River had been identified by the Japanese as the main defensible position in central Malaya, and recognising the preparatory defensive works being undertaken the IJAAS, bombed and strafed the Brigade's position, attacking both visible targets and the jungle bordering roads and railways where they knew troops would be situated. Under near constant air attack, much of the Brigade's work had to be carried out at night.[72] Similar attacks took place on the 28th Brigade positions. Although the IJAAS strafing attacks against troops at the Slim River did not achieve significant material damage, low-level bomber attacks had greater effect and they impaired the preparation of defensive positions.[73] Moreover, the already fatigued troops were deprived of sleep and were increasingly demoralised by the seemingly continuous IJAAS air attacks. This greatly reduced their fighting efficiency and ability to withstand the rapid envelopment shock tactics of the Japanese army.[74]

On 7 January fierce fighting ensued at Slim River before Japanese tanks and troops, supported by aircraft, overran the line. The defending forces suffered severe losses; the 12th and 28th Brigades losses exceeded three-quarters of their original strength of 5,000. Japanese air support was significant in this major Allied defeat. The failure to hold the position on Slim River was the result of several features, including the British anti-tank guns being unprepared for the nature of the attack and poorly placed road obstacles. The fatigue and exhaustion of the division was, however, a major

72 Wigmore, *Japanese Thrust*, p.193.

73 AWM: 54-553/3/2: Major General A.S. Allen and Brigadier Berryman, Operations in Malaya, May 1942.

74 Colonel Deakin, 5/2nd Punjab, in Kirby, *Loss of Singapore*, p.378; Wigmore, *Japanese Thrust*, p.193.

contributing factor and this was furthered by the direct cooperation and interdiction attacks of the IJAAS.[75]

The Japanese army had identified the British forces' dependence on fixed positions and firepower, and that a successful attack on such positions would require the neutralisation of that firepower.[76] At Slim River, British artillery was targeted by the IJAAS, both when firing and during its movement between positions. The effect was that guns moved up to artillery positions, fired briefly, and then withdrew to a new position – with almost all road movements made at night time.[77] Thomas Pounder, a gunner with 88th Field Regiment, Royal Artillery (RA), recalled that his battery 'very seldom moved during the day because the Japanese aircraft were overhead.'[78] William Notley, a driver with 155th Field Regiment, RA, recalled that the British forces 'just couldn't cope' with Japanese air bombing and strafing attacks.[79] The IJAAS air attacks helped to offset the advantage that the British forces' artillery established over the Japanese artillery.[80] This represented a continuation in the pattern of operations that the IJAAS had established during the first days of the Japanese advance in Malaya. The Japanese Army's experience in China had demonstrated that close air support could offer a replacement to heavy artillery particularly when frontline positions were near one another.[81] IJAAS doctrine reflected the experience gained in China, and close air support was identified as a way to offset the Japanese army's relative weakness in artillery support.

The IJAAS counter-air operations, and their continued focus on maintaining air superiority, ensured that the RAF was unable to directly intervene in ground operations during 5–7 January, and was therefore absent from the Battle of Slim River. Between 8 and 12 January, to assist the ground campaign the RAF's limited resources were employed against interdiction targets in Thailand.[82] After 8 January, the retreating ground forces in the west of Malaya were making urgent requests for air support, principally however, this was not for limited attacks on frontline positions. Instead, based on their previous experience of Japanese coastal infiltrations, requested were made for the RAF's support against small craft along the Malacca coastline. Along with reconnaissance missions, the RAF's limited resources were therefore fully tasked on priority targets away from

75 Kirby *Loss of Singapore*, pp.281–283.
76 TNA: AIR 40/1880: Directorate of Intelligence, Allied Air Forces, South West Pacific Area, 'Intelligence Information Memorandum No. 31: the Japanese Character in War, citing captured Japanese instruction on "Ways and Methods of the Enemy"', 8 October 1943, p.5.
77 IWM: Audio/22926: Fergus Gordon Anckorn, Reel 2, 00:14:20.
78 IWM: Audio/4887: Thomas Pounder, Reel 1, 00:12:30.
79 IWM: Audio/16670: William Notley, Reel 1, 00:22:00.
80 AWM: 54-553/3/2: Major General A.S. Allen and Brigadier Berryman, Operations in Malaya, May 1942.
81 TsAMO RF: Ф.500 оп.12451 д.213: OKH-Abteilung Fremde Heere, Referat III: Studie – Erfahrungen und Betrachtungen aus dem japanisch-chinesischen Feldzug 1937–1938, 1938, p.21.
82 Shores, *Bloody Shambles*, pp.283–87.

close support of ground forces. Increasingly, as the Japanese advanced down the Malaya peninsula, the RAF's priority switched to the defence of seaborne convoys, loaded with reinforcements, on which any hope of maintaining Singapore depended. This prioritisation of air operations was driven by the needs of the ground forces and reflected the preferences of both local forces and General Sir Archibald Wavell, Supreme Commander American-British-Dutch-Australian Command (ABDACOM).[83]

Following victory at Slim River, 25th Army's lines of communication were tenuous and still reliant on facilities in Thailand, extended over some 500 kilometres. The extended supply lines risked comprising the speed of advance. To offset this threat, Yamashita wanted to prevent the withdrawal of British forces and, through air support, offset the army's relative lack of artillery and its shell expenditure. However, the operations of 3 *Hikō Shudan* were not concentrated against a single decisive objective. Supporting 25th Army on either side of Malaya, across several axes of advance, air operations in this period included control of the air, reconnaissance, long-range bombing of Singapore and its airfields, close support to ground operations and interdiction attacks. This diffusion of effort was not opposed by Yamashita.[84] The IJAAS employed bombing and strafing with the aim of disrupting the movements of transports on the limited road network, and at the relatively few crossing points for motor transports.[85] Strafing and bombing attacks were also made on trains by Japanese aircraft.[86] Crucially, however, the effort to interdict the British forces was not concentrated. Instead, units assigned to support the army frequently self-selected targets of opportunity within the overall area of operations, and large formations were not employed en masse to interdict the main transport nodes on the withdrawal route. As a consequence, attacks on any one formation were sporadic and whilst delays were caused, the IJAAS was unable to concentrate the retreating forces and allow 25th Army to engage them decisively.[87] Further interdiction could also have targeted road movements at night, a role the IJAAS was unprepared to meet because of a lack of pilots trained for operations at night.[88] Despite persistent IJAAS interdiction attacks on the roads and railways they were unable to prevent the withdrawal of troops and transports. Wavell would later write that 'had the Japanese used their air superiority effectively there would have been a complete disaster.'[89]

83 TNA: AIR 23/4714: 'Directive from ABDACOM to Wes Group, Singapore', 18 Jan. 1942.
84 Miyako, *Japanese Monograph 55*, pp.87–9; Allen, *Singapore*, p.174, pp.187–8; Farrell, *Defence and Fall*, pp.336–7; Kirby, *Loss of Singapore*, p.411.
85 IWM: Audio/10813: Ian Howard Wethey, Reel 3, 00:16:5; IWM: Audio/22926: Fergus Gordon Anckorn, Reel 2, 00:23:00; IWM: Audio/18362: Ronald Delavigne, Reel 1, 00:10:00.
86 IWM: Audio/4748: Harold Lloyd Payne, Reel 1, 00:20:00.
87 Kirby, *Loss of Singapore*, p.391.
88 TNA: AIR 40/2137: Director of Air Tactics, 'Replies to questionnaire on Japanese Air Tactics'.
89 TNA: CAB 106/38: General Sir Archibald Wavell, Despatch on 'Operations in Southwest Pacific, 15 January 1942 to 25 February 1942', 1948.

Despite such views, the IJAAS did meaningfully contribute to the Japanese breakthrough at Slim River and the subsequent pursuit of British forces. In addition to concentrating troops of 11th Division sufficiently to allow the 25th Army to inflict losses on the formation of more than 75 percent, the IJAAS made repeated low-level attacks on artillery batteries immediately behind the frontline during the retreat. These attacks destroyed guns and towing lorries, delayed the movement of artillery, and reduced the time batteries could fire before having to relocate their positions. This reduced the artillery fire support that the rearguard received during the retreat. The defeat at Slim River resulted in the rapid loss of central Malaya and reduced the likelihood that southern Malaya could be held long enough to allow reinforcements to reach Singapore in time to influence the outcome of the campaign.

Battle of Muar

The withdrawal into northern Johor, on 14 January, temporarily shifted the focus of air operations for both sides further towards close support for the ground forces. The defence of northern Johore coincided with the arrival of air reinforcements. Wavell hoped that these reinforcements would enable close support to be provided to the defending troops. Nonetheless, a tension existed between this aspiration, the need to regain air superiority and the priority assigned to air cover over the convoys bringing reinforcements into Singapore.[90] As a result, when Percival issued orders to Bennet for the defence of Johor, he noted that effective air support for the infantry could not be provided. This was despite it being recognised that if the position in Johore was lost then Singapore would fall. In comparison, Japanese air attacks in support of the ground campaign were now increasing in tempo.

The defence of Johore rested on positions on the two main road arteries in west Malaya. The British distributed their forces in the areas of Muar and Gemas. To defend Muar, the 45th Indian Brigade were ordered to take up an extended line, with troops deployed both sides of the Muar River towards Segamat – which sits behind Gemas. The defence of Gemas included the 27th Australian Brigade in a forward position at a bridge leading towards Gemas, seeking to ambush the Japanese advance. The first encounters between the fresh Australian troops and the Japanese offered some hope for the defence of Singapore. The ambush before Gemas had inflicted heavy casualties to the Japanese 5th Division. Despite these successes, pressure increased as the Japanese reinforced their attacks and after pausing on 16 January, ground was gained on 17 January. Against the 45th Brigade, the Japanese had greater success, and, on the night of 15 January, they were able to cross the Muar River. This followed successive bombing attacks on Muar which had begun on 11 January, and which aided the Japanese 4th Guards Regiment to occupy the

90 Wigmore, *Japanese Thrust*, pp.201–213.

defending forces whilst the 5th Guards Regiment crossed the Muar River. In the following days the IJAAS made numerous low-level attacks against defensive positions and successfully interdicted movements.

During the advance into Johor, the IJAAS actively supported the Japanese Army. Tenang rail station – on the route leading from Yong Peng to Segamat – and Segamat – a valuable interdiction target with river crossing and strategically important crossroads – had been bombed on 11 and 13 January.[91] On 14 January, the IJAAS again attacked targets in Segamat, during which they achieved a direct hit on 9th Indian Division Headquarters.[92] The main IJAAS focus, prior to 15 January, was, however, directed against troops defending the town of Muar which was kept under constant attack on 11 and 13 January, but not on 12 January when heavy rain curtailed operations. RAF fighters were able to provide only limited air cover to the troops at Muar whose AA provision was minimal and, dating from 1918, was considered 'practically worn out'.[93]

On the morning of 15 January, Gemas was heavily bombed by the Japanese, following close air reconnaissance the previous afternoon.[94] Further air attacks were made in direct support of the ground battle, with 2/30th Australian battalion headquarters and company areas being bombed. Japanese dive bombers targeted anti-tank gun and field artillery pieces. Early in the afternoon, the Japanese looked to advance, using their armour to push through the defences, and the assault was supported by air attack.[95] During IJAAS attacks, if Allied troops began to direct small arms fire against the aircraft, the Japanese ground forces looked to take advantage of the diversion of firing targets by launching their attacks. [96] Although this attack was unsuccessful, aerial activity and artillery fire from the forces clashing at Gemas grew in intensity during the afternoon.[97] Counterattacks regained limited ground, but they lacked effective artillery support because an IJAAS Sentai of 12 aircraft, directly cooperating with ground units, were strafing and bombing artillery positions. A gun tractor was amongst several vehicles destroyed in these attacks.[98] With mounting pressure, the Australians pulled out, a movement hindered by IJAAS aircraft strafing transports as they withdrew.[99] Owing to the damage done to the artillery's vehicles, and the boggy ground conditions, three 25-pounder artillery pieces had to be abandoned. The 8th Indian Brigade, in positions behind the 27th Australian Brigade, also received heavy air attacks. Muhammad Khan, an officer in 2/10th Battalion Baluch Regiment, 8th

91 AWM: 52-4/1/15/4: Royal Australian Artillery Headquarters (R.A.A.HQ), 8 Australian Division AIF Malaya, War Diary January–February 1942, 11–13 Jan 1942.
92 IWM: Documents/3396: Goodman, Diary, 14–15 Jan. 1942; AWM: 52-4/1/15/4: R.A.A.HQ, 14–15 Jan 1942.
93 AWM: 52-4/1/15/4. R.A.A.HQ, 10-13 Jan 1942; Kirby, *Loss of Singapore*, p.414.
94 AWM: 52-4/1/15/4: R.A.A.HQ, 14 Jan 1942; Kirby, *Loss of Singapore*, p.413.
95 Wigmore, *Japanese Thrust*, pp.218–219.
96 IWM: Audio/6011: James Ronald Gregory, Reel 1, 00:15:00.
97 AWM: 2020.22.30: Austin Ellerman Yeats, Diary, 15 Jan 1942.
98 AWM: 52-4/1/15/4: R.A.A.HQ, 15 Jan 1942.
99 Wigmore, *Japanese Thrust*, p.220.

Brigade, recalled that in mid-January the Battalion had been under 'extraordinary air bombardment'.[100] On 17 January, the IJAAS conducted harassment raids in areas immediately behind the frontline, bombing Yong Peng, Buloh Kasah, Segamat, and Batu Anam. These operations, in increasing strength, were continued the following days with increasing attacks on Segamat and Labis.

Attempting to stymie the flow of forward reinforcements, the RAF undertook operations to interdict Japanese movements on the Gemas road. Ground operations were now within range of fighter squadrons based in Singapore and efforts in support of the forward positions began to increase.[101] Contributing to the increase in air support was the arrival in theatre of Air Vice-Marshal Paul Maltby who from 12 January assumed the role of Assistant Air Officer Commanding Air Headquarters Far East, RAF. In 1940–41, Maltby had commanded No. 71 Group (Army Co-Operation) in the United Kingdom and in the summer of 1941 had studied 'air support bombers' operating in close coordination with ground forces whilst observing the American Louisiana Manoeuvres.[102] During the latter Maltby had noted that 'most of the more successful missions were directed against targets by the air force commander and his staff, based on the Army Commander's general plan and directions in keeping with the development of the battle and not in response to requests from army troops or formations in the forefront of the battle.'[103] Maltby's arrival coincided with RAF resources being used to a greater extent in the land battle, with Squadrons operating with less prescriptive instructions but within the structures of the general plan of operations and wider battlefield developments. Requests from forward troops were, however, often refused because the targets requested for attack were unsuitable.

The combination of a more coherent integration of air assets in the ground campaign and the proximity of the battlefield increased the effectiveness of the air support that the RAF provided.[104] In the morning of 16 January, 12 RAAF Buffalo fighters strafed a long and concentrated Japanese convoy on the Gemas road. In the afternoon a small force of bombers, along with a fighter escort, repeated the attack. Following the bombing, the convoy received further strafing attacks. During the attacks on the Gemas Road on 16 January, fighter aircraft alone expended 17,000 rounds.[105] These operations achieved notable success in one of the rare instances where ground and air forces achieved effective coordination and Japanese motor transports were attacked, with sixty vehicles reported destroyed.[106] Reconnaissance sorties over the area of Gemas on 16 January also undertook strafing of enemy ground troops. Air interdic-

100 IWM: Audio/11748: Muhammad Ismail Khan, Reel 5, 00:03:50.
101 RAFM: AIR 41/63: AHB, Malaya, p.134.
102 G. Patrick Murray, 'The Louisiana Manoeuvres: Practice for War', *Louisiana History: The Journal of the Louisiana Historical Association*, 13:2 (1972), pp.117–38.
103 RAFM: AC73/15/3/1: Air Vice-Marshal Paul Maltby, American Diary, 18 Sept 1941.
104 Wigmore, *Japanese Thrust*, p.223.
105 AWM: 54-81/4/140: Lyster, *First Narrative*, p.72.
106 AWM: 52-4/1/15/4: R.A.A.HQ, 16–17 Jan 1942; RAFM: AIR 41/63: AHB, Malaya, pp.95–96; Kirby, *Loss of Singapore*, p.413.

tion attacks were also made on the route through Gemas and, in the course of these sorties, a Japanese formation headquarters was observed and bombed.[107] On 17 and 18 January, the RAF repeated strafing and bombing attacks on troops' movements and marshalling yards at Gemas.[108] As well as interdicting road movements during this period, Japanese troops' movements along the coastline and rivers of Malacca were attacked. RAF support for the ground forces on the west coast, however, left insufficient forces for similar operations in the east where the priority remained maritime patrols and anti-shipping attacks, with the latter being undertaken at the request of the Army on several occasions during this period. As well as guarding against a threatened landing in south-east Malaya, the RAF was also instructed that all available air effort was to be directed to destroying Japanese convoys looking to pass south of Singapore.[109] Therefore, despite the gravity of the military situation that was unfolding during this period, the majority of sorties undertaken by squadrons equipped with the Lockheed Hudson, a twin-engined bomber and maritime reconnaissance aircraft, were directed to reconnaissance off the east coast of Malaya.

In response to the increased activity and effective attacks being made by RAF forces in support of the ground campaign, the IJAAS increased its air superiority sorties. Having increased their air cover for the movement of the Japanese army on the Gemas road, the resources available for strafing attacks in support of the ground forces was reduced. Air support for Japanese ground forces was therefore reduced during the second half of January but IJAAS bombers continued to actively support the advance.

On 20 January, the IJASS continually bombed the forward positions of 27th Brigade as well as undertaking close reconnaissance of the lines which aided Japanese artillery fire. RAF fighter units operating from Singapore, as well as being engaged in morning and afternoon patrols to counter Japanese bombing of Singapore, were directed to patrol north, up the Malaya peninsula. The patrols would conduct strafing or other army support operations but to those conducting them it felt as though the main purpose was 'showing their aircraft to the troops.'[110] Despite the decisive nature of the battle in Johor, and the morale of the defending forces being worsened by a perceived lack of air support, close air support was not the most important contribution that the RAF could provide during the fighting. Interdiction attacks, such as those on the Gemas road, offered a meaningful opportunity to influence the ground campaign.[111] So, too, did operations which reduced IJAAS air support for 25th Army and RAF counter-air operations continued in January. On 20 January, for instance, attacks on congested IJAAS units occupying airfields Kuala Lumpur and Kuantan destroyed five aircraft and damaged a further

107 AWM: 52-4/1/15/4: R.A.A.HQ, 17 Jan 1942.
108 AWM: 54-81/4/140: Lyster, *First Narrative,* p.73, p.77.
109 AWM: 54-81/4/140: Lyster, *First Narrative,* p.82.
110 IWM: Audio/15577: James A. Sandeman Allen, Reel 1, 00:17:05–00:19:40.
111 Tsuji, *Japan's Greatest Victory*, p.162.

six.[112] Given the limited size of the forces available to the RAF, however, the overall effect of any operation remained limited.

On 20 January, the 45th Indian Brigade were ordered to withdraw as their positions south of the Muar River were at risk of being outflanked by the Japanese advance along the coast of the Johor Straight. Earlier in the battle, at 1000 hours on 19 January, the IJAAS had delivered an effective attack against the Brigade's Headquarters which resulted in the death of all but one of the staff officers and destroyed it as a command centre.[113] The situation was serious and the Army began making urgent demands for air support to counter the incessant low-flying and dive-bombing IJAAS attacks being made against the forces at Muar. Coordinating this air support was difficult, formations were dispersed and wireless was subject to geophysical interference, and it was not until mid-afternoon, at 1518 hours, that Buffalo fighters took off to provide much needed air cover. Arriving over the 45th Indian Brigade, these fighters intercepted six IJAAS Army 97 bombers and drove off their attacks. The following day would bring yet more urgent calls for air support, principally air cover, but also ground attack and air supply. The RAAF escorting fighters, three Buffalo, undertook strafing of Japanese troops when no IJAAS opposition was encountered. The head of the retreating column reached the bridge at Parit Sulong but found it was already held by the Japanese. So urgent was the need to support the ground forces' attempt to push through the Japanese that two Fairey Albacore biplane torpedo bombers were bombed up and despatched to attack troops at the bridge. The attack was not, however, made in close cooperation with the ground forces and although relatively successful, it did not enable the crossing to be forced. Only limited further air support could be provided and the 45th Brigade, compressed into an increasingly restricted area, was forced to defend against Japanese attacks supported by both low-level air attacks and artillery fire directed by aircraft. Dispersing through the jungle, 1,000 troops succeeded in returning to the British lines, but the 45th Brigade was destroyed as an effective force.[114] Japanese air support and interdiction attacks played a contributory part in this success.

On 21 January, the 27th Australian Brigade, holding Yong Peng and subject to numerous attacks by the IJAAS, began to make calls for air support. The RAAF and the Australian ground forces had effectively liaised on the nature and requirements for air cooperation on the east coast of Malaya since 7 January.[115] By mid-January, however, the RAF and RAAF were required to prioritise the protection of convoys arriving into Singapore with reinforcements.[116] The result was that the IJAAS was able to make attacks which kept continual pressure on 27th Brigade whilst Japanese ground forces tried to infiltrate and outflank their positions. As the pressure increased

112 RAFM: AIR 41/63: AHB, Malaya, p.112.
113 Wigmore, *Japanese Thrust*, p.233.
114 Kirby, *Loss of Singapore*, p.428.
115 Bennett, *Why Singapore Fell*, p.83.
116 TNA: AIR 23/4714: 'Directive from ABDACOM to Wes Group', Singapore, 18 Jan 1942.

on 22 January, Albacores were once more despatched to undertake tactical bombing missions in support of the forward line, this time accompanied by a Blackburn Shark, a biplane which was in theatre as a target-towing aircraft – a job it was considered unsuitable for owing to its lack of speed.[117] This scratch force successfully bombed a Japanese motor transport column moving up to Yong Peng from Muar.[118] On 23 January, a composite force which comprised all available Albacores, Sharks and CAC Wirrays – a single-engine monoplane, with a crew of two, predominantly used in a training role – was despatched to make interdiction attacks on the Japanese lines of communication. On 24 January, 14 single-engine biplane torpedo bombers, both Vickers Vildebeest and Fairey Albacores, were despatched in a night attack designed to interdict movements on the Gemas-Yong Peng road.[119] As the Japanese advanced into southern Malaya, these outdated types were called on to delay the arrival of supplies and reinforcements, even if only briefly, in order to ease the pressure on the withdrawal back to Singapore.

The IJAAS was also able to achieve success against transport columns in their attacks. The effect over these attacks was aided by the poor route control and discipline of the newly-arrived reinforcements in Malaya. Motor convoys which moved towards the front prior to the fighting at Muar were closely packed across the route of advance, including the highly vulnerable and prominent crossroads, with the result they were often vulnerable targets for air attack.[120] Throughout the withdrawal from Muar the IJAAS divebombed the packed transports of the British forces as they travelled along the limited road network.[121]

Small units were also subject to attack and had their withdrawal from forward positions towards the main forces harassed by aircraft.[122] These attacks were not undertaken by large formations but, possessing air superiority, Japanese bombers could operate at low level immediately behind the frontline. Under air attack, the largely inexperienced freshly arrived units became dispersed and there were lengthy delays before columns were able to assemble and continue movements.[123] On both 22 and 23 January, the IJAAS made attacks on Australian troops in forward battle area. Throughout 23 January, the IJAAS bombed at least five different major crossroads immediately behind the frontline, as well as making repeated strafing and bombing attacks on the withdrawal along the major roadways. These attacks were in addition to further close reconnaissance and air support over the frontline which continued on 24 January. The IJAAS also made attacks against the artillery batteries supporting the British forces.[124] Throughout the morning of 25 January, III Corps found that

117 RAFM: AC73/15/3/11: Maltby, 'Notes on Norgroup'.
118 RAFM: AIR 41/63: AHB, Malaya, p.112.
119 RAFM: AIR 41/63: AHB, Malaya, p.113.
120 Colonel James Thyer in Wigmore, *Japanese Thrust*, p.228.
121 IWM: Audio/10813: Ian Howard Wethey, Reel 3, 00:16:50.
122 AWM: 2020.22.30: Austin Ellerman Yeats, Diary, 15 Jan 1942.
123 IWM: Audio/6171: Berthold Wells Key, Reel 3, 00:04:00.
124 AWM: 52-4/1/15/4: R.A.A.HQ, 23–24 Jan 1942.

Brewster Buffalo Mk II (WP-F, WP-N, WP-O, WP-Y, WP-U, WP-W, WP-K, WP-B and four others), of 243 Squadron, in formation flight over Singapore, 2 February 1942. (RAF Museum: P007759)

movements on the route behind Yong Peng were being repeatedly divebombed by the IJAAS. Urgently, calls were made for air cover over III Corps, and the RAF met these in the afternoon of 25 January. Twelve Buffalo fighters were despatched and, with the IJAAS attacks having abated, and the request having changed to offensive support, these made a sweep to the west of III Corps to interdict Japanese movements towards Yong Peng.[125] On 27 January, Australian troops were subjected to numerous air attacks, both bombing and strafing, as the IJAAS continued to harass and interdict movements behind the frontlines.[126] The roads were under almost continual air attack for prolonged periods, and, with signal wires and telegraph lines having been cut and wireless prone to interference, this delayed the relaying of orders and intelligence between units and headquarters.[127] The IJAAS also targeted forward ground positions, with 2/26th and 2/30th Battalions, and 2/15th Field Regiment RA receiving notable attacks, whilst the headquarters of 27th Brigade and 9th Indian Division were bombed.[128]

125 RAFM: AIR 41/63: AHB, Malaya, pp.113–114.
126 AWM: 2020.22.245: Major John William Cardwell Wyett, Diary, 27 Jan 1942.
127 TNA: AIR 20/5576: Wing Commander Cave, 'Report by Command Signals Officer, Far East Command, RAF, on Malayan Operations, 1941–42', Dec 1945.
128 AWM: 52 4/1/15/4: R.A.A.HQ, 27 Jan 1942.

On the east coast, on 15 January, from 0930 until dark and continuing throughout the next day, IJAAS bombers were in operation against positions near Endau. On 18 January, as British forces moved up from Endau to the frontline, the IJAAS attacked the area with the aim of interdicting the movement of reinforcements. Forward positions at Endau were then bombed on 19–20 January.[129] British troops advancing to reinforce the line around Batu Pahat against an outflanking manoeuvre by the 5th Guard Regiment were also strafed and bombed as the IJAAS targeted positions behind the frontline to disrupt troop movements.[130] The IJAAS also targeted major crossroads behind the forward line on the east coast towards the end of January.[131]

As the Allies withdrew back to Singapore, a strong combined action by the Japanese forces could have caused complications to the British withdrawal to Singapore through the bottleneck of Johor Bahru, and across the Johor causeway. These operations and the final withdrawal from Malaya on 31 January were, however, subject to only minimal interference by either Japanese ground forces or the IJAAS. Following a week of preparations 25th Army crossed the straights of Johor and the IJAAS was active throughout the fighting in Singapore until its surrender on 15 February 1942.[132]

The extent to which the IJAAS actively supported the ground battle is suggested by their aircraft losses during the Malaya campaign. Given the limited extent the RAF could contest air superiority after the initial battle, the IJAAS losses were considerable. In the first month of combat the IJAAS lost 209 aircrew in operations in Malaya, 72 of whom were pilots. Excluding transport types, over half of the IJAAS's original air strength was damaged during the campaign in Malaya. Reconnaissance and bomber types suffered damage in excess of 66 percent between 8 December and 15 February.[133]

Conclusion

The Malayan Campaign starkly illustrates that the effective integration of air power on the battlefield is not defined by the material damage to the enemy created by air strikes on ground positions. It is, instead, the extent to which these strikes support the wider objectives of the ground campaign.

129 AWM: 2019.22.96: Arthur Leslie Varley, Diary, 19–20 Jan 1942.
130 IWM: Audio/23812: Cyril Doy, Reel 8, 00:03:30.
131 AWM: 2019.22.96: Arthur Leslie Varley, Diary, 26–31 Jan 1942.
132 AWM: 52-8/4/16/1: Special Reserve Battalion AIF (Malaya), War Diary, February 1942; IWM: Audio/6011: James Roland Gregory, Reel 1, 00:15:00, 00:26:50; IWM: Audio/6042: Geoffrey Pharaoh Adams, Reel 2, 00:00:50; Kirby, *Loss of Singapore*, p.513, p.521, p.534.
133 TNA: WO 208/1023: Air Headquarters Section No. 7, Translation of Captured Japanese Documents, 'Summary of Losses (and Percentage of Losses) of 3 Flying Division During Early Stages of Operations', 1 Sept 1942; Miyako, *Japanese Monograph 55*, p.95.

The initial heavy losses suffered by the RAF and RAAF squadrons limited the air support they could provide ground forces in Malaya. The attempted counter-air operations against targets in Thailand, conducted without local air superiority, were misguided. They resulted in further losses in operations that could not materially change the course of the campaign. The losses in the first stages of the campaign meant that the RAF could not afford to dissipate its remaining effort, but this occurred because of the inefficient organisation for Army cooperation. Operations in northern Malaya were characterised by targets of opportunity and request for air support either being unmet or attacked after such delay that the air support provided was no longer of value. The arrival of Maltby helped stabilise the staff work in Air Headquarters Far East and led to less prescriptive orders being issued to aircraft undertaking air support operations and armed reconnaissance sorties. Increased flexibility in the operational orders to aircrews allowed these sorties to be more responsive to the operational needs of the ground forces. As the campaign continued down the Malaya peninsula, and particularly as the fighting moved into range of fighter cover from Singapore, the RAF's operations in support of the ground forces increased in effectiveness. The reduced size of the air force meant, however, that the effect remained limited.

The IJAAS fought an exemplar air power campaign in support of the Japanese Army's ground campaign, whose ultimate objective was the capture of Singapore. The greatest obstacle to this objective was first the threat of interference from the RAF. After this was the need to keep British ground forces sufficiently off-balance that their relative strengths could not be effectively employed against the Japanese advance. At the outset of the campaign the IJAAS therefore prioritised counter-air operations and it entirely achieved its first aim, air superiority. Having done so, the IJAAS then persistently attacked the British ground forces. Attacks behind the battlefield interdicted the British forces on the limited road and rail network within Malaya. Opportunities did arise where the IJAAS might have sought to switch their full concentration to air interdiction, and which might potentially have offered 25th Army the opportunity to ensure the decisive defeat of the defending forces in Malaya. Instead, the IJAAS maintained its focus on air superiority and the decisive defeat of British forces was achieved in Singapore. The IJAAS's cooperation with 25th Army was, however, a key enabler in the rapid defeat of the British forces in Malaya. The morale effect of these attacks was pronounced on inexperienced British ground troops who rapidly became tired, fatigued, and demoralised by the course of the campaign. The IJAAS's direct cooperation with the Japanese army meaningfully contributed to the success of the latter's 'driving charge'. The IJAAS also consistently targeted artillery batteries and thereby restricted the fire support available to the infantry. Japanese air support, coordinated with ground operations and in close proximity to the battlefield, made a valuable contribution within the Malayan Campaign.

The campaign in Malaya demonstrates the value of close air support, conducted in close proximity to the battle and in coordination with ground forces. The IJAAS's direct cooperation operations consistently supported the ground forces to achieve their wider strategic objective. This was achieved by the psychological effect of its air strikes on and in close proximity to the battlefield, rather than causing physical destruction or large losses to British forces. The IJAAS achieved this by coordinating closely with the army at the outset of the campaign, and thereafter maintaining local coordination. The IJAAS was therefore able to provide tactical fire support at important points in the campaign, and to maintain a persistent pressure on British forces. It was not, however, able to consistently concentrate its forces against the battlefield. Instead, the IJAAS concentrated its limited forces on securing air superiority. Having done so, the IJAAS was then able to support the ground campaign. The RAF, unable to contest air superiority for much of the campaign, was able to have only an isolated influence on the battlefield despite the work it undertook to improve cooperation with ground forces. The campaign in Malaya therefore demonstrates both the importance of air power on the battlefield, an importance which cannot be measured solely by the physical destruction caused, and that an essential prerequisite of close air support is control of the air.

7

'Air Power in the Land Battle': Montgomery and Close Air Support

John Alexander

Introduction

In August 1942, the British Army, led by the Chief of the Imperial General Staff (CIGS), General Sir Alan Brooke, continued to demand the Chiefs of Staff agree an Army Air Arm or an RAF command whose sole task was to provide air support for the Army.[1] In doing so, it perpetuated Group Captain John Slessor's characterisation of the Army's view of army-air cooperation, in 1939, as 'the subordination of the Air Force to the Army'.[2]

Yet when Brooke's protégé and nominee to takeover British Eighth Army, Lieutenant General Bernard Law Montgomery, arrived at its forward Headquarters on Ruweisat Ridge on 13 August 1942, he 'asked where was the Air Force HQ [?]. He was told they were many miles back.'[3] They were forty miles away on the coast at Burg-el-Arab.[4] As he noted in his diary:

> When I took over command, Army HQ was right forward, and Air HQ Western Desert was right back near the landing grounds. The Army was fighting its battle and the RAF was fighting its battle. There was no combined HQ, with the two commanders and the two staffs completely in each other's pockets. I gather they

1 The National Archives, Kew (TNA): CAB 80/37: COS (42) 364 Continental Operations D43. Operational Organisational & System of Command dated 1 August 1942.
2 TNA: AIR 8/272: 'Note by D. Plans on General Staff Memorandum, June 1939'. Employment of Bombers, Fighters, and A.A. Defences in France: Minutes and Memoranda, 1939.
3 Montgomery of Alamein, Bernard Law Montgomery, *The Memoirs of Field-Marshal the Viscount Montgomery of Alamein* (London: Collins, 1958), p.99.
4 Francis Wilfred De Guingand, *Operation Victory* (London: Hodder and Stoughton, 1947), p.130.

> had been in close touch in the past. But the arrival of Auchinleck and Dorman-Smith at Army HQ seems to have altered that; the RAF had no use of either of these two, and Army HQ and the two staffs seem to have drifted apart. I decided to remedy this at once and move Army HQ back to Air HQ and invite the AOC and his senior staff officers into my mess. This was a good move, and from that moment we never looked back.[5]

Montgomery's 'method' from arriving in the desert to the German surrender is well known. To paraphrase John Buckley, it was to win with minimum casualties while maintaining morale through an organised battle, comprising a simple, efficient and well understood plan, 'with careful allocation of artillery and air power' to maximise fire power, with great consideration given to logistics.[6] Yet the literature, perhaps distracted by Montgomery's personality and other controversies, largely fails to recognise Montgomery's exceptional air-mindedness or explain it, though some contemporaries, including Brian Horrocks, Slessor, and Arthur Coningham noted it at the time. Hamilton's hagiographic biography of Montgomery, largely reliant on Montgomery's curated papers, occasionally picks out his consideration of air power whereas Barnett's *Desert Generals* revisionist criticism of Montgomery barely mentions the RAF.[7] More recently Hall's history of the development of British tactical air power from 1919 to 1943 notes Montgomery was the exception to the rule in his understanding of air power, without examining the underlying reasons.[8] Fennel has emphasised the important relationship of air power and morale during the North African Campaign, and Montgomery's understanding of it.[9] Despite recent excellent research on Montgomery's combined arms doctrine, there is, however, no monograph or research article that examines Montgomery as a proponent of air support.[10]

This chapter considers Montgomery's grasp of the essential character and importance of air power in support of the land battle, and its integration at army level, as he took over Eighth Army and examines how his understanding was different from other British Army generals at the time, and why that may have been. It starts therefore by

5 Nigel Hamilton, *Monty: The Making of a General 1887–1942* (Sevenoaks: Coronet, 1984), p.638.
6 John Buckley, *Monty's Men: The British Army and the Liberation of Europe* (Yale University Press, 2014), pp.29–30; See also Shelford Bidwell and Dominick Graham, *Fire-Power: The British Army Weapons and Theories of War 1904–1945* (Pen & Sword Books Limited, 2005), Book IV, The Second Round.
7 Correlli Barnett, *The Desert Generals*, 2nd ed (London: G. Allen & Unwin, 1983), p.22, p.41, p.191, p.233.
8 David Ian Hall, *Strategy for Victory: The Development of British Tactical Air Power, 1919–1943* (Westport, Conn: Praeger Security International, 2008), p.144.
9 Jonathan Fennell, 'Air Power and Morale in the North African Campaign of the Second World War', *Air Power Review*, 15:2 (2012), pp.1–17.
10 See for example: Charles James Forrester, *Monty's Functional Doctrine: Combined Arms Doctrine in British 21st Army Group in Northwest Europe, 1944–45*, Wolverhampton Military Studies (Helion & Company Limited, 2018).

The Western Desert Air Force used aircraft such as the No 2 Squadron South African Air Force Curtiss P-40 pictured here to provide air support to Eighth Army before Montgomery's arrival, but it lacked army/air force level coordination. (RAF Museum: PC77/5/821)

considering his understanding of integrating land and air power at the time he took over Eighth Army rather than what has subsequently been written. The chapter then examines the evidence of the development of Montgomery's understanding of joint air-land power, seeking to explain his air-mindedness.

Monty's air-mindedness

Montgomery made his understanding of the characteristics and importance of air power clear on taking over command of Eighth Army, just twenty-four hours after his arrival in Egypt. His aircraft landed at Cairo early on the morning of 12 August and he met with General Sir Claude Auchinleck, who was to hand over the Army's Middle East Command to General Sir Harold Alexander on 15 August. Auchinleck told Montgomery to spend two days with Eighth Army before taking over on 15 August. Montgomery then met with Alexander and Major General John Harding, the Deputy Chief of the General Staff, GHQ Middle East. At 0700 hours the following day, Montgomery picked up Brigadier Freddie de Guingand, a fellow Warwickshire Regiment officer he had previously patronised, who briefed him on the drive to Main HQ Eighth Army at Ruweisat Ridge. According to de Guingand the brief included the dislocation of the Army and Air Headquarters, the habit of fighting in dispersed 'Jock Columns', and the unsatisfactory headquarters set-up.[11] Montgomery told de Guingand he wanted to speak to all HQ staff that night. Thus, on arrival at HQ Eighth Army, Montgomery had yet to meet either Air Marshal Sir Arthur Tedder, the Air Officer Commanding-in-Chief (AOC-in-C) RAF Middle East Command, or Air Vice-Marshal Arthur Coningham, Air Officer Commanding (AOC) Air HQ, Western Desert.

Arriving at 1100 hours, at 1400 Montgomery announced by signal that he had taken command, two days early. That night, after visiting Lieutenant General Sir Bernard Freyberg and the New Zealand division, he gathered the HQ staff together. He told them he did not like the general atmosphere he found. The defence of Egypt lay here on the Ruweisat Ridge. There would be no further withdrawal; all plans and instructions dealing with further withdrawal were to be burnt at once. The Army would stand and fight, and if they could not stay there alive, they would stay there dead. There would be no bellyaching. He assured them he was quite sane and told them: 'The first thing to do is to move our HQ to a decent place where we can live in reasonable comfort and where the Army Staff can be together and side by side with the HQ of the Desert Air Force.'[12] Chapter three notes how the collocation of Army formation HQs and allocated RAF brigades had been standard practice in 1918 and to collocate was extant doctrine, although as Montgomery noted, like much doctrine it had not been consistently practiced in the desert.[13] Montgomery made de Guingand his chief of staff and de Guingand arranged the move of the HQ to Burg-el-Arab.

Montgomery thus first met Coningham on 16 August when their HQs collocated. Montgomery and Coningham agreed on the importance of air superiority as a prerequisite for effective air support and the merits of a joint command system. Coningham was most impressed, telling Air Vice-Marshal Tommy Elmhirst, the Air Officer Administration, 'Tommy, I have now been with the Army in this desert for over a year and have seen three Army Commanders and two Corps Commanders come and go, but we now have a man, a great soldier if I am any judge, and we will go all the way with him.'[14]

A few days later, Montgomery, when visiting his protégé and newly arrived corps commander Lieutenant General Brian Horrocks, gave him a glowing account of the Desert Air Force while they were sheltering from a Stuka attack. Montgomery told Horrocks, 'And you know the Army and RAF must fight hand in hand.' Horrocks later wrote Montgomery was the most air-minded general he ever met.[15] On 21 August Coningham, Elmhirst and Harry Broadhurst attended Montgomery's first

11 De Guingand, *Operation Victory*, p.135.
12 TNA: CAB 106/703: 'Western Desert: Copy of an Address to Officers of Headquarters 8th Army by General B.L. Montgomery', 13 August 1942.
13 TNA: AIR 10/1889: Royal Air Force Manual of Army Co-Operation 2nd Edition Amendment Lists: 1-8 1937 (Reprint), Chapter III.
14 Vincent Orange, *Coningham: A Biography of Air Marshal Sir Arthur Coningham* (London: Methuen, 1990), p.106.
15 Brian Horrocks, *A Full Life*, [Rev. ed.] (London: L. Cooper, 1974), p.122.

Air Officer Commanding and Staff Officers, Burg-el-Arab, 10 August 1942, six days before Montgomery moved HQ Eighth Army to join them; Air Vice-Marshal Coningham is in the centre, seated. (RAF Museum: X002-7488)

corps commanders' conference where the plans for the defensive Battle of Alam Halfa were worked out jointly.[16]

Montgomery's first battle in the desert, the Battle of Alam Halfa, from 30 August to 6 September 1942, according to the RAF's official history of air support during the war, 'set the seal on the procedure and organisation for air support.' It exemplified 'the use of air power on efficient and economical lines, when used in direct support of an army in the field.'[17] Tedder and Coningham had been organising unrelenting air attacks on Rommel's forces all year, but often previously in isolation from Eighth Army. Now, as Air Marshal Sir Arthur Barratt, AOC-in-C Army Cooperation Command, reported, after visiting during the battle, Montgomery and Coningham worked together, and Montgomery attributed the victory to the joint army-air plan drawn up in the joint army-air HQ.[18] The Desert Air Force first gained air superiority. Its continuous air interdiction meant the enemy was launching an offensive with only 20 percent of the fuel it required. Nine days before the enemy attacked, RAF medium bombers attacked enemy columns moving forward, and during the battle light bombers attacked enemy formations, forcing the feared German 88mm guns into the AA rather than anti-tank role.[19] This was a victory for RAF theory, with the air force being integral to the Army plan and not an ancillary, and air superiority was the key. Montgomery reminded Eighth Army before Second Alamein started on 23 October 1942 that they were backed up by 'the finest air striking force in the world', recognising it was not an ancillary air arm.[20]

Montgomery continued to consolidate his thoughts on air power in the land battle, eventually in 1945 pronouncing air power as the first principle of war, notwithstanding his increasingly difficult relations with Tedder and Coningham in north-west Europe. A month after Alamein, Montgomery published the pamphlet *Some Notes for Senior Officers on the Conduct of Battle*, which gives an clear indication of his prioritisation of air support.[21] The first section highlighted the importance of selection and maintenance of the aim, the second of morale (both principles of war), and the third the importance of air-land coordination, of securing airfields, of involving the RAF in planning from the start, and of the employment of fighters, bombers, and reconnaissance aircraft, as well as close support, before outlining his concept of land battle. Using J.F.C. Fuller's principles of war, adopted in the 1920s by both the Army and RAF, Montgomery went on to highlight in the pamphlet the importance of concentration, cooperation of all arms, simplicity, and speed of action.[22]

16 Orange, *Coningham,* pp.106–7.
17 Air Historical Branch (AHB), *Air Publication 3235. The Second World War, 1939–1945, Royal Air Force, Air Support* (London: Air Ministry (AHB), 1955), p.69.
18 TNA: AIR 20/3093: Middle East: 'Report on Visit by Air Marshal Barratt', 1942.
19 AHB, *Air Support*, pp.70–1.
20 Montgomery of Alamein, *Memoirs*, p.128.
21 RAF Museum: AIR 69/968: Some Brief Notes for Senior Officers on the Conduct of Battle by General BL Montgomery, C-in-C 8th Army, December 1942.
22 Alaric Searle, 'Inter-Service Debate and the Origins of Strategic Culture: The "Principles of War" in the British Armed Forces, 1919–1939', *War in History*, 21:1 (2014), pp.4–32.

Lieutenant General B.L. Montgomery in the Western desert before El Alamein, soon after taking over Eighth Army, n.d. (RAF Museum: PC95/46/12)

Montgomery's address to his Tripoli lessons conference in early 1943, soon after its capture, was published as *Some Notes on High Command.*[23] The aim of the conference was to learn lessons from the recent victory at Second Alamein and the subsequent pursuit, and was partly aimed at the commanders of the newly arrived Anglo-US forces in Algeria. Air power, strategical, tactical and army, is listed first. In the pamphlet, Montgomery also noted that understanding air power was a necessity for all aspiring army commanders. Subsequently Coningham's address to the same conference was published in the UK as *Air Power in the Land Battle*, a note by the Chief of the Air Staff.[24] It stated all land operations were land-air operations which must be jointly planned and conducted by the army and air force commanders together. Called the Montgomery-Coningham system, this doctrine was also adopted by the US Army and US Army Air Forces in early 1943.[25]

The success of the Montgomery-Coningham system was such that it was adopted in the UK for the invasion of Europe against the War Office's resistance, holding out

23 General Sir B.L. Montgomery, *Some Notes on High Command in War*, second edition (Italy: Eighth Army, 1943).
24 TNA: AIR 20/4582: Army/Air Cooperation: 'Air Power in the Land Battle.' 1943 Feb–June.
25 United States. War Department, *FM 100-20 Command and Employment of Air Power 1943* (Washington, U.S. Govt. Printing Office, 1943).

for a separate Army Cooperation Command. A composite, multifunctional, unified group like the Desert Air Force, collocated with the Army HQ was proven in Exercise *Spartan* in March 1943. On 29 April, the Chief of the Air Staff, Air Chief Marshal Sir Charles Portal, proposed to the Chiefs of Staff the formation of an Expeditionary Air Force that would operate on the model of the Eighth Army and Desert Air Force.[26] It was accepted two days later. Tedder noted in a letter to Portal: 'I suggest CIGS [Brooke] is now caught in a cleft stick. He cannot disown Monty, but he must choose to repudiate Monty's views, which are founded on battle, or himself be a minority voice.'[27]

Slessor was later to note it was:

> ...difficult for older officers to adjust their mentality to the new concepts of a land campaign as a joint venture, rather than one on which the RAF was in a position entirely subordinate to the army. Montgomery understands that brilliantly, but for some time he was almost a lone voice crying the in the wilderness.[28]

The beginnings of Montgomery's exceptionalism

Montgomery's air-mindedness is evident soon after the First World War when he went out of his way to include aircraft in his sub-unit training schemes. Thus when commanding A Company, 1st Battalion Royal Warwickshire Regiment in May 1925, he arranged for an RAF officer to be attached for a week and for No. 2 (Army Cooperation Squadron) RAF to give a demonstration 'showing the various ways in which aircraft can cooperate with infantry in war.'[29] The squadron, equipped with Bristol Fighters and based at RAF Manston, was commanded by Squadron Leader R.E. Saul who was to be a student at Camberley in 1927 when Montgomery was Directing Staff (DS). It is possible other company commanders did the same but at the time one Army Cooperation Squadron was assigned to each division. Although this allocation of squadrons to divisions was twice that of 1918, there were thirty-six companies in each division which made such cooperation exceptional. Later, as an acting brigade commander on an exercise in Egypt in 1932, when de Guingand was his brigade major, Montgomery appropriated RAF Army Cooperation aircraft to support his brigade when they were allocated to the division.[30] These actions indicate

26 TNA: CAB 80/69/24: C.O.S. (43) 224 (O), 'The Organisation of the RAF. for Continental Operations. Memorandum by the Chief of Staff Committee', 1943, p.1; TNA: CAB 79/60/41: COS (43) (O), 91st 1 May 1943 2. 'Organisation of the RAF for Continental Operations'.

27 Hall, *Strategy to Victory*, p.150.

28 John Slessor, *The Central Blue: Recollections and Reflections* (London: Cassell, 1956), pp.418–19.

29 Nigel Hamilton, *Monty: The Making of a General 1887–1942* (Sevenoaks: Coronet, 1984), p.185.

30 Nigel Hamilton, *Monty: The Making of a General*, p.185.

Montgomery was convinced of the utility of air power on the battlefield, albeit obsolete army cooperation aircraft, and was determined to include it in his formation training.

Montgomery's First World War experience as a staff officer seems to have been key to his development not only into an outstanding staff officer and trainer of men, but also because his staff officer experience involved air-land coordination. Whereas his contemporaries such as Viscount Gort, Alexander and Richard O'Connor distinguished themselves during the First World War in battalion or brigade command – or his airmen contemporaries such as Tedder, Coningham and Trafford Leigh-Mallory in command of squadrons – Montgomery witnessed rather than experienced command.[31] In his memoirs Montgomery noted that 'by the time the 1914–18 war was over it had become very clear to me that the profession of arms was a life-study.'[32] By the inter-war period Montgomery realised all arms integration included air-land.

In the First World War as a general staff officer (GSO) in a formation HQ, Montgomery was responsible for operations, intelligence, and training staff duties, and it was at corps and army HQs where air-land cooperation was practiced. Unlike the hated 'ground strafing' – described in earlier chapters – artillery observation and tactical reconnaissance Royal Flying Corps (RFC) squadrons were allotted to corps (and called corps squadrons). By 1918 air power was essential to what Jonathan Bailey calls the birth of the modern system of warfare, which transformed the linear battlefield of 1914, familiar to Napoleon or Wellington, to the three-dimensional battlefield of 1918, recognisable to us now.[33]

The evidence suggests, therefore, Montgomery's time at Headquarters IX Corps on the Western Front from July 1917 until July 1918 will have been influential. As Hamilton's authorised biography highlights, Montgomery, as the IX Corps GSO2 Training, issued a typical forty-page preparatory instruction prior to its involvement in British Second Army's attacks at the Third Battle of Ypres.[34] Montgomery's instructions included the use of aerial photographs and intelligence provided by No. 53 Squadron RFC as the corps squadron.[35] General Sir Herbert Plumer's bite and hold tactics, using steel rather than blood, the concentration of force at decisive points and the rapid consolidation and use of artillery on the inevitable German counterattacks made a lasting impression on Montgomery.[36] Furthermore, Montgomery would

31 See John Keegan, *Churchill's Generals* (Weidenfeld and Nicolson, 1991).

32 Montgomery of Alamein, *Memoirs*, p.36.

33 Jonathan B. A. Bailey, 'The First World War and the Birth of Modern Warfare', in MacGregor Knox and Williamson Murray (eds), *The Dynamics of Military Revolution, 1300–2050*, 1st edn (Cambridge University Press, 2001), pp.132–53.

34 Hamilton, *Monty: Making of a General*, p.127.

35 H.A. Jones, *The War in the Air: Being the Story of the Part Played in the Great War by the Royal Air Force*, History of the Great War Based on Official Documents by Direction of the Historical Section of the Committee of Imperial Defence, 6 vols (Oxford: Clarendon Press, 1935), Volume iv, p.181.

36 Hamilton, *Full Monty*, pp.125–27.

have seen that 'the good weather allowed the RFC a clear view of the enemy's depth and German counter-attacks, which … collapsed against the concentrated artillery fire against them.'[37]

Later Montgomery experienced operating without air superiority and therefore without air support. This experience, one Hamilton omits from his biography, occurred during the Third Battle of the Aisne, at the end of May 1918, when Montgomery was GSO1 (chief operations staff officer) for IX Corps. Here the five battered divisions of IX Corps reconstituting on the Chemin-des-Dames in the quiet Champagne sector were part of the French Sixth Army under General Denis Aguste Duchêne. Duchêne ignored General Philip Petain's call for elastic defence and placed most of his sixteen divisions, including the five British on a forward slope lacking the depth to face the German *Operation Blucher* offensive.[38]

The IX Corps RAF squadron, No. 52, reported clouds of dust caused by infantry and artillery on 22, 23 and 24 May but this intelligence was not acted upon. It was also not recorded in the HQ War Diary signed off by Montgomery. No. 52 Squadron flew continuous patrols from 24 May and, as there was no German air activity, they were able to fly low but found no further evidence of the forthcoming attack.[39] When the German attack came on 27 May, it was accompanied by the German Air Service gaining air superiority. For example, in one combat report from 1 June 1918, Lieutenant Illsley's Royal Aircraft Factory RE.8 was attacked by eight Halberstadts.[40]

Montgomery witnessed the unhappy experience of the RE.8s of No. 52 Squadron, who had struggled to integrate with the French air service and therefore had no protection for reconnaissance. Their detection of the enemy was ignored and they were swept from the skies.[41] The attack shattered the Allied lines and the German Army advanced 22 kilometres, the largest single day's advance of the War.[42] By the end of the battle IX Corps was reduced to little more than one division.

In contrast during the earlier Battle of Lys against the German *Georgette* offensive in April 1918, IX Corps was supported by No. 3 Squadron RAF, operating under Allied air superiority and the fighters' (or scouts') 'ground strafing' played a key role

37 Jeremy Pughe-Morgan, 'The Third Battle of Ypres (Passchendaele)', in Mungo Melvin (ed), *The First World War Battlefield Guide. the Western Front Volume 1 Volume 1*, 2nd edn (Andover: Creative Media Design, Army Headquarters, 2015), pp.107–14 (p.111).

38 David T. Zabecki, *The German 1918 Offensives: A Case Study in the Operational Level of War* (London: Routledge, 2006), p.216.

39 TNA: AIR 1/677/21/13/1887: Air Operations, the Western Front. 1918 May–Nov. AHB Narrative, p.2, p.6; TNA: WO 95/837/1: IX Corps Headquarters Branches and Services: General Staff War Diary, May 1918, pp.6–7.

40 TNA: AIR 1/1223/204/5/2634/73: Air Combat Reports: 52 Squadron Royal Air Force, June 1918, 'Combats in the Air,' 1 June 1918.

41 TNA: AIR 1/675/21/13/1265: 'The German Attack on 27th May 1918, by Member of 52 Squadron'.

42 Zabecki, *The German 1918 Offensives,* p.219.

in delaying the German attacks.[43] Furthermore, as the GSO1 Operations of 47th Division during the later Hundred-days Campaign, Montgomery was less involved with air-land as the coordination was normally at Corps HQ, but he routinely received air reconnaissance reports and included air reconnaissance in his orders to the division. He was therefore aware and receptive to the value of air power in the land battle.[44] From his battle experience in a formation HQ, Montgomery saw at first hand the importance of gaining control of the air to enable subsequent aerial reconnaissance and attack. Thus, Montgomery's staff experience was significantly different from commanding a battalion in the line.

Exposure to air power thinking at Staff College

It is difficult to assess on the available evidence Montgomery's understanding of air power from his time as a student at Camberley in 1920 and when DS at Camberley from 1926–1929. RAF instruction was, however, increasingly part of the curriculum. The Chief of the Air Staff, Air Chief Marshal Sir Hugh Trenchard, selected the early RAF DS. For example, Wing Commander Leslie Gossage was the RAF DS in 1925, having attended the course in 1923, was an expert in Army Cooperation, joining from commanding the School of Army Cooperation, and before that he had been selected as Trenchard's personal staff officer at the Cairo Conference which decided how Mandate Iraq was to be governed and gave the RAF military control. Gossage later published a book on air power and retired as an air marshal.[45] His successor, O.T. Boyd had the same Army Cooperation pedigree and would have been Deputy AOC-in-C Middle East in 1940 instead of Tedder had his Vickers Wellington not landed in Sicily rather than Malta. Boyd's lectures, which survive, were based on CD22 and the new AP 1300 but were so uninspiring that the CIGS General Sir George Milne wrote to Trenchard requesting his early replacement.[46]

Montgomery had left Camberley before Boyd's replacement, Wing Commander Trafford Leigh-Mallory, arrived as DS in 1930, as he did not do the course beforehand, and before John Slessor arrived as a student in 1931. Leigh-Mallory and Slessor were up-and-coming air-land thinkers, and both were widely published. Trenchard's

43 TNA: WO 95/836/4: IX Corps, Headquarters Branches and Services: General Staff War Diary, 1918. 'Order of Battle, 7 April 1918; H. A. Jones, *The War in the Air*, Volume iv, pp.366-404.

44 TNA: WO 95/2705/3: 47th Division General Staff War Diary, 1918.

45 Ernest Leslie Gossage, *The Royal Air Force* (W. Hodge & Co Ltd, 1937).

46 Joint Services Command and Staff College (JSCSC), Shrivenham: Staff College 1929, Junior Division Year's Work; Staff College 1929, Senior Division Year's Work; *CD22 Royal Air Force Operations Manual*; *Air Publication 1300. Royal Air Force War Manual. Part I: Operations* (London: HMSO, 1928); TNA: AIR 5/280: 'CAS to CIGS', 10 December 1928. Minutes of conference held on 13 February 1923 between CAS and CIGS on Army co-operation.

patronage of Leigh-Mallory and Slessor and their subsequent careers somewhat contradicts the idea that the RAF was not interested in air support of the Army between the Wars. Nevertheless, the teaching of air power probably reflected the doctrine of the time, and Army cooperation predicated on tactical reconnaissance would have been taught rather than a joint air-land campaign.[47] Wing Commander Arthur Capel, who took over from Slessor as the RAF DS at Camberley, inheriting his lesson plans, thought Camberley amateurish and not forward-looking.[48]

Chief Instructor at Quetta

According to Hamilton, Montgomery began to teach the importance of joint air-land operations when Chief Instructor at the Indian Army Staff College at Quetta from June 1934 to June 1937.[49] He was at Quetta at the same time as Slessor was commanding No. 3 (India) Wing RAF at the airfield there and writing his seminal book *Air Power and Armies* based on his Camberley RAF DS lectures.[50] Montgomery does not mention Slessor at Quetta in his memoirs and Slessor's memoirs mention Montgomery only once, when he arrived at the airfield for a staff ride, and, realising the extent of the earthquake damage, helped with the rescue.[51] The Quetta curriculum mirrored Camberley's and therefore focused on Army Cooperation but as Quetta did not have an RAF DS, the RAF student normally taught these lessons.

Nevertheless, it seems Montgomery and Slessor discussed joint air-land integration in the few months they overlapped at Quetta before the earthquake forced the redeployment of Slessor's wing. Slessor's papers reveal that he lectured Montgomery's Junior Division in 1935, Slessor's Wing hosted various Staff College combined operations exercises and demonstrations, which included presentations by Slessor, and that Slessor was critical of Quetta teaching Army cooperation and not land-air operations.[52] It seems highly likely Slessor would have used his Camberley lecture notes to teach from, teaching what was later published as *Air Power and Armies*, emphasising the need for a joint air-land campaign, predicated on control of the air, and that interdiction was the most efficient use of air attack in support of the land battle. Possibly because of Montgomery's focus on 'first class war' and not imperial policing,[53] Slessor thought his wing had become overly focused on major war 'because of constant schemes and

47 Edward Smalley, 'Qualified, but Unprepared: Training for War at the Staff College in the 1930s', *British Journal for Military History*, 2:1 (2015), p.18.
48 Imperial War Museum (IWM): Audio/3166: Interview Capel, *Arthur John*, Reel 4.
49 Hamilton, *Monty: Making of a General*, p.254.
50 John Slessor, *Air Power and Armies*.
51 Slessor, *The Central Blue*, p.110.
52 TNA: AIR 75/35: RAF Staff College, Quetta: No 3 (Indian Wing) RAF, 1934.
53 John Gooch, '"A Particularly Anglo-Saxon Institution": The British General Staff in the Era of Two World Wars', in David French and Brian Holden Reid (eds), *British General Staff* (Routledge, 2004), pp.170–79.

Survivors of Wing Commander J.C. Slessor's No. 3 (India) Wing RAF bury some of their 56 comrades and children killed in the earthquake, June 1935, when Montgomery was Chief Instructor at the Quetta Staff College. (RAF Museum: X001-2351/009)

exercises with the Staff College' rather than current operations on the Frontier.[54] Finally, Slessor recalled discussing air-land integration with Montgomery, but that Montgomery was not interested.[55]

Two years later on the way home from Quetta, Montgomery captured his thinking on modern land warfare in what became three articles on the encounter battle with enemy armoured formations and air striking forces, rather than the methodical battle of 1918.[56] In his *Army Quarterly* article, Montgomery highlighted the requirement for the weight of the RAF effort to support the army and attack enemy concentrations before the encounter, which the Allies had evidently failed to do before German Spring Offensive in 1918. These articles demonstrate advanced thinking about modern war and air support for ground forces, rather than extant doctrine, and echo Slessor's lecture notes and his *Air Power and Armies*.

54 TNA: AIR 75/29: India and Pakistan: Frontier Operation, 1933; Slessor, *The Central Blue*, p.94.
55 IWM: Audio/3176: Interview Slessor, John, Reel 3.
56 B.L. Montgomery, 'The Problem of the Encounter Battle as Affected by Modern British War Establishments', *Royal Engineers Journal*, 1937, pp.339; Bernard Law Montgomery, 'The Problem of the Encounter Battle as Affected by Modern British War Establishment', *Canadian Defence Quarterly*, 15:1 (1937), pp.13–25; Bernard Law Montgomery, 'The Major Tactics of the Encounter Battle', *Army Quarterly*, 36 (1938), pp.268–72.

Palestine

Montgomery commanded the 8th Division in northern Palestine from late 1938 until mid-1939 towards the end of the Arab Revolt which had started in 1936. One feature of the campaign had been the RAF's strikingly modern use of fighter aircraft to provide close air support called for by wireless communications. Air Commodore Arthur Harris, Air Officer Commanding Palestine and Transjordan, later wrote 'I had had there a busy year [1938–39] teaching the British army the advantages, and the rebels the effectiveness of air power.'[57] Harris, who was at Camberley in 1928–9 when Montgomery was DS, wrote, 'I always pride myself that Monty, who is only too willing to learn anything new and learns at speed, got his first real understanding of air cooperation from me, during his very short term of office in Palestine in 1939.' Furthermore, when Montgomery was taken ill, Harris 'thought with dismay that we were to lose a man whom I considered to be one of our best generals.'[58] Yet Harris' RAF Staff College lecture admitted the importance of air support in Palestine was inversely proportional to number of British troops and Britain had flooded Palestine with troops after Munich, using Montgomery's 8th Division and Richard O'Connor's 7th Division to resolve the conflict.[59] Montgomery hardly mentions the RAF in his correspondence at the time, whereas future CIGS Lieutenant General Jack Dill praised it highly in 1936 when British forces were under greater pressure.[60] Instead, Montgomery seems focused on war in Europe, calling Palestine first-class training for small units in a second-class war.[61] It would seem Harris was wrong, and that Montgomery learnt little from him on air-land integration.

Second World War

France 1940

While there is no question that Montgomery's experience in the Battle of France in 1940 greatly influenced his thinking on army command, he makes no explicit reference to air power either in his subsequent memoirs or in his evidence to the Bartholomew Committee. Montgomery's evisceration of Gort's command of the BEF is remarkable for its insight and clarity. Notwithstanding the rush to form and

57 Arthur Travers Harris, *Bomber Offensive* (London: Collins, 1947), p.9.
58 Harris, *Bomber Offensive,* p.30.
59 RAF Museum: AIR 69/18: 'Staff College Lecture on Royal Air Force Operations in Palestine during the Arab Rebellion 1936–1939.'
60 TNA: WO 191/75: Lt Gen Dill, 'Preliminary Notes of the Lessons of the Palestine Rebellion', 1939.
61 TNA: WO 216/111: Maj Gen B L Montgomery GOC 8th Division, 'Palestine Notes for CIGS February 1939', 1938; James Barker, 'Monty and the Mandate', *History Today*, 59:3 (March, 2009); TNA: WO 191/75: Lt Gen Dill, 'Preliminary Notes of the Lessons of the Palestine Rebellion', 1939.

equip the BEF, Montgomery's memoirs criticise Gort for going along with Gamelin's risky strategy, for the flawed Anglo-French command arrangements for the BEF, for the lack of BEF exercises, and for rushing forward in a command post without communications or his principal advisers.[62] Although Montgomery does not mention it, the air-land arrangements were also problematic, as Montgomery must have realised. Gort and Barratt (commanding British Air Forces France) were not co-equals. Gort commanded ten percent of the land force, reported to the French Western Front commander (Georges) not the Army group commander (Billote) and for the first twelve days of the campaign did not speak to them. Barratt commanded around half the Allied air forces in France, could call on the metropolitan RAF, reported to the Air Ministry and was collocated with the French regional air commander. Air Vice-Marshal Charles Blount, Gort's Air Component Commander, was based in BEF Rear (not the main or advanced HQ) and had to go looking for Gort in an autogiro. The BEF had no dedicated communications for tasking the Air Component, which although it had no Stukas, did have Bristol Blenheims and Westland Lysanders. Both were only used for ground attack after they were withdrawn to the UK. Hawker Hurricanes were used for ground strafing on their final sorties from French airfields.[63]

Montgomery's command of the 3rd Division in France in 1940 reinforced his reputation. His highly realistic training of the Division to advance to the River Dyle and also to retreat from it had, in the words of one of his staff officers, 'almost exactly prefigured what the division was called to do once the Germans invaded Belgium.'[64] After a series of remarkable manoeuvres, it marched into the Dunkirk perimeter retaining its cohesion and discipline.[65] Montgomery's training had emphasised the German air threat, the need for concealment, night manoeuvre and 'filling the air with bullets'.[66] Division exercises included exercising with No. 51 Wing RAF's Lysanders in the tactical and artillery reconnaissance roles according to the Army Cooperation doctrine of the day.[67] The 3rd Division War Diary mentions slight German air interference on 16 and 17 May when withdrawing to the River Dendre and some air attacks on 31 May on the Dunkirk perimeter, but otherwise there is no mention of air attack.[68] A divisional operation order issued for the advance to the Dyle mentions RAF fighter

62 Montgomery of Alamein, *Memoirs*, pp.43–58.

63 Group Captain John Alexander, 'Chapter 18: The War Was Not Going to Be Won by Fighter Squadrons but by the Fight on the Floor': British Air/Land Integration in France, 1940', in Maj Paul Knight (ed) *Ex Parabellum Gelb Read Er; Background Reading*, (Warminster: Land Warfare Centre, 2022), pp.231–32.

64 Nigel Hamilton, *Monty: Making of a General*, p.338; C.P. Dawnay, 'Inside Monty's Headquarters', in T.E.B. Howarth (ed), *Monty at Close Quarters: Recollections of the Man* (London: Leo Cooper in association with Secker & Warburg, 1985), pp.1–18 (p.3).

65 Robin McNish, *Iron Division: The History of the 3rd Division* (London: I. Allan, 1978), p.89.

66 IWM: Bernard Law Montgomery (BLM) 15: Training Instructions Issued by Me When GOC 3rd Division in France during the Period of the 'Phoney War', Feb–May 1940.; IWM: BLM 17: 3rd Division Exercises, Nos 3 & 4, 6–8 & 29–31 Mar 1940.

67 IWM: BLM 16: 3rd Division Exercises, Nos 1 & 2, 13–15 & 19–21 Dec 1939, pp.11–2.

68 TNA: WO 167/218: 3 Division General Staff War Diary, May 1940, pp.1–3.

protection and tactical reconnaissance provided by No. 4 Squadron RAF but otherwise there is little mention, positive or negative, of the RAF.[69] When Montgomery gave written evidence to the Bartholomew Committee, he reinforced the need for all arms air defence and other passive defence measures, but, unlike other witnesses, without mentioning the impact of German or Allied air support.[70]

Home Command

Montgomery was one of the first corps commanders to practice close support bombing using the tentacle method developed in the Wann-Woodall experiments.[71] When commanding South East Command in Exercise *Tiger* in mid-1942, his post exercise debrief showed his thinking just before taking over Eighth Army:

> The Air Force must therefore be involved not just in response to army requests for support, but at the highest staff levels from the very beginning, when the army plans were actuality formulated. The Air Staff at HQ of Army formations should be regarded as part of the general staff and not as something separate dealing in black magic.[72]

Conclusions

This chapter has demonstrated Montgomery's air-mindedness on taking command of Eighth Army using contemporaneous records. It shows that in 1942 Montgomery understood all modern land campaigns were air-land campaigns. He understood the strategic, operational, and tactical levels of air power, and the need to win control of the air. There is no evidence that Montgomery understood the detail of interdiction and close air support, but he recognised its importance. He left the detail of air support to the airmen with whom he planned the campaign jointly, and with whom Montgomery was determined to be collocated.

The chapter has also shown the evolution of Montgomery's air-land thinking was an extension of his thinking about preparing for a 'first-class war' as he put it, a war in Europe. His air-mindedness was part of his 'method'. Thus, he was keen to use Army cooperation aircraft in his unit exercises between the wars. His writing about modern encounter battles included air-land on his return from Quetta. Once in a position to do so in Home Command after 1940, he ensured air power was embedded in his exercises. A proponent of Fuller's principles of war, increasingly he regarded air power

69 IWM: BLM 14: 3rd Division Operation Instructions, p.15.
70 TNA: WO 106/1775: Bartholomew Committee Report on Lessons to Be Learnt from Operations in Flanders: Evidence, Report and Action Arising, 1940. 'Montgomery, 3rd Division'.
71 Hamilton, *Monty: Making of a General*, p.443, p.450, p.532.
72 Hamilton, *Monty: Making of a General*, p.443, p.450, p.532.

as a principle of war, and by 1945 listed it as the first principle, although intriguingly this was not adopted more widely.

It may be his First World War air-land experiences on corps and division staff, particularly in defeat at the Third Battle of the Aisne where the lack of air superiority made his own corps squadron impotent, influenced his thinking. Likewise, he may have been influenced by Slessor when they briefly served together at Quettta, although, as this chapter reminds us, Montgomery was renowned for his independent thinking.

8

Operations *Strangle* and *Diadem*: Assessing the Impact of Tactical Air Power in Support of the Allied Ground Forces, Central Italy, March–June 1944

Bill Pyke

> *The Mediterranean theatre has been the primary crucible for the development of tactical air power and the joint command between the Allies.*
>
> Lieutenant General Ira C. Eaker, USAAF,
> C-in-C Mediterranean Allied Air Forces, June 1944

Initial hopes and plans that the Allied armies would advance rapidly northwards up the Italian peninsula foundered during the last two months of 1943. Italy was proving to be anything but 'the soft underbelly of Europe' with experienced and determined German troops holding a defensive line 75 miles south of Rome. It became known as the *Gustav Line*, and it extended across the peninsula from the Adriatic coast south-westwards to the Tyrrhenian Sea.

Following several Allied ground force attempts to breach the Gustav Line between January and early March 1944, the senior air commanders of the Mediterranean Allied Air Forces (MAAF) had already been planning to use air power through both tactical and strategic attacks behind the German frontline. The specific objective of these attacks was the interdiction of German lines of supply from Northern Italy which would weaken the German ability to maintain their defensive posture north of the *Gustav Line*. Although the original objective of Operation *Strangle*, as it was named, was never achieved, this initial operation did lead to paralysing the movement of the defending German forces. Together with the follow-on operation, *Diadem*, MAAF continued with both air interdiction and close air support missions that ultimately enabled Allied ground forces to finally breach the *Gustav Line* and to advance north towards Rome.

This chapter assesses the impact of this first major attempt to interdict supply to an army not actively engaged in battle using tactical airpower. It also addresses the operational interrelationship between air superiority, air interdiction and close air support in Central Italy between March and June 1944.

Setting the scene: The Allied and German military dispositions on the Gustav Line, November–December 1943

Since the start of Operation *Husky* in July 1943, the Allies had advanced through Sicily and up the Italian peninsula only to meet continual and strong resistance from battle-hardened units of the German Army. Having foreseen the threat to his southern front, Hitler had already ordered the redeployment of additional troops from France and Yugoslavia to strengthen a defence line south of Rome. By December, 18 German divisions were stationed in Northern and Central Italy under the command of the well-regarded *Generalfeldmarschall* Albert Kesselring.[1]

Under Kesselring the German ground forces reinforced this natural defence line at this narrowest part of the Italian peninsula. It became known as the *Gustav Line*. Topography gave the Germans a natural defence line with mountainous terrain, and steep-sided ravines, many of which were considered impassable. Worse still, the weather between November 1943 and March 1944 was atrocious. The military historian, John Terraine, wrote:

> The [Allied] armies found themselves trapped in battlefields either deep in snow, or deep in mud, or both, inescapably and ominously recalling the doomed landscape of the Western Front in 1916 and 1917. Soldiers and airmen suffered the depression of feeling that they were now caught in a secondary theatre where they would have to go on fighting and suffering casualties, but no longer for prime purposes.[2]

Monte Cassino became the lynchpin of the *Gustav Line*. Towering above the Liri valley to the west, and the Garigliano and Rapido rivers to the south, the Germans held the high ground from a vantage point 1,700 feet above the river valleys from which they had a clear and complete view of any attempted moves by the Allied armies.

The south-eastern entrance to the Liri valley would be seen as the obvious place to breach the *Gustav Line*. But between November 1943 and early March 1944 nothing could have been further from the truth. This low-lying ground was covered by flooded fields, swollen, fast-flowing rivers, concealed strong points, machine gun nests, mortars, and artillery batteries that were ranged west to east across the entrance to the valley. Everywhere in this area, Allied troops, tanks and road vehicles continually became bogged down in the glutinous mud.

1 Lieutenant Colonel Howard D. Belote, *Once in a Blue Moon: Airmen in Theater Command: Lauris Norstad, Albrecht Kesselring, and Their Relevance to the Twenty-First Century Air Force*, CADRE Paper No. 7 (Maxwell AFB, AL: Air University Press, 2012), pp.32–5; Wing Commander Andrew Brookes, 'The Northern Mediterranean 1943–1945', *Royal Air Force Historical Society, 46* (2009), pp.14–5.

2 John Terraine, *A Time for Courage* (London: Macmillan, 1985), p.585.

The failed attempts to breach the Gustav Line, January–March 1944

General Sir Harold Alexander felt confident that he could dislodge the Germans on the *Gustav Line*. He considered the two ways to get to Rome: either through the Liri Valley, or alternatively to invade by sea southwest of Rome. Alexander chose both options with a plan to attack simultaneously in January 1944. The objective was to outflank the German defences together with a frontal attack on the *Gustav Line* by the Allied forces across the Rapido and Garigliano rivers, expecting to catch the German defenders off-balance. The two Allied forces would then join up to encircle the retreating German troops and then advance towards Rome. Initially, there was resistance to Alexander's proposal from the American high command. They considered it an overly ambitious plan with an undermanned invasion force and an anticipated shortage of amphibious landing craft. The American commanders had already issued an order to redeploy landing craft to England in preparation for Operation *Overlord*, the invasion of Normandy. It was only the direct intervention of Winston Churchill that changed the thinking. He managed to persuade President Franklin D. Roosevelt to back Alexander's plan.

With the President's support and the agreement of General Dwight D. Eisenhower, who at the time was still the Supreme Commander-in-Chief of the Allied Expeditionary Force, the plan was now scheduled for late January. It went ahead as Operation *Shingle*, a combined Anglo-American invasion force under the command of the American Major-General John P. Lucas to land near Anzio, a coastal port located thirty miles southwest of Rome. Initially it was a success, and the landing was unopposed. It had caught the Germans by surprise. However, because of Lucas' overly cautious attitude, the advancing troops were ordered to stop seven miles inland to await further supplies and reinforcements. It was a major tactical blunder. With the loss of the element of surprise, Kesselring rapidly redeployed his reinforcements south of Rome. In late January, Kesselring had only two divisions deployed south of Rome. By early March, seventeen divisions were in position in that area. With an ensuing bloody stalemate, the Allied forces remained hemmed into the narrow bridgehead for a further four months. Churchill was to write after the war that he 'had hoped we were hurling a wildcat on to the shore, but all we got was a stranded whale.'[3]

To make matters worse, there were several other attempts to breach the *Gustav Line*. One attempt was made in mid-February to take Monte Cassino, a key objective which was dominated by the sixth century Benedictine monastery built near the top of the mountain. During the period between late December and early February, the British, New Zealand and Indian troops who had been pinned down by both German artillery fire and snipers on the flanks of Monte Cassino were erroneously convinced that the monastery was a strongpoint that was being used by Panzer units. In 1954, Marshal of the Royal Air Force (RAF) Sir John Slessor, who was Deputy Commander

3 Winston Churchill, *The Second World War, Volume V. Closing the Ring* (London: Cassell, 1951), p.432.

of MAAF in 1944, met General von Senger und Etterlin, the former commander of the XIV *Panzerkorps*. General Senger was a devout Catholic, and he told Slessor that the monastery was not used by his troops prior to the bombing. Slessor believed there was no doubt that the general spoke the truth.[4]

Nevertheless, with increasing losses, the New Zealand commander, Lieutenant General Sir Bernard Freyberg VC, requested that aircraft from the strategic and tactical components of the MAAF be used to carry out an air raid to destroy the monastery.[5] The use of air power at this point was now considered necessary to break the deadlock. However, the air commanders did not support the raid. They were overruled by General Sir Henry Maitland Wilson, the Supreme Commander Allied Command Mediterranean (ACMED), and Alexander, who was now Commander-in-Chief of Allied Armies in Italy. On 15 February over 500 tons of bombs were dropped by 254 aircraft of the American Twelfth and Fifteenth Air Forces reducing the monastery to a shattered ruin that the Germans then, for the first time, used as a strongpoint. A month later, on 15 March, a repeat of heavy bombing of the town of Cassino also failed to dislodge the defending German troops. In April, Slessor wrote to the Chief of the Air Staff, Marshal of the RAF Sir Charles Portal, emphasising that '*the bomber is not a battlefield weapon*'.[6] The heavy bombing did not enable the Allies to achieve a breakthrough on the *Gustav Line*. Every attempt had ended in failure. The Allied ground forces were repelled repeatedly by the well-trained, seasoned units of the German army: panzers, panzer grenadiers, and paratroopers.

Set against this, the Allies had one distinct advantage: air superiority. The MAAF had a ten-fold dominance in air assets over the *Luftwaffe* in this theatre of operations and had gained almost complete control of the air. Plans were put in place to utilise tactical air power to break the deadlock on the *Gustav Line*.[7] Senior commanders at the MAAF had already proposed a plan to interdict the German lines of communication to deny German ground forces of supplies necessary for them to maintain their defensive posture north of the *Gustav Line*.

The Mediterranean Allied Air Force

Following undertakings made at the Casablanca Conference in January 1943, a formal decision was taken in December of that year to establish the MAAF, to replace Mediterranean Air Command, with an organisational structure that

4 MRAF Sir John Slessor, *Central Blue* (London: Cassell, 1956), p.577; Terraine, *Courage*, p.589.
5 Denis Richards and Hilary St. George Saunders, *Royal Air Force 1939–1945: Volume 2 The Fight Avails* (London: HMSO, 1954), p.358.
6 Slessor *Central Blue*, p.573. Author's italics.
7 W.F Craven and J.L. Cate (eds), *The Army Air Forces in World War II, Vol III, Europe: Argument to V. E. Day January 1944 to May 1945* (University Chicago Press: Chicago, 1951), pp.373–7.

would ensure that this coalition of air forces would operate harmoniously and successfully. In mid-January 1944 Lieutenant General Ira C. Eaker was appointed as Commander-in-Chief MAAF with Air Marsal Sir John Slessor as his Deputy. It was an unprecedented undertaking in coalition air warfare on a scale that had never previously been attempted. The MAAF operated through three key air combat roles: strategic, tactical, and coastal components. By March 1944 the MAAF could field over 4,000 combat aircraft to commence a major and comprehensive interdiction campaign with the specific intention of cutting the German lines of communication: to literally strangle the transport of troops and war materiel south of Florence.

The Mediterranean Allied Strategic Air Force (MASAF)

Strategic operations were undertaken primarily through the American Fifteenth Army Air Force. Though it was based in southern Italy, its primary role was to maintain the strategic offensive against Germany together with the Eighth and Ninth Army Air Forces, based in England. These three American strategic air forces now had the range and capability to reach all areas of Italy, Germany, Romania, Hungary, and Bulgaria. This component was based at several airfields in the Foggia region of south-east Italy. On occasion, its secondary role was its availability for operations against major targets in northern and central Italy.

The Mediterranean Allied Tactical Air Component (MATAF)

In January 1944 the Mediterranean tactical air forces could field 1,800 aircraft and this component was to play the prominent role in air interdiction, and later in close air support operations, during Operations *Strangle* and *Diadem*. The American Twelfth Army Air Force provided a major part of the tactical air forces with 53 squadrons. The RAF provided 27 squadrons, including its Desert Air Force. Other national air forces that provided squadrons included the Australians, Canadians, South Africans, the Free French, Polish, and the co-belligerent Italians. During May, the tactical air forces fielded 94 squadrons of fighters, fighter-bombers, and medium bombers that were stationed in the Naples area, Sicily, Brindisi, and the Mediterranean islands of Corsica and Sardinia.

The Mediterranean Allied Coastal Air Force (MACAF)

Coastal operations were primarily conducted by the RAF's squadrons against enemy ships using coastal routes, in addition to carrying out attacks on port facilities used for the storage of the enemy's supplies.

The plans for Operation *Strangle*: moving from theory to practice

When plans were drawn up for Operation *Strangle* there was a sharp division between those who favoured bombing railway infrastructure and those who wanted to focus

North American B-25J Mitchell (336099 82 and 336061 86) of the 319th Bomber Squadron, US Twelfth Air Force, in formation flight over Castelnovo, 18 November 1944, after Operation *Diadem*. (RAF Museum: P012914)

on bridges, viaducts, road junctions and tunnel entrances.[8] On 11 February 1944, and prior to the launch of Operation *Strangle*, Slessor wrote a memorandum to Brigadier-General Lauris Norstad, the American Director of Operations at the MAAF, as follows:

> There are now some seventeen German divisions in Italy south of Rome. I do not believe the Army – even with our support – will move them. But I think it more than possible that the Hun, by concentrating all this force so far south, has given us – the Air Forces – an opportunity. He has been able up to now just to support his smaller armies on the present line in spite of our air attacks on his communications. I find it hard to believe that, by increasing those forces, he has not put a load on his communications which they will not be able to stand if we really sustain a scientifically planned offensive *against the right places* in his L. of C. [Lines of Communication].[9]

Slessor's memorandum reflected his own thinking on air interdiction – the disruption of the enemy's supplies and movements behind the frontline. This was very much Slessor's idea. He had lectured on the concept at the British Army's Staff College at Camberley during the early 1930s his ideas on the interaction between ground and air forces were published in 1936 in his seminal work *Air Power and Armies*.[10] Slessor had examined examples of First World War operations that involved bombing behind the enemy's frontline. His investigations convinced him that with war now possible in the third dimension that, 'Air may stop men and supplies arriving at the battlefield at all.'[11] The American air power historian Phillip S. Meilinger credited Slessor with writing 'perhaps the best air power treatise written in English before World War II' and wrote of his importance in the genesis of interdiction. Slessor wrote *Air Power and Armies* at a time when very few air power thinkers were considering tactical air power in a battlefield context. As Meilinger wrote, 'Slessor recognized that effective interdiction required cooperation between air and ground units, reasoning that there were occasions when ground should support the air effort – a heretical belief among ground officers at the time.'[12] In early 1944, however, Slessor's ideas had not been tested on this scale. Central Italy was now to provide the crucible of experimentation for tactical air interdiction and close air support that would provide important learning experiences. They would subsequently be applied with considerable success in numerous tactical air operations.

8 Craven and Cate, *The Army Air Forces in World War II,* p.371–3.
9 Slessor, *Central Blue*, p.568.
10 Wing Commander John C. Slessor, *Air Power and Armies* (Oxford: Oxford University Press, 1936), p.35.
11 Slessor, *Air Power and Armies*, p.200.
12 Philip S. Meilinger, foreword: Sir John Cotesworth Slessor, *Air Power and Armies* (Tuscaloosa: The University of Alabama Press, 2010), pp.i–xi; Phillip S Meilinger, 'John C Slessor and the Genesis of Air Interdiction', *The RUSI Journal*, 140:4 (1995), pp.43–8.

Group photograph of RAF personnel, Sicily, circa 1943, including Solly Zuckerman, seated second left. (RAF Museum: PC71/19/1182)

Prior to Slessor taking up his post at the MAAF, Air Chief Marshal Sir Arthur Tedder, who had commanded Mediterranean Air Command (MAC), recommended that Slessor should meet Professor Solly Zuckerman who had been Tedder's scientific adviser in the Mediterranean during 1943. Before the War he was a professor of Zoology at Oxford. He came to prominence as an expert in operational research having studied the efficacy of bombing during the London Blitz.[13] Zuckerman held a strong view that success would only come with sustained air attacks on Italy's rail infrastructure: major railway centres, marshalling yards, large concentrations of locomotives and rolling stock, and signalling and repair facilities. Slessor met Zuckerman in London during early January 1944 and had no argument with his ideas. Of course, none of this was new to Slessor who also believed that there were no simplistic, empirical solutions with air interdiction, and that one method should not be adopted to the exclusion of all others.[14] He considered it important to adapt 'one's thinking to the conditions at the time and to the developing capacity of aircraft and weapons, making

13 Craven and Cate, *The Army Air Forces in World War II*, p.372
14 Slessor, *Central Blue*, p.568.

full use of the flexibility of air power to attack the enemy transportation system in the way that seemed most likely to be profitable in the conditions with which we were faced, and with the resources we had at our disposal.'[15]

Zuckerman did not share Slessor's views on flexibility on the choice of targets, and he had the distinct advantage of strong backing from both Tedder and the Air Ministry. He continued stick to his ideas for a rail transportation plan, and he had a somewhat myopic and negative view regarding bridges and viaducts. He insisted that, 'railway and road bridges are uneconomical and difficult targets, and in general do not appear to be worth attacking except where special considerations demand it in the tactical area.'[16] But Zuckerman certainly did not appreciate the rapidly evolving air power tactics and techniques employed by high performance fighter-bombers, particularly with the dive-bombing of bridge targets by Republic P-47 Thunderbolts.[17] Furthermore, neither Zuckerman nor his operational research team working in London fully appreciated the complexities of road and rail transport in some of the difficult terrain of central Italy.

Prior to the start of *Strangle*, Kesselring had 19 divisions deployed in Central Italy. The German Fourteenth Army was deployed south of Rome to prevent an Allied breakout from the Anzio bridgehead, with additional divisions in reserve in case of a further Allied landing from the sea north-west of Rome. The German Tenth Army was deployed to maintain defence on the *Gustav Line*.

Operation Strangle, 19 March–10 May 1944

On 19 March the air directive was issued that embodied the initial objective as Operation *Strangle*: 'to reduce the enemy's flow of supplies to a level which will make it impractical to operate his forces in Central Italy.'[18] However, in the first few weeks, with both strategic and tactical air interdiction sorties focused on railway infrastructure, it was becoming increasingly obvious that interdiction sorties were not preventing the German supply movements. The adverse weather conditions during that first month had been a highly limiting factor in carrying out successful interdiction missions. At that time, and with little effective damage to the rail infrastructure, the German high command still had a variety of options; by redirecting transport to alternative parts of the rail network and by increasing the usage of motor transport on the road network.

In frustration, General Eaker wrote to the American Lieutenant General Jacob. L. Devers, the Deputy Supreme Commander ACMED as follows:

15 Slessor, *Central Blue,* p.568.
16 Craven and Cate, *The Army Air Forces in World War II*, pp.371–2.
17 Craven and Cate, *The Army Air Forces in World War II*, pp.377–83.
18 Craven and Cate, *The Army Air Forces in World War II*, p.570.

> All our experience in attacks on communication in this theater has shown that even the most successful bombardment of a marshalling yard does not cut traffic for more than a few hours. Attacks on marshalling yards are valuable because they destroy concentrations of goods, rolling stock and repair facilities. We have found that a more permanent way to cut lines is by attacks on bridges and viaducts which are more difficult to repair.[19]

On the British side, Slessor was equally frustrated. A month into the operation he wrote to Portal on 16 April as follows: 'we are not going to succeed in doing what I had hoped with some confidence we should do, namely, make it impossible by the end of April for the Hun to maintain an army of seventeen odd divisions south of Rome.'[20] Slessor also noted 'we are not forcing him to expend fuel or ammunition.' Slessor made the case for melding both interdiction plans, and as the RAF official historians Richards and Saunders wrote, 'he succeeded in blending the two opposing designs [the attacks against rail infrastructure versus bridges, viaducts, roads and motor transport] into a single plan.'[21]

As the weather improved in late April and early May, the Allied tactical air forces increased their attacks on all the supply routes south of Florence. Their sorties were now focused on a wider range of targets. Simultaneous attacks on road junctions, bridges, and viaducts were already starting to paralyse the well-recognised quality of German tactical improvisation and mobility. The squadrons of medium bombers based in Sardinia and Corsica attacked bridges and viaducts, while the fighters and fighter-bombers based in southern Italy attacked ships, motor vehicles, trains, tunnel entrances and road junctions.

It was the use of fighter-bombers, and notably the P-47 Thunderbolt, that made a major contribution through successful tactical interdiction sorties.[22] The P-47 proved to be an ideal tactical fighter-bomber for missions in Central and Northern Italy between early 1944 and the end of the War in May 1945. Powered by an eighteen-cylinder Pratt and Whitney engine, it could deliver 2,300 horsepower. It was an incredibly robust aircraft that could also sustain major damage from flak and cannon shells.[23] It was armed with eight 0.5 calibre machine guns, 500lb bombs, and rockets. The pilots flying P-47s gained notoriety for taking out road and rail bridges through its excellent dive-bombing capabilities. Since December 1943 the American Twelfth (Tactical) Air Support Air Force component of the MAAF had been taking delivery

19 Frederick M. Sallagar, *Operation STRANGLE (Italy, Spring 1944): A Case Study of Tactical Air Interdiction* (Santa Monica, CA: RAND Corporation, 1972), p.33.
20 William Pyke, *Air Power Supremo: A Biography of Marshal of the Royal Air Force: Sir John Slessor* (Barnsley: Pen & Sword Military, Kindle e-book, 2022), p.247.
21 Richards and Saunders, *The Royal Air Force*, p.363
22 Eduard Maximilian Mark, *Aerial Interdiction: Air Power and the Land Battle in Three American Wars* (Maxwell, AL: Center for Air Force History, 1994), pp.157–8.
23 Michael McCarthy, *Air-to-Ground Battle for Italy* (Maxwell AFB, Ala: Air University Press, 2004), p.77.

Ground view of pilot in cockpit of Kittyhawk Mk III or Mk IV, No. 112 Squadron RAF, Italy, circa 1944 at the time of Operations *Strangle* and *Diadem*. P-47s had replaced P-40 variants in USAAF usage by this time. (RAF Museum: PC032305)

of P-47D Thunderbolts that were now entering squadron service in the Mediterranean theatre in large numbers. To demonstrate the effectiveness of the aircraft, the MAAF allowed William Wyler, a successful Hollywood director, to make a documentary about the activities of a squadron based in Corsica between March and May 1944.[24] The documentary recorded the air interdiction attacks on bridges, railways, large road transport vehicles and ammunition dumps. Three squadrons of P-47s from the Twelfth's 57th Group had the distinct geographical advantage of being only twenty minutes' flying time from their airbase in Alto, located on the northeast coast of Corsica, to the Italian mainland. That area was still under German control, with a high number of interdiction targets.

The 57th Group flew numerous sorties, sometimes as many as eight or nine per day, and often revisited old targets to ensure that the enemy was unable to repair and rebuild previously destroyed road and rail bridges. The incessant attacks by the P-47s and the other MAAF tactical units ensured that by mid-April all rail links south of

24 *Thunderbolt*, dir. by William Wyler and John Sturges (Monogram Pictures, and Carl Krueger Productions, 1947). See also *Thunderbolt, 1945*, National Archives Video Collection, 2017 https://www.youtube.com/watch?v=eXEKEc9lnTM, accessed 30 April 2024.

Florence were blocked.[25] The enemy was then compelled to rely solely on mechanical transport (MT) to continue to supply the frontline. This put an exceptional strain on German logistic planning to satisfy both the need to maintain supply with both a diminishing number of suitable road vehicles, and the increasing scarcity of fuel supplies. The MATAF continued to attack both individual vehicles and road convoys ferrying troops and supplies.

The Fourteenth Army War Diaries for 19 April 1944 recorded that 'rail transportation had been completely eliminated and wave after wave of Allied air attacks on the Army rear degraded the supply situation … many transport vehicles were disabled, and the mobility of German Army units was eliminated.'[26] Even before the start of *Diadem* 1,800 heavy road vehicles had been destroyed or damaged by the continual attacks by fighters and fighter-bombers.[27] The German Tenth Army records for early May revealed that 'unremitting Allied fighter-bomber activity makes movement or troop deployment almost impossible … fighter bombers maintain constant patrol over all roads … daytime movement is paralyzed.'[28] The fighter-bomber strafing attacks often terrified the German troops and depressed their morale. These sorties were now delivering impressive results.

During *Strangle* the tactical air forces of the MAAF flew 21,688 sorties in the interdiction zone between Pisa and Rome.[29] Even before the end of *Strangle*, German quartermasters' reports were expressing their increasing concern about the shortage of fuel and motor transport at the front.[30]

Operation *Diadem*

On 11 May a major Allied artillery barrage marked the opening of Operation *Diadem*. The air interdiction campaign continued as far north as the Po Valley, but two significant things changed with the opening of *Diadem*:

25 *Thunderbolt*, dir. by William Wyler and John Sturges (Monogram Pictures, and Carl Krueger Productions, 1947). See also *Thunderbolt, 1945*, National Archives Video Collection, 2017 https://www.youtube.com/watch?v=eXEKEc9lnTM, accessed 30 April 2024.

26 Robert E. Schmaltz, 'The Uncertainty of Predicting Results of an Interdiction Campaign', *Aerospace Historian*, 17:4 (1970), pp.150-53.

27 Wesley Frank Craven and James Lea Cate, *The Army Air Forces in World War II, Vol. III, Europe: Argument to VE Day, January 1944 to May 1945* (Washington, DC: Office of Air Force History, 1983), p.383.

28 Maj. Robert A Renner, USAF, 'Allied Air Power comes of Age: The Roles and Contributions of Air Power to the Italian Campaign', *Air Power Review*, 6:3 (Autumn 2003), pp.79–89 (p.82).

29 Brookes, *Air War over Italy*, p.84.

30 Mark, *Aerial Interdiction,* p.174.

1 With the Allied forces advancing north and breaching the *Gustav Line*, the Germans were now expending their ammunition and other supplies at an alarming rate. They were also running out of fuel and access to MT.
2 The MAAF had started to liaise with the ground forces to coordinate tactics and to agree on the selection of interdiction and air support targets at daily meetings. With almost complete control of the air, both close air support and battlefield air interdiction up to twenty miles behind the German lines was now paralysing their movement.

Since starting air interdiction operations in the Western Desert, the RAF and the British Army had been coordinating joint air-ground operations to identify targets immediately behind the enemy's frontline. By the time they reached Salerno they had evolved a system which came to be known as 'Rover David', which was used for the first time in October 1943. The Americans adopted the British Rover system naming their system as 'Rover Joe'. Group Captain David Heysham was the first Rover air controller and identified German targets along the Sangro river in October 1943. Subsequent Rover operations were thus named after him. 'Rover Joe' was not named after any individual, but instead after the universal term for the American soldier: G.I. Joe. The name 'cab rank' was taken from its comparison to rows of London taxicabs lined up outside hotels, theatres, and train stations.[31]

The system worked on the basis of a mobile ground command vehicle which was manned by an RAF officer (controller) and an Army liaison officer (ALO). These vehicles were positioned close to the frontline and equipped with two-way VHF radios that enabled them to be in constant communication with: (1) forward ground observation points (OPs), near the battlefront or on high ground; (2) aerial observation posts (AOPs) in the form of small RAF spotter aircraft flown by Royal Artillery pilots; and (3) the ever-present Allied fighter-bombers that were 'roving' in their area.

A critical element of the Rover system involved the assembly over areas of the frontline of a 'cab rank' of fighter-bombers that were present on a continual basis during daylight.[32] Those aircraft took off at regular thirty-minute intervals from their airfields having already been briefed on their pre-selected target list. However, before attacking those targets, those aircraft 'roved' for a period of twenty minutes awaiting a possible call from the ground command vehicle. Newly identified targets could then either be marked immediately by Allied artillery smoke shells or alternatively the air controller would give the pilot of the fighter bomber the target coordinates and a description of nearby physical features. Many of those targets were road vehicles. The Rover system had the unique advantage of locating and catching 'fleeting' targets which could then be destroyed within minutes.

31 Maj. Paul Johnson (RCAF), 'The Question of British Influence on U.S. Tactical Air Power in World War II', *Air Power History*, 6:3, (Autumn 2003), p.82.
32 Major Robert A. Renner, USAF, 'Air Power Comes of Age: The Roles and Contributions of Air Power to the Italian Campaign', *Air Power Review*, Vol.6, No.3 (Autumn 2003), p. 3.

By 14 May a German Tenth Army report recorded that they were 'practically empty of fuel on their right flank' and by 24 May the *Oberquartiermeister* had started to fear that the mobility of the entire Army had been called into question.[33] The following selected extracts from the Tenth Army's war diaries reveal the deterioration of the German defences and their inevitable collapse over the first two weeks of *Diadem*:

> 16 May: Ceaseless air attacks day and night on all access roads. Heavy fighter-bomber support for enemy ground forces … Ammunition situation in L-1 Corps is tenuous because of movement difficulties, created by constant fighter-bomber attacks and destruction of roads.
>
> 18 May: With strongest fighter-bomber support and heaviest artillery fire, enemy immediately smashes any movement in our lines. Constant unremitting Allied fighter-bomber activity makes movement or troop deployment almost impossible, while enemy can move his reserves freely and without hindrance.
>
> 22 May: Tenth Army again suffered today from the effects of enemy air supremacy. In addition to strong fighter support for enemy ground attack, large fighter-bomber and bomber formations attacked our access roads, especially where they knew our redeployments from left to right Army wing were taking place.
>
> 30 May: All divisions exhausted, especially 305th which arrived without its logistics train. Most divisions lack hot food because field kitchens not available. Despite availability of ample supplies resupply difficulties have increased during retreat. Corps is dependent on a few roads through mountains which are almost hourly blocked through incessant air attacks.[34]

Slessor visited the ground forces following up the Allied advance after the start of *Diadem* and wrote later 'that they found that the actual numbers of tanks, guns and vehicles wrecked or burnt out on the roads exceeded the claims we had made', adding, 'Lord Trenchard has said that all land battles are confusion and muddle, and the job of Air is to accentuate that confusion and muddle in the enemy's Army to a point when it gets beyond the capacity to control.'[35] He concluded that, 'German mobility was paralyzed by his enormous losses in mechanical transport and the catastrophic conditions of his roads.'[36]

33 Sallagar, *Operation STRANGLE*, p.72.
34 Sallagar, *Operation STRANGLE*, pp.68–9.
35 Slessor, *Central Blue*, 'Notes on operations leading to the Capture of Rome', p.583.
36 Slessor, *Central Blue*, 'Notes on operations leading to the Capture of Rome', p.584.

Conclusions: assessing the impact of *Strangle* and *Diadem*

The directive issued at the start of Operation *Strangle* on 19 March 1944 had the specific objective of interdicting supplies and transport infrastructure behind the German frontline to a point at which it would be impractical to continue to maintain its forces in Central Italy. There can be no doubt that this initial objective was never achieved. Taken literally, this directive implied that the use of air power alone would compel the German defending forces on the *Gustav Line* to retreat, and therefore eliminate the need for Allied ground force combat. Some air commanders may have believed this, but it was always an unrealistic and overly ambitious plan. The initial mission of the air interdiction campaign was primarily focused on the destruction of the Italian rail infrastructure between Florence and Rome.

Central Italy had thus become the testing ground for a coalition of both strategic and tactical air forces on a scale never previously attempted. Consequently, there was a steep learning curve in its application. Mistakes were made, and notably in the areas of intelligence and operational research in assessing the capabilities and tenacity of a first-class enemy on the defensive. The interdiction operations of *Strangle* succeeded *but not for the objective specified on the 19 March directive*. The steady and continual bombing of targets in the interdiction zone degraded both the rail and road transport network to such an extent that shortages – transport, fuel, tyres and other spare parts – were already causing concern to the German quartermasters as early as the final week of April. The increasing dependence on mobility compelled the German commanders to reassign vehicles initially earmarked for their vital tactical mobility to be transferred for logistic support duties.[37] That fatal decision only exacerbated the problem by drastically reducing their capability of tactical mobility.

Some commentators and military historians have criticised the official air history accounts for what they saw as exaggerations of the impact of tactical air operations in Central Italy. There were also lukewarm and negative responses from some senior Allied Army commanders. General Alexander himself gave 'tepid praise to the operation as "aiding" the breakthrough of his armies from the *Gustav Line*. Lieutenant General Mark W. Clark, frustrated by dogged resistance on his drive to Rome, flatly declared all air interdiction, including *Strangle*, "a flop".'[38] The German supply statistics available for the period between March and May revealed that, in many cases, the inventories hardly changed, often averaging 4,000 tons a day, and in some cases they increased. But those supply depot statistics only reveal part of the story. Even before the end of *Strangle* there were already increasing and widespread shortages of key items, as discussed previously. In the *Diadem* phase the challenge for the German forces was to transfer key supplies and troops from the rear areas of the battlefield up

37 Schmaltz, 'The Uncertainty of Predicting Results of an Interdiction Campaign', pp.150-53; Sallager, *STRANGLE*, p.24; Mark, *Aerial Interdiction*, pp.159-161.

38 Jeff Pattern, 'Operation "Strangle": First Great Air Interdiction Campaign', *War History Network* (Summer, 2015), pp.54–64.

to the frontline. Those movements came under constant attack from Allied fighters and fighter-bombers that were now providing close air support.

But the most convincing evidence of the success of tactical operations is provided by the enemy's reports of Allied air interdiction and close air support. As we have seen, the contemporary war diary entries of the German logistics officers in the Tenth and Fourteenth Armies consistently reported their frustration of diminishing supplies and their freedom to move during the latter stages *Strangle* through to *Diadem*. In 1972, and nearly thirty years after *Strangle* and *Diadem*, the RAND analyst Frederick M. Sallagar published a comprehensive analysis of *Strangle*. He concluded that whereas interdiction never succeeded in preventing the flow of German supplies to the front, he also concluded that even by early May, and prior to operation *Diadem*, air interdiction had already degraded German mobility on the battlefield.[39] By early June the defending German forces had lost nearly all their mobility and were then incapable of manoeuvre.

Sir John Slessor wrote in his post-operation report shortly after the *Strangle/Diadem* interdiction campaign as follows:

> Above all, perhaps, the enemy was deprived by the impossibility of rapid and coherent movement, of that flexibility which has always been such an admirable quality in German defensive fighting, his ability to pick up a battalion here, the contents of a leave train there, a machine-gun *abteilung* from one division and a couple of batteries from another, and fling them in as an improvised battle group to save a local situation.[40]

If the entire *Strangle/Diadem* episode is judged against the criteria of what might be called an effects-based operation, then its overall impact of the tactical air operations was successful. Concentrating on the metrics of one interdiction parameter (in this case, the transport of recorded tonnage of supplies/day to the front) to the exclusion of others can lead to a failure to recognise the other effects that interdiction may have had (in this case, the interdiction of mobility). During *Strangle* and *Diadem* the MAAF continued with its interdiction of supply doctrine, little realising at the time the paralysing effect it was having on the German Army's ability to move and manoeuvre. Sallagar noted this when he wrote that 'the critical importance to the enemy of tactical mobility may not have been appreciated in MAAF headquarters which remained more concerned with supplies than troop movements. But at least one Allied air commander, though equally interested in supply denial, was fully aware how much the Germans depended on tactical mobility: Sir John Slessor.'[41]

Both *Strangle* and *Diadem* laid the foundations for numerous subsequent and successful interdiction and air support operations. But as Sallagar cautioned in his

39 Sallagar, *Operation STRANGLE,* p.xiii.
40 Slessor, *Central Blue*, p.584.
41 Sallagar, *Operation STRANGLE*, p.62

1972 report, 'if there is one lesson to be drawn from this case study it is that the term interdiction is not limited to a single kind of air campaign. It covers a variety of missions that may serve different objectives … there is no such thing as a universally applicable interdiction doctrine.'[42]

42 Sallagar, *Operation STRANGLE*, pp.xiii-xiv.

9

'Flying Artillery': The Development and Employment of Aerial Rocket Artillery Helicopters by the US Army, 1963–1972

Clive Richards

Introduction

Although the phrase 'flying artillery' has often been used in connection with the provision of close air support to ground forces, as is noted in the introduction to this work, air forces are not artillery. However, during the 1960s the US Army would deploy armed rotary-wing aircraft that would occupy the no man's land between conventional tube artillery and close air support (CAS) aircraft. Two units would justify the appellation 'flying artillery' – the Aerial Rocket Artillery (ARA) battalions that formed part of the US Army's two airmobile divisions. This paper will consider those factors that drove the development and employment of an Aerial Rocket Artillery capability by the Army, the degree to which this infringed on the United States Air Force's (USAF's) CAS function and the factors that led ultimately to the disappearance of these battalions in the 1970s.

Sky Cavalry

The establishment of the helicopter as a significant component in the US Army's inventory during the 1950s reflected the increased emphasis placed on mobility in the decade following the conflict in Korea. For the Army, 'the Eisenhower era' was 'one of continuing crisis. New technology, changing views on the nature of war, and the fiscal principles of the Eisenhower administration produced widespread doubts about the utility of traditional land forces.'[1] In response to the conventional might of the USSR and to the rapid development of nuclear arsenals on both sides of the Iron Curtain,

1 A.J. Bacevich, *The Pentomic Era: The US Army Between Korea and Vietnam* (Washington, DC: National Defense University Press, 1986), p.3.

many advocated the development of 'a new model army of wide ranging, dispersed forces, maneuvering [*sic*] to avoid the Red Army steamroller, quickly striking its rear and flanks with small-yield, precisely targeted atomic weapons, concentrating to suppress resistance, and then dispersing to begin the process anew.'[2]

Although it was envisaged that aircraft would furnish much of the required mobility, two schools of thought emerged during the 1950s as to the way it should be achieved. On the one hand were those who argued for the use of air and ground vehicles in combination. Major General James M. Gavin was an early champion of such an approach. Whilst serving in the Department of the Army as Assistant Chief of Staff G-3, he had penned an article that appeared in the April 1954 issue of *Harper's Magazine* in which he called for the restoration of the 'mobility differential' that cavalry had traditionally exerted over the Army's other combat arms.[3] Gavin's revamped cavalry, however, would not be mounted on horseback, but on something much more modern. The means to restore 'the mobility differential we lack will be found in the air vehicle', he argued. 'Fully combined with the armoured division, it will give us real mobility and momentum.'[4] Contemporary cavalry would operate 'helicopters and light aircraft, to lift soldiers armed with automatic weapons and hand-carried antitank weapons, and also lightweight reconnaissance vehicles, mounting antitank weapons the equal or better of the Russian T-34s.'[5]

The first field test of Gavin's 'Sky Cavalry' concept (SkyCav I) took place within Exercise *Sage Brush* at the end of 1955. A second trial (SkyCav II), involving 1st Armored Division, formed part of Exercise *Sledge Hammer* in the spring of the following year.[6] Although 'the earlier test reports were not encouraging', support for Sky Cavalry continued at the highest level. One proponent was General Maxwell D. Taylor, US Army Chief of Staff between 1955 and 1959.[7] He referenced Sky Cavalry's potential in an address to the sixty-ninth annual meeting of the US Armor Association, which took place at Fort Knox, Kentucky (home of the US Army Armor School) in May 1958. Following a firepower demonstration that included both armed and unarmed helicopters, Taylor told his audience that he was 'tremendously impressed with that combination of fire and movement, of the inherent built in mobility which we have in our armored formations':

2 Brian McAllister Linn, *Real Soldiering: The US Army in the Aftermath of War, 1915-1980* (Lawrence, KS: University Press of Kansas, 2023), p.129.
3 Major General James M. Gavin, 'Cavalry, and I Don't Mean Horses,' *Harper's Magazine*, 208:1247 (April 1954), pp.54–60 (p.54).
4 Gavin, 'Cavalry, and I Don't Mean Horses,' p.60.
5 Gavin, 'Cavalry, and I Don't Mean Horses,' p.54.
6 Lieutenant Colonel John T. Collier, 'Cavalry of the Sky,' *Army Information Digest,* 12:11 (November 1957), p.27.
7 Christoper C.S. Cheng, *Air Mobility: The Development of a Doctrine* (Westport, CT: Praeger, 1994), p.135.

> I often have an occasion to say that the Germans almost won World War II by the combination of the Stuka dive bomber and armored formations on the ground. Working together they broke through fortified fronts and destroyed armies in the field in an incredibly short period of time. I think we have today the germ of a new team as suggested and demonstrated to a degree in the exhibitions which we saw this morning. I feel that in the future your armored formations on the ground, accompanied by Sky Cavalry – which in turn carries small, light atomic weapons – offer a great possibility for any Blitzkrieg of World War III – or the Blitzkrieg of any limited war.[8]

Recommendations put forward by the Armor School led the US Continental Army Command (USCONARC) to examine 'Army Aircraft and Ground Forces Mobility'. This in turn resulted with the Armor School being tasked by USCONARC 'to develop an advance plan Table of Organization and Equipment, plan of troop test, and training text' for an 'Aerial Reconnaissance and Security Troop', the first example of which 'was troop tested' at Fort Stewart, Georgia, during January 1960.[9] By 1961, this initiative had matured into the 'Air Cavalry Troop'.

Airmobility

However, interest in the potential use of both aircraft to further the Army's battlefield mobility extended beyond the Armor branch. Notably, trials were also being conducted by the Army Aviation School. The School transferred from Fort Sill, Oklahoma, to Fort Rucker (Fort Novosel), Alabama in 1954, and here it came together with the Aviation Test Board and the Aviation Combat Development Center to form the Army Aviation Center.[10] A report published by *Aviation Week* in November 1957 described the Army Aviation Center's ongoing efforts to establish 'operational flying cavalry' units consisting of 'reconnaissance elements equipped with small two-man helicopters, troop carrier groups with much larger equipment, weapon sections of large helicopters with their whole payload devoted to missile and machine gun armament, and resupply and evacuation groups of large helicopters.'[11]

The difference between the Sky Cavalry concept and the work being done at Fort Rucker was touched upon in review of future developments in armoured warfare that

8 'Address of General Maxwell D Taylor before the United States Armor Association,' *Armor,* LXVII:4 (July-August 1958), p.11.

9 General Herbert B. Powell, 'Air Cavalry Troop,' *Army Information Digest,* 17:2 (February 1962), pp.68–9.

10 Charles R. Shrader, *History of Operations Research in the United States Army, Volume II: 1961–1973* (Washington, DC: Office of the Deputy Under Secretary of the Army for Operations Research, United States Army, 2008), p.262.

11 'Army Evaluates Armed Helicopter Units,' *Aviation Week,* 67:18 (4 November 1957), pp.78–9 (p.78).

followed Maxwell's May 1958 address to the US Armor Association. While acknowledging 'the initiative and imagination shown by the Army Aviation School in what we might refer to as the "basic research" in aviation concepts', a presenter from the Armor Center at Fort Hood (now Fort Cavazos) nevertheless noted that that 'their currently proposed organization, consisting solely of armed aircraft and air-landed troops, does not conform to Armor's concept of SKYCAV which is a combination of both surface and air elements.'[12]

Although Lieutenant General Hamilton H. Howze, Commanding General XVIII Airborne Corps (and previously the first Director of Army Aviation) had been able to add an addendum to the Army Aircraft Requirement Board (the Rogers Board) 1960 report considering 'The Requirement for Air Fighting Units', he and other the advocates of airmobility would have to wait for another two years for the opportunity to press their case in earnest.[13] The catalyst would be Secretary of Defense Robert McNamara. Noting 'that air vehicles, operating in the environment of the ground soldier but freed from the restrictions imposed by the earth's surface, may offer the opportunity to acquire quantum increases in mobility, provided technology, doctrine, and organization potentials are fully exploited', on 19 April 1962 McNamara directed the Army to undertake 'an extensive program of analyses, exercises and field tests to evaluate revolutionary new concepts of tactical mobility and to recommend action to give the Army the maximum attainable mobility in the combat area.'[14]

The following month saw the establishment at Fort Bragg (now Fort Liberty) of an 'Army Tactical Mobility Requirements Board', presided over by Howze, to consider the question: 'to what extent may aircraft properly be substituted for ground vehicles to provide combat and logistical mobility for the Army?'[15] Following trials held at Fort Bragg during the summer of that year, the Howze Board's final report was submitted to the Secretary of the Army on 20 August 1962. It came to 'a single, general conclusion: adoption by the Army of the airmobile concept ... is necessary and desirable. In some respects, the transition is inevitable, just as was that from animal mobility to motor.'[16]

The Howze Board recommended the creation of thirteen new airmobile units by the end of 1967. Five were Air Transport Brigades. A further three would be Air Cavalry Combat Brigades. Intended to act as 'an air fighting unit which destroys or punishes the enemy by aerial maneuver, surprise and heavy application of firepower delivered from rotary wing, light attack helicopters, and by air delivered riflemen

12 'Armor of the Future,' *Armor,* LXVII: 4 (July–August 1958), pp.16–7.
13 Hamilton H. Howze, *A Cavalryman's Story: Memoirs of a Twentieth Century Army General* (Washington, DC: Smithsonian Institution Press, 1996), p.235.
14 US Army Tactical Mobility Requirements Board, *Final Report: Army Tactical Mobility Requirements Board* (Fort Bragg, NC, 20 August 1962), Inclosure [*sic*] 1, 'Directives', p.1.
15 US Army Tactical Mobility Requirements Board, *Final Report*, p.1.
16 US Army Tactical Mobility Requirements Board, *Final Report*, p.95.

and tank killer teams', during simulations of 'conflict in highly developed areas, such as Europe, the air cavalry combat brigade proved most effective as a supplement to ground divisions.'[17]

The final five would be fully-fledged Air Assault Divisions. 'The Army division', the Board's final report argued, 'is a well established basic unit, being the smallest organization which encompasses all combat arms and services and which, when proper administrative support is provided by higher echelons, is capable of sustained independent operation.'[18] Although based on the US Army's standard infantry division, as revised by the Reorganization Objectives, Army Divisions (ROAD) initiative, the new divisions were intended to capitalise on 'the opportunity for increasing tactical mobility in the battle area through the use of helicopters.' To facilitate this, the Board conceded that 'considerable organizational surgery was necessary to switch reliance for mobility from ground to air vehicles.'[19] This applied not only to the division's three constituent infantry brigades, but also to its supporting artillery.

The ARA requirement

It was recognised from the outset that air assault divisions would need to be able to call upon copious amounts of supporting fires. In part, this could be supplied by making artillery units airmobile. It had been recognised for some time that the helicopter held 'considerable promise as a means of providing mobility, both on and off the battlefield for light cannon and missile field artillery elements.'[20] Central to a ROAD Division's Divisional Artillery (Divarty) were three direct support battalions, each armed with 18 105mm towed howitzers, and techniques for airlifting these weapons by helicopter had been well established by 1962.

The issue of providing heavier artillery support to the new air assault divisions, however, remained. ROAD divisions were provided with a single general support battalion, armed with 155mm howitzers, that 'augmented and extended the range of the three 105-mm. battalions.'[21] However, with a travelling weight of 12,700lbs the M114 155mm howitzer then in service was significantly heavier than either the M101 105mm howitzer (4,980lbs) or the lighter M102 105mm howitzer then under development (3,338lbs).[22] This was significantly beyond the lift capability of the helicopters

17 US Army Tactical Mobility Requirements Board, *Final Report*, p.40.
18 US Army Tactical Mobility Requirements Board, *Final Report*, p.35.
19 US Army Tactical Mobility Requirements Board, *Final Report*, p.38.
20 *Tactical and Technical Trends in Artillery Instruction (*Fort Sill, Okla: United States Army Artillery and Guided Missile School, February 1958), p.13
21 Major General David Ewing Ott, *Field Artillery 1954–1973*, Vietnam Studies, (Washington, DC: Department of the Army, 1995), p.86.
22 Weapons Department, *Field Artillery Cannon Weapons Systems and Ammunition Handbook*, (Fort Sill, Okla: Army Field Artillery School, 1983), pp.1-5.

then in service; even the new CH-47A Chinook could only carry the 155mm howitzer by 'breaking it down into two separate loads.'[23]

Moreover, even if it had been possible to lift heavy guns, it nevertheless appeared to many senior officers that tube artillery would be unable to provide all the support airmobile formations would require. For example, as part of the work of the Howze Board the chair wrote to several senior US Army commanders in June 1962 to garner their opinions 'on the application of air vehicles to provide land warfare mobility.' Given 'the vulnerability of aerial vehicles to hostile ground fire' it would be necessary to develop 'a proper mix of air and surface fire support weapons so organised that echelons no higher than the Division can expeditiously plan and execute air mobile assault operations', observed the head of US Military Assistance Command, Vietnam (MACV), General Paul D. Harkins. He continued:

> In addition to conventional artillery weapons, I visualize the provision of a family of armed aerial vehicles capable of effectively supporting aerial transport vehicles throughout the movement to and from the objective area as well as providing fire support for the forces in the objective area. Initially such fire support aerial vehicles can be provided by adaptation of presently available fixed and rotary wing aircraft.[24]

The answer to both issues, in the view of the Howze Board, was the armed helicopter. Accordingly, it therefore suggested that 'an aerial rocket battalion of 36 HU-1B (AH-1B) helicopters' should substitute for the 155mm howitzer battalion in the air assault division.[25]

ARA in Vietnam

The headquarters of an experimental air assault division – 11th Air Assault Division (Test) – was activated at Fort Benning (now Fort Moore), Georgia, on 7 February 1963.[26] Subsequently, on 18 July 1963 the 3rd Battalion, 377th Artillery was activated at Fort Benning as the first ARA battalion.[27] The next two years would see the new, understrength division undertake a series of intensive trials and exercises. By the middle of 1965 the worsening situation in Vietnam would spur

23 Ott, *Field Artillery 1954–1973*, p.55.
24 US Army Command and General Staff College, Fort Leavenworth, KS: Ike Skelton Combined Arms Research Library Digital Library: N18967.3-A: Letter from Harkins to Howze, undated (c. June-July 1962).
25 US Army Tactical Mobility Requirements Board, *Final Report*, p.39.
26 John B. Wilson, *Armies, Corps, Divisions, and Separate Brigades*, Army Lineage Series, (Washington, DC: Center of Military History, United States Army, 1999), p.253.
27 Janice E. McKenney, *Field Artillery, Part 2*, Army Lineage Series, (Washington, DC: Center of Military History, United States Army, 2010), p.1371.

further changes. In July of that year, the 1st Cavalry Division, then in Korea, was redesignated the 2nd Infantry Division; and the 2nd Infantry Division as the 1st Cavalry Division (Airmobile). Personnel for the latter were drawn both from the previous 2nd Infantry Division and the 11th Air Assault Division (Test), which was inactivated. The same month would also see 3rd Battalion, 377th Artillery inactivated, to be superseded as the divisional ARA battalion by 2nd Battalion, 20th Artillery. On 28 July President Johnson announced publicly that the division was to be despatched to Vietnam, and in September the division's artillery personnel arrived in theatre.

Within two days of arriving the 2/20th flew its first combat sorties. Whilst in Vietnam, the battalion would become known by its radio callsign, *Blue Max*. The battalion's primary armament in theatre during the Bell UH-1B era was the XM-3 weapons system. According to a report submitted by the Army Concept Team in Vietnam in July 1964, the system comprised 'two pods of 2.75-inch rockets mounted one on each side of the UH-1B':

> Each pod contains 24 rockets. The system is aimed from the right seat using the fixed Mark VIII infinity reflex sight and fired by a trigger switch on the right hand cyclic stick. It may also be fired by the trigger switch on the left cyclic stick. The maximum useful range ... is 2500 meters. Effective fire was occasionally delivered at ranges up to 4000 meters. Unit aviators believed, however, that it was most effective at approximately 1500 meters. The system permits firing in pairs and ripples of pairs at the rate of six pairs per second.[28]

In 1968, the 2/20th exchanged its UH-1s for Bell AH-1G Huey Cobras. Being 'specifically designed for aerial weaponry', the new type afforded 'significantly increased rocket helicopter speed, range and firepower.'[29] Other changes in that year would also lead to the 2/20th being joined in Vietnam by a second ARA battalion. The conversion of 101st Airborne Division to airmobile status (as 101st Air Cavalry Division) on 1 July 1968 would lead in turn to the reactivation of 4th Battalion, 77th Artillery at Fort Sill as the division's ARA battalion, and it subsequently joined the 101st in theatre. Two years later, the designation of both battalions would be changed from 'Aerial Rocket Artillery' to 'Aerial Field Artillery'.[30]

28 Army Concept Team in Vietnam, *Airmobile Company in Counterinsurgency Operations* (San Francisco, CA: Joint Research and Test Center, 1964), p.45.

29 Major Warren E. Mullen, 'Aerial Rocket Artillery,' *US Army Aviation Digest*, 14:12 (December 1968), p.24.

30 The term 'Aerial Field Artillery' was introduced to replace ARA in the revised edition of U.S. Army, *Field Manual FM 6-102 'Field Artillery Battalion, Aerial Field Artillery'* (Washington DC: Headquarters, Department of the Army, 1970); *United States Army Aviation Digest*, 16:4, (April 1970), p.5.

US Army Bell HU-1B-BF Iroquois (60-3589), armed with a prototype of the XM-3 weapon system. Development testing of the XM-3 was conducted at Fort Rucker by the US Army Missile Command, in conjunction with the US Army Aviation Board and the US Air Force, during 1962. The HU-1B was redesignated the UH-1B with effect from 18 September 1962. (RAF Museum: PC75/2/6016)

Bell HU-1A-BF Iroquois (57-6097), firing an AGM-22 (anti-tank guided weapon) from side mounting. The AGM-22 was used in only limited numbers by the ARA battalions in Vietnam. (RAF Museum PC75/2/6017)

The ARA role

The UH-1, AH-1, and 2.75 inch rocket were by no means employed solely by the ARA/AFA battalions. These units were distinguished not by their equipment, but rather by the way in which they operated. While conceding that they were 'capable of providing armed aerial escort, reconnaissance and security' in common with other gunships, a study of 'the capabilities and techniques for co-ordinated employment of combinations of the fire support means available to the 1st Cavalry Division (Airmobile)' circulated by the latter's artillery headquarters in April 1969 cautioned against using ARA batteries 'in roles other that [*sic*] their specific assigned mission', given that to do so 'reduces [their] responsiveness, availability and effectiveness.'[31]

Central to their 'specific assigned mission' was the status of the battalions as *artillery* units. According to the revised 1970 edition of *Field Manual FM 6-102*, AFA was 'employed to provide aerial fire support to all maneuver forces throughout all areas of operations and may be assigned any of the standard tactical missions for field artillery.'[32] It went on to define the AFA's operational concept as being to 'deliver fires from the aircraft in flight, employing speed, agility, and responsiveness to achieve surprise and destroy targets':

> Aerial field artillery provides a means of extending the fire support capabilities available to the force commander. Aerial field artillery possesses mobility characteristics which provide for artillery support in many situations in which the mobility characteristics of other types of field artillery are less suited. It is capable of rapidly maneuvering and massing fires in any type of terrain despite the wide dispersion required for survival on the modern battlefield.[33]

The battalions emphasised their artillery identity. 'All of the battalion's commissioned officers are artillery branch trained' noted an article on the 2/20th in the February 1966 issue of *Army Aviation*. Although their enlisted pilots were not similarly branch qualified, they too would appear to have quickly adopted the artillery ethos. 'Even our warrant officers get to feel that they are artillerymen after a while', asserted the then battalion commander, Lieutenant Colonel Nelson Mahone. 'Many people tend to class all armed helicopters as "gun ships", but we consider ourselves a breed apart, and our success with artillery tends to support this.'[34] Lieutenant General John J.

31 Headquarters 1st Cavalry Division Artillery (Airmobile), 'Coordinated Employment of Fire Support Means', 5 April 1969, Annex A 'Design Capabilities and Limitations of Individual Fire Support Means'; attached to Department of the Army, Office of the Adjutant General, 'Senior Officer Debriefing Report: MG George I Forsythe, CG, 1st Cavalry Division (Airmobile), Period 19 August 1968 to 23 April 1969', 15 May 1969, p.76, <https://apps.dtic.mil/sti/tr/pdf/AD0501952.pdf>, accessed 10 Oct. 2024.

32 U.S. Army, *Field Manual FM 6-102* (1970), p.1.

33 U.S. Army, *Field Manual FM 6-102* (1970), pp.1-2.

34 'Vietnam's ARA', *Army Aviation,* 15:2 (1966), p.5.

Tolson III would later note that 'some officers considered aerial rocket artillery to be a nuisance on the battlefield, and they could not understand why its method of employment should be any different than the armed helicopter which escorted the tactical troop lift':

> Fortunately, the aggressive spirit of the aerial rocket artillery battery demonstrated that it could and should be used in mass. While the other armed helicopters were preoccupied by pinpoint targets, the aerial rocket artillery could deliver area fire with the same responsiveness (and through the same communication channels) that tube artillery had done in the past.[35]

Tolson went on to outline the preferred method of deploying ARA:

> Aerial rocket artillery, in contrast to the roving gunship, generally stayed on the ground with one section having a two-minute alert time. They were positioned so to be only a matter of minutes away from any potential target. Two minutes after a fire mission was received, they were airborne, and, in a matter of a few minutes more, on target. As soon as the first section departed, a second section moved from a five-minute alert to the two-minute alert status, and another standby team moved to the five-minute alert. By this method, continuous and accurate firepower could be delivered. Aerial rocket artillery was so effective in the 1st Cavalry Division that the artillery commanders had to constantly remind the Infantry to use tube artillery when appropriate rather than call automatically for aerial rocket artillery support.[36]

ARA and CAS

As the USAF historian John Schlight noted, Tolson's description of ARA best practice 'replicated that which Air Force fighters were using.'[37] The employment of ARA battalions served to highlight differing Army and Air Force perceptions of what CAS could and should do – and, moreover, who should provide it.

While the task of providing CAS to US Army units in combat rested primarily with the US Army Air Force up to the end of the Second World War, the post-war period would see significant shifts in the delivery of such support. The initial impetus came from two measures enacted on 26 July 1947. The first was the National Security Act of 1947. Section 208 of this Act established formally a separate USAF

35 Lieutenant General John J. Tolson, *Airmobility 1961–1971*, Vietnam Studies, (Washington, DC: Department of the Army, 1999), p.122.
36 Tolson, *Airmobility 1961–1971*, p.122
37 John Schlight, *Help From Above: Air Force Close Air Support of the Army 1946–1973* (Washington, DC: Air Force History and Museums Program, 2003), p.345.

and provided for the transfer of most of the Army's existing aviation structures and assets – including those hitherto used to provide CAS – to the new Service.[38] On the same day, President Harry S. Truman signed Executive Order 9877 outlining the 'assignment of primary functions and responsibilities to the three armed services.' This order stipulated that one of the 'specific functions of the United States Air Force' was 'Air support to land forces and naval forces.'[39]

Just what this would mean in practice was considered when Secretary of Defense James V. Forrestal met with the Joint Chiefs of Staff (General Omar N. Bradley, US Army; Admiral Louis E. Denfeld, US Navy; and General Carl Spaatz, USAF) at Key West, Florida, in March of the following year. The result (entitled 'Functions of the Armed Forces and the Joint Chiefs of Staff' but known informally as the 'Key West Agreement') was approved by Truman on 21 April 1948. In 1954 this document was revised and reissued as Department of Defense Directive DoDD 5100.01 'Functions of the Armed Forces and the Joint Chiefs of Staff' (although it has continued to be referred to as the 'Key West Agreement'), and later revisions of the DoDD 5100.01 have followed up to the time of writing.[40]

While recognising that 'the Air Force has primary interest in all operations in the air' and that providing 'close combat and logistical air support to the Army' was one of its primary functions, the Key West Agreement and its successors did not deny the Army certain organic air capabilities, such as the operation of light aircraft for artillery observation and liaison.[41] Wolf has described 'the prevailing attitude in the Air Force' at this time as being 'to acquiesce to the Army expanding into support roles for its organic aviation, as the Air Force pursued nuclear capabilities for its tactical forces as well as its strategic ones.'[42] Nevertheless, divisions between the two services with regard to provision of CAS continued to run deep and the USAF remained sensitive to any suggestion that the Army might seek to trespass upon their responsibilities. When testifying before the US Senate Armed Services Committee's Subcommittee on the Air Force on 24 May 1956, Howze (then Director of Army Aviation) was asked 'what is organic aviation?' He defined the term as describing an 'aircraft which belong to the Army and does not operate as a part of another service in support of the Army.'

38 Richard I. Wolf, *The United States Air Force: Basic Documents on Roles and Missions* (Washington, DC: Office of Air Force History, United States Air Force, 1987), pp.74–6.

39 Wolf, *The United States Air Force: Basic Documents on Roles and Missions*, p.87, p.90.

40 For an overview of the antecedents and subsequent iterations of DoDD 5100.01 up to 2020, see Office of the Secretary of Defense, Chief Management Officer, Organizational Policy and Decision Support, 'White Paper: Evolution of Department of Defense Directive 5100.01 "Functions of the Department of Defense and Its Major Components"' (2020), <https://dml.armywarcollege.edu/wp-content/uploads/2022/12/DoD-CMO-White-Paper-Evolution-of-5100.01-2020-Update.pdf>, accessed 10 Oct. 2024.

41 Wolf, *The United States Air Force: Basic Documents on Roles and Missions*, p.163.

42 Wolf, *The United States Air Force: Basic Documents on Roles and Missions*, p.241.

Howze went on to note that an organic aircraft 'will be painted brown ... and have the Army name on it.'[43]

For their part, Army leaders in the Pentagon were keen to reassure both politicians on Capitol Hill and their USAF counterparts that the new airmobile initiatives were not an attempt by their Service to acquire their own air force. While 'aviation that operates continually in the ground soldier's environment should be responsive to his immediate command and should therefore be organic to the Army', on 18 February 1963 Secretary of the Army Cyrus Vance told a subcommittee of the House of Representatives Committee on Appropriations that 'the Army plans neither to organize an Army Air Corps not to duplicate tactical air support missions that are the responsibility of the Air Force.' [44] Later that same day the US Army's Chief of Staff, General Earle Wheeler, reiterated that his Service's 'air mobility concepts do not infringe in the Air Force missions or responsibilities.' While hailing the 'unique and distinctive service to the Army and the Defence tri-service team' exercised by the Howze Board 'by exploring the possibilities of applying Army aircraft to the natural evolutionary development of improved firepower and mobility systems for the Army', Wheeler also acknowledged 'the continuing requirement for Air Force fighter-bomber aircraft, operating in close support of the ground battle, to counter enemy aircraft, and for interdiction, deep reconnaissance, and close air support missions. I feel very strongly about this.'[45]

To many, however, it appeared that the Air Force's priorities in terms of its ground support commitments did not correspond to those of their Army colleagues. This viewpoint was reflected in the June 1963 issue of *Army* magazine. Although 'the three missions of the Tactical Air Command' were achieving air superiority over the battlefield, CAS, and interdiction', according to 'Perry Poe' – a pseudonym used by the magazine's own staff – 'the Air Force tends to fuse these three missions into one.' In support of this contention, the article cited comments made before a Congressional committee by General Curtis E. LeMay, the USAF's Chief of Staff between 1961 and 1965:

> General LeMay in telling why Air Force close air support was perfectly adequate said, 'In Korea no soldier lost his life in enemy air action. I think this is a pretty

43 Major General Hamilton H. Howze, Director of Army Aviation, Office, Deputy Chief of Staff for Operations, 24 May 1956, in United States Senate Committee on Armed Services, *Hearings before the Subcommittee on the Air Force, Airpower* (Washington, DC: U.S. Government Printing Office, 1956), p.794.

44 Hon Cyrus E. Vance, Secretary of the Army, 18 February 1963, in United States House Committee of Appropriations, *Hearings before Subcommittee , Department of Defense Appropriations for 1964* (Washington, DC: US Government Printing Office, 1963), p.100.

45 Testimony of General Earle E. Wheeler, Chief of Staff, US Army, 18 February 1963, in United States House Committee of Appropriations, *Hearings before Subcommittee, Department of Defense Appropriations for 1964* (Washington, DC: US Government Printing Office, 1963), p.125.

Douglas A-1E Skyraider, USAF, 1st Air Commando Group, 34987 during a CAS mission, Vietnam. (RAF Museum: PC75/2/7164)

> good record.' It is indeed. It speaks well of TAC's performance in achieving air superiority over enemy air, but it has nothing to do with the adequacy or inadequacy of TAC's attacks on enemy ground targets that are in close combat with our own ground forces.[46]

Dissatisfaction in the USAF's CAS efforts led some Army officers on the ground in Vietnam to compare it to that furnished by their ARA counterparts. At least some members of 1st Cavalry Division would appear to have preferred the latter. The relative merits of both were considered in an exchange on the pages of *Army* in 1966–7. 'In the midst of all the praise by the Army for the close air support the Air Force is providing in Vietnam', Captain Ramon Antonio 'Tony' Nadal wrote in a letter published in November 1966, 'I would like to raise a dissenting voice.'[47] During his time as the commander of Alpha Company, 2nd Battalion, 7th Cavalry, Nadal stressed that he 'had occasion to call for TAC air and to see its results up close.' While acknowledging that troops in the field were 'getting better close air support, I am sure, than we had ever had before', he nevertheless argued that 'with a bit more effort on the part of the Army and the Air Force, close air support can be better than it is now.'

46 'Perry Poe', 'How's Air Mobility', *Army*, 13:11 (June 1963), p.28.
47 Captain Ramon A. Nadal, 'Front & Center: Dissent on Close Air Support', *Army*, 16:11 (November 1966), pp.14–6.

Nadal's critique of USAF CAS revolved primarily around its 'insufficient responsiveness to the specific needs of the infantry.' He highlighted three issues. The first was timeliness. 'The Air Force seldom placed fighter aircraft on combat air patrol over an operational area', Nadal charged. 'Instead the aircraft were on strip alert. The time it took to get a TAC air strike after the request was usually 30 minutes. This is too long.' The second related to a lack of responsiveness to communications. 'The platoon', in Nadal's view, 'should be able to communicate with the aircraft making the strike.' Although the attachment of Forward Air Controllers to units was useful, 'many times it would be easier and faster to let the pilot flying the strike talk to the man who needs it.'

His final criticism centred upon 'aircraft armament and accuracy of fire.' During his time in Vietnam, he had found that 'too many times the aircraft had arrived with the wrong load' – 750lb or 1,000lb bombs, rather than cluster bombs and napalm. 'The bursting radius of the big bombs,' according to Nadal:

> [...]coupled with the lack of close accuracy of the aircraft/pilot system forced on us a safety zone that invariably was beyond the VC [Viet Cong] who crowd in so close and usually are only 50 or 100 metres ahead of our troops. We in the infantry need closer air support than that. We need air strikes that hit 100 meters ahead of our positions. And the ordnance ought to be designed for this job.

Nadal contrasted the USAF's failings with the success of ARA. 'Invariably', in his judgement, 'when we became engaged the best close fire support we received was from the armed HU-1B's [*sic*] of the 2/20 Artillery.' His reasons were fourfold. In contrast to CAS aircraft, the ARA helicopters 'were readily available; two of them flying over the general area of the battlefield, and the rest laagered far enough that they could support in a short period of time.' Communication with the ARA crews proved more straightforward. Although 'the ARA were normally requested and controlled by the artillery FO (forward observer) attached to the rifle company ... when needed any infantryman with a radio could control them.' Thirdly, they did not require the same degree of separation from the enemy that their fixed-wing counterparts needed. 'We could call them in, and did on many occasions, to fire 40 to 50 meters to our front,' Nadal recalled. Finally, he praised the ARA's constancy. 'You could count on the ARA to fly in almost any weather, day or night.'

A counterpoint to Nadal appeared in *Army* two months later. The author, Captain Richard A. Dixon, opened his letter with the confession that he had previously 'shared his [Nadal's] opinions along with many other ground commanders who collectively evince an ignorance of tactical air support procedures.' However, Dixon's outlook had 'changed soon after being assigned to G3 Air in the 1st Cavalry Division.' Here, he had been 'able to learn the tac air business first-hand.'[48]

48 Captain Richard A. Dixon, 'Airborne FAC the Key', *Army*, 17:11 (January 1967), p.6.

Dixon contested Nadal's statements as to the delay in providing CAS, claiming that 'the 1st Cavalry Division received continuous air support during the during the entire Bong Son operation' with 'at least two Air Force fighters on station over the operational area at all times during daylight.' Dixon 'had flown with the airborne forward air controller (FAC) on many of the missions' and in his experience they 'had the capability of striking at any time within five minutes except that it usually required at least 20 minutes to sort out the friendlies from the VC within the target area. On several occasions we would receive word from the ground commander that an area was clear only to discover on closer observation that friendlies were present within the target area.'

To Dixon, bypassing the FAC as advocated by Nadal would be counterproductive. 'The airborne FAC is the key to good, close air support,' he argued. 'He has eyeball contact with the fighters and visual contact with ground forces through marking devices such as smoke. He has radio contact with all elements in the air and on the ground to include forward observers and platoon leaders when necessary.' By contrast, 'all the contact between the commander in the ground and the fighter pilot is useless. Trying to control the air strike from the jungle floor is like trying to adjust artillery fire by sound alone. Captain Nadal might as well recommend direct communication between the ground commander and each piece of tube artillery firing in his support.'

Captain Dixon also differed in his appreciation of the bombloads carried by USAF CAS aircraft. They were required to carry 'a variety of weapons tailored to fit the wide variety of terrain'; although the cluster bombs and napalm favoured by Nadal were 'very effective in open terrain', both were 'relatively ineffective in dense foliage.' Here he believed that the CAS aircraft held a definite advantage over their ARA counterparts. While expressing 'a healthy respect' for the latter, he noted that 'their stock or ordnance is limited' and consequently ARA's 'effectiveness was minimal in densely foliated areas. On several occasions in my experience,' Dixon continued, 'tac air was called in with heavier ordnance because the aerial rocket artillery could not penetrate the jungle canopy.'

'I think this is the worst way to do it'

A further argument raised against the use of helicopters on the battlefield centred upon their vulnerability. From the outset, voices from both within and beyond the Army had questioned whether they were too slow, cumbersome, and fragile for this task. One outspoken critic was LeMay. While appearing before a House of Representatives committee in February 1963, Le May offered two reasons why the armed helicopters were unsuitable for the battlefield support role. The first related to their viability as weapons platforms. Vibration was a major problem. 'We have not been able to get a smooth-flying one. Some are smoother than others, but they all vibrate,' he told the assembled Congressmen. 'We have never been able to get a good firing platform out of a chopper.'[49]

49 General Curtis E. LeMay, Chief of Staff, US Air Force, 25 February 1963, in United States House Committee of Appropriations, *Hearings before Subcommittee , Department of Defense Appropriations for 1964* (Washington, DC: US Government Printing Office, 1963), p.485.

The second was their vulnerability to ground fire. 'I think you have to have high performance in order to do this job properly,' LeMay argued. Although the USAF at first used F-51 Mustangs for close air support tasks during the Korean War, 'this didn't last very long. As soon as the automatic weapons got to work on them this became an improper pastime and we had to pull propeller airplanes off and put jets on the mission. You need performance.' While conceding that it might be possible 'to get more performance out of the helicopters', LeMay nevertheless suggested that armed helicopters would need to deliver their weapons while hovering:

> You don't want to go in over any area and stand there in order to shoot the target. This is not healthy. You don't even do that on the ground. A doughboy doesn't do that. He is moving around all the time or he doesn't live very long. You have to have flexibility.

There are better ways than doing it than with choppers,' LeMay concluded. 'As a matter of fact, I think this the worst way to do it at the present time.'[50] Later in the same session LeMay acknowledged that helicopters would be 'useful in Vietnam' but reiterated his view that 'you cannot take them into combat where you will be shot at. You have to keep them out of the field of fire.'[51]

While LeMay's protestations appear overstated, nevertheless the skies over Vietnam did prove a hostile environment. In 1968 alone, for example, the US Army lost 866 helicopters of all types.[52] While contemporaneous studies do not differentiate between ARA helicopters and other gunships, it is nevertheless clear that flying any form of armed helicopter in combat was dangerous. An investigation of casualty statistics relating to US Army fixed and rotary-wing aircraft between 1962 and 1967 concluded that 'the weapon threat was approximately 85 percent Caliber .30 type, 10 percent Caliber .50 type, and 5 percent miscellaneous, including booby traps and land mine detonations, usually in the landing zone.'[53] While the average number of flying hours per casualty for all US Army aircraft in Vietnam during the period in question was calculated as being 1,100, and 9,400 per fatality, the equivalent figures

50 General Curtis E. LeMay, Chief of Staff, US Air Force, 25 February 1963, in United States House Committee of Appropriations, *Hearings before Subcommittee , Department of Defense Appropriations for 1964*, p. 486.

51 General Curtis E. LeMay, Chief of Staff, US Air Force, 25 February 1963, in United States House Committee of Appropriations, *Hearings before Subcommittee, Department of Defense Appropriations for 1964*, p. 495.

52 Testimony of General Henry A. Miley, Deputy Commanding General, US Army Material Command, 1 August 1969, United States Senate Committee on Armed Services, *Hearings on Military Posture* (Washington, DC: US Government Printing Office, 1969), p.4032.

53 Ballistic Research Laboratories, *Report No. 2030: US Army Casualties Aboard Aircraft in the Republic of Vietnam, 1962 through 1967* (Aberdeen Proving Ground, MD: US Army Aberdeen Research and Development Center Ballistic Research Laboratories, March 1970), p.11.

for armed UH-1B and C helicopters were just 400 (+/-150) and 2,900 (+/-400) respectively. Transport UH1-D and H helicopters, by contrast, flew 1,150 hours per casualty (+/-250) and 9,500 hours per fatality, while for OV-1A/B/C Mohawks (the fixed-wing US Army type with the highest risk factor) the figures were 2,000 per casualty and 22,200 per fatality. The report indicated 'that the risk of casualty (and fatality)' was 'related to the "aggressiveness" of the missions assigned to the various classes of aircraft. Armed UH-1B/C and OV-1A/B/C, in the rotary-wing and fixed-wing classes, fly the highest-risk missions.' It attributed the 'significantly lower risk per casualty in the fixed-wing aircraft' primarily to the latter's 'ability to overfly the main threat (which is small caliber weapons in Vietnam) and fewer personnel on board (usually).'[54]

A second study found that between February 1968 and April 1969 'during an average day, gunships flew 2,487 sorties or 1,229 hours.' Operational losses amounted to 199 aircraft (49 AH-1s and 150 UH-1s) – one every two and a half days – 'for an average of one armed helicopter every 5,700 sorties.' The original US Army study went on to compare this with 'an analysis by the Directorate of Operations, DCS/Plans and Operations, Hq [*sic*] USAF, in April 1969 which showed USAF losses at one "attack" or reconnaissance aircraft per 3,000 sorties'; although, as the USAF author went on to note, Army and Air Force definitions of 'sortie' differed significantly.[55]

After Vietnam

The early 1970s saw the US Army embark upon several exercises intended to record and analyse its recent performance in south-east Asia. One such was the 'Vietnam Studies', a series of monographs written by senior serving US Army officers. Included in this series was a volume by Lieutenant General John H. Hay, Jr devoted to *Tactical and Material Innovations*. In Hay's judgement, ARA represented 'one of the major artillery innovations of the Vietnam War.'[56]

For all their apparent success in the field, however, the ARA battalions did not long survive the end of that conflict. Following the return of 1st Cavalry Division to the United States, 2nd Battalion 20th Artillery was inactivated on 10 April 1971.[57] The 101st Airmobile Division's ARA battalion was redesignated as a field artillery battalion on 1 September 1971, and it was eventually inactivated at Fort Campbell,

54 Ballistic Research Laboratories, *Report No. 2030: US Army Casualties Aboard Aircraft*, pp.18-19.

55 HQ Pacific Air Forces, Directorate, Tactical Evaluation, CHECO Division, 'Project CHECO Report, Army Aviation in RVN – A Case Study', 11 July 1970, pp.41-2, <https://apps.dtic.mil/sti/pdfs/ADA486929.pdf>, accessed 10 Oct. 2024.

56 Lieutenant General John H. Hay Jr, *Tactical and Material Innovations*, Vietnam Studies, (Washington, DC: Department of the Army, 2002), p.32.

57 Janice E. McKenney, *Field Artillery, Part 1*, Army Lineage Series, (Washington, DC: Center of Military History, United States Army, 2010), p.578.

Kentucky, on 21 January 1978.[58] In part, the fate of the ARA battalions also reflected that of their parent formations. During the 1970s, US Army doctrine was revised with the aim of moving 'the Army out of the rice paddies of Vietnam and … on the Western European battlefield against the Warsaw Pact.'[59] This reorientation was guided, in large part, by the US Army Training and Doctrine Command (TRADOC), which had been established in 1973 with General William E. DePuy at its head. 'TRADOC,' according to Linn, now 'became the center of a concerted effort to build a new model army, one that rejected the Vietnam experience and looked toward (or, more accurately, back to) the repulse of a Soviet attack on NATO.'[60] Although advocates of airmobility sought to emphasise that the concept was neither inspired by nor tied to counterinsurgency in the first instance, doubts as to their utility in the context of the defence of Europe's Central Front nevertheless undermined the continued relevance of the airmobile divisions.

It can also be attributed to the belief that for all its utility, ARA was seen as something of a stopgap and did not represent a sustainable substitute for conventional artillery. 'Aerial artillery support is extremely critical in airmobile operations outside normal artillery range,' Lieutenant Colonel Carl M. Putman conceded in the May–June 1970 issue of *Armor*. However, he went on to contend that 'as a direct fire, point target weapons system, the attack helicopter cannot accomplish the classic artillery mission of delivering heavy tonnages of sustained area fire':

> The gunship can fill only partly such an artillery mission in delivering a concentration of explosive rockets on a specified area in a specified time. This is a useful capability only when tube artillery is not in range. Thus, at best, the gunship is only an expedient substitute for artillery. There is no obvious gain in efficiency of employment when attack helicopters are controlled by the Field Artillery. The opposite, in fact, would appear to be true since a veto authority is introduced between the supported commander and his gunships.

While acknowledging 'the success of aerial rocket artillery in the airmobile divisions', Putman saw 'the precedent established by the two current aerial rocket artillery battalions' as having 'the aura of a tactical expedient pending development of true aerial artillery capability. The functional parallel between attack helicopter fire and artillery fire is less convincing than the parallel between attack helicopter fire and that

58 McKenney, *Field Artillery, Part 2*, p.898.

59 David Fitzgerald, *Learning to Forget: US Army Counterinsurgency Doctrine and Practice from Vietnam to Iraq*, Stanford Security Studies, (Stanford, CA: Stanford University Press, 2013), p.43.

60 Linn, *Real Soldiering: The US Army in the Aftermath of War*, p.159.

delivered tanks, recoilless rifles, and other direct fire support means integrated and co-ordinated by the maneuver unit commander.'[61]

Ultimately, however, the demise of the ARA battalions reflected a doctrinal shift in the way armed helicopters were utilised by the US Army. Writing in the March 1981 issue of the *US Army Aviation Digest*, the US Army Field Artillery School's then Commandant (Major General Edward A. Dinges) and Senior Maneuver Instructor (Major Joseph F. Pullano) noted that 'the closest aviation organization to what is now the attack helicopter company was the old aerial rocket artillery battalion, later called an aerial field artillery battalion.' However, while the latter had 'functioned exactly like artillery units and operated in the divarty communications net,' the primary mission of the attack helicopter company was now 'to destroy tanks and other armoured vehicles in concern with other members of the combined arms team.'[62] This change in the status of the armed helicopter from fire support to manoeuvre system marked the end of aerial rocket artillery.

61 Lieutenant Colonel Carl M. Putman, 'Proponency of Aerial Fighting Vehicles,' *Armor*, LXXIX:3 (1970), p9.

62 Major General Edward A. Dinges and Major Joseph F. Pullano, 'Fire Support for the Attack helicopter,' *US Army Aviation Digest*, 27:3 (1981), p.3.

10

'Suddenly like cavalry': British Close Air Support in the Falklands Campaign

John Alexander

Introduction

> 2 Para [2nd Battalion, Parachute Regiment] were stuck on a forward slope, in daylight, being engaged by 35mm AAA [anti-aircraft artillery] at 2000 metres range, something to which they had absolutely no answer. Suddenly like cavalry came three Harriers, which promptly took out the guns and turned the tide of the battle.[1]

Thus, Brigadier Julian Thompson, who commanded the Landing Force and 3 Commando Brigade during the Falklands Campaign, described the impact of close air support (CAS) at the Battle of Goose Green at a Royal Air Force Historical Society seminar twenty years after the event. His intervention followed Air Chief Marshal Sir Peter Squire, then Chief of the Air Staff, who in his seminar paper on commanding No. 1 (Fighter) Squadron RAF in the campaign had described his Hawker Siddeley Harrier Ground Attack and Reconnaissance Mark 3s (GR3s) as 'having a significant effect on the outcome of that battle.'[2] Thompson had been ordered to capture Goose Green and defeat its Argentine garrison because of the British government's political imperative for an early victory and when the attack faltered, Harrier CAS turned the battle.[3] Yet there were few other instances of decisive Harrier GR3 CAS despite the absence of Argentine fighters over the Islands, No. 1 Squadron's expertise in its specialist role, and the limited organic fire support available to the British infantry

1 'Falklands Campaign', *Journal of the Royal Air Force Historical Society*, 30 (2003), p.115.
2 Air Chief Marshal Sir Peter Squire, 'Harrier Operations – No 1 Sqn', *Journal of the Royal Air Force Historical Society*, 30 (2003), pp.102–9 (p.106).
3 Julian Thompson, *No Picnic: 3 Commando Brigade in the South Atlantic, 1982* (London: L. Cooper in association with Secker & Warburg, 1985), p.200.

force. According to Headquarters 5 Infantry Brigade, which joined 3 Commando Brigade to form a divisional formation called Land Forces Falklands Islands (LFFI), there 'was an absence of CAS in this operation.'[4] Neither was CAS mentioned in the Chief of Defence Staff's (CDS's) note on principal lessons of the campaign.[5] Yet four of the 14 Harrier GR3s deployed were lost, three to Argentine surface-to-air fire, and all were damaged by ground fire, while conducting offensive air support. No.1 Squadron flew 123 sorties in 58 missions over 25 days in the conflict, although few were CAS.[6]

The historiography largely overlooks British CAS in the campaign. As the British official historian, Lawrence Freedman, explains, 'the central story of air power and the Falklands concerns Britain's determination to limit the risks its forces faced in the course of the amphibious landing.'[7] His official history therefore focuses on the air battle between Argentine attack aircraft and British Sea Harriers and surface-based air defences. He notes a role for the RAF in the campaign was initially unforeseen. It subsequently included the Vulcan bomber *Black Buck* raids, which arguably dominate the RAF historiography of the campaign, Nimrod maritime patrols, and a huge air-to-air refuelling and air transport effort, including forty C-130 air drops to the Task Force, each a 24-hour round trip from Ascension Island. In addition, 10 RAF Harrier GR3s were initially sent as Sea Harrier attrition replacements, subsequently switched to offensive air support and later reinforced by another four aircraft. Freedman briefly notes two of the three Harrier GR3 were shot down re-attacking, and the strained command arrangements in theatre, including the absence of a joint theatre commander and the limited capacity to coordinate offensive air support, a NATO doctrinal term explained below. While many other appraisals of air power in the Falklands omit the offensive Harrier GR3 role,[8] recent assessments by David Jordan and John Shields both introduce various challenges for CAS in the campaign.[9] The most enlightening Harrier GR3 memoir is by Jerry Pook, one of Squire's flight

4 *Ex Atlantic Legacy Study Guide Operation CORPORATE*, Study Guide, Feb/Mar 2018 (Warminster: Land Warfare Development Centre), p.113.

5 The National Archives, Kew (TNA): DEFE 71/653: Operation Corporate (Falklands Conflict) Lessons Learned; Presentations' 1982, 'The Principal Military Lessons of the Falkland Islands', dated 15 December 1982.

6 TNA: DEFE 58/270: 'AOIC Central Trials and Tactics Organisation Report on Tactical Lessons Learned from Air Operations during the Falkland Islands Conflict', 1982, p.F–7.

7 Lawrence Freedman, 'Air Power and the Falklands', in John Andreas Olsen (ed), *A History of Air Warfare*, 1st edn. (Washington, DC: Poole: Potomac; Chris Lloyd distributor, 2010), pp.157–74, (p.161).

8 Phillip Grove, 'Falklands Conflict 1982 – The Air War: A New Appraisal', in Steven Badsey, Rob Havers, and Mark Grove (eds), *The Falklands Conflict Twenty Years On* (Frank Cass, 2004), pp.265–81.

9 David John Jordan and John Harris Shields, '"In at the Deep End": RAF Harrier Operations During the Falklands War', *The RAF Air Power Review*, 21:2 (2018), pp.110–29; John Shields, *Air Power in the Falklands Conflict: An Operational Level Insight into Air Warfare in the South Atlantic* (Barnsley: Air World, 2021).

commanders, an uncompromising critique of the impact of the 'shabby treatment the [No.] 1 (F) Squadron pilots had received at the hands of senior Royal Navy officers', published, as the historian David Jordan warns, some time after the campaign.[10]

This chapter offers a fresh perspective on British CAS in the Falklands Campaign and the perennial issue of the prioritisation of CAS vis-à-vis other air power roles by examining the command arrangements for air support during the campaign. The chapter draws heavily on raw contemporary official reports, some only recently released. One reason the Falklands Campaign could be seen as an anachronism is that it occurred during what one air power scholar calls a 'doctrinal vacuum' of British air power doctrine, fought as it was between the withdrawal Air Publication (AP) 1300 4th Edition and the first edition of AP 3000 *Air Power Doctrine* in 1991.[11] The chapter starts therefore by considering the doctrine the RAF used at the time. Moreover, the campaign occurred before the institutionalisation of the operational level, operational art, mission command, the manoeuvrist approach, and 'jointery', which began with the publication of *Design for Operations, British Military Doctrine* in 1989. Hence, notwithstanding a painting of the landing at San Carlos on the latter's cover, Hew Strachan omits the Falklands Campaign from his study of *Operational Art and Britain, 1909–2009.* Nevertheless, British command demonstrated A.A. Svechin's notion of operational art linking the steps between strategy and tactics, later codified in *Design for Operations*, as the second part of the chapter highlights while examining Freedman's observation of the absence of a joint operational command in theatre and its subsequent impact on air-land integration.[12] The bulk of the chapter focuses on the impact of these command arrangements on Harrier GR3 offensive air support during the campaign, before concluding.

Offensive air support

Notwithstanding the apparent absence of British air power doctrine at the time, the RAF, focused on NATO's Central Region, used NATO tactical air power doctrine in the campaign and to frame its immediate post-campaign assessments. NATO tactical

10 Jerry Pook, *RAF Harrier Ground Attack – Falklands* (Barnsley: Pen & Sword Aviation, 2007), p.8; Jordan and Shields, 'In at the Deep End', p.119.

11 Viktoriya Fedorchak, *British Air Power: The Doctrinal Path to Jointery*, Bloomsbury Collections (London: Bloomsbury Academic, 2018), p.2; Gp Capt Christopher Finn, 'British Thinking on Air Power: The Evolution of AP 3000', *Air Power Review*, 12:1 (2009), pp.56–68 (pp.56–7).

12 Hew Strachan, 'Operational Art and Britain, 1909–2009', in John Andreas Olsen and Martin van Creveld (eds), *The Evolution of Operational Art: From Napoleon to the Present* (Oxford: OUP, 2010), pp.96–136; Aleksandr A. Svechin, *Strategy*, trans. by Kent D. Lee (Minneapolis: East View, 1992), p.269; Chief of the General Staff, *Design for Military Operations: The British Military Doctrine*, D/CGS/50/8 Army Code 71451 (London: HMSO, 1989).

air power doctrine emphasised the philosophy of centralised control and decentralised execution, the necessity of joint air-land planning at all levels and included CAS as part of offensive air support. The British had increasingly used the term offensive air support for air support on the battlefield since the end of the Second World War and had convinced NATO to use it when NATO started codifying tactical air power doctrine in the 1970s. Furthermore, offensive air support included tactical air reconnaissance, CAS, and battlefield air interdiction. This was 'air action against hostile surface targets which are in a position to directly affect friendly forces and which required joint planning and co-ordination', whereas CAS was in close proximity and therefore required integration.[13] The RAF had used today's NATO definition of CAS defined in the book's introduction from at least 1963.[14] NATO subsequently removed offensive air support and battlefield air interdiction from its doctrine in 1999, leaving just CAS and air interdiction.[15] Tactical air reconnaissance also fell into NATO disuse as a term with specialist Intelligence, Surveillance and Reconnaissance platforms increasingly used for reconnaissance rather than fighters.

Strategic direction

The strategic direction of the campaign was set when Admiral Sir Henry Leach, the First Sea Lord, when looking for the Secretary of State for Defence, John Nott, on 31 March joined a meeting between the Prime Minister and Nott discussing the British government's possible reactions to the imminent Argentine invasion of the Falkland Islands. In the absence of both the CDS, Admiral of the Fleet Sir Terrance Lewin, and the acting CDS, the Chief of the Air Staff, Air Chief Marshal Sir Michael Beetham, Leach told the meeting when asked about assembling a task force:

> I said, yes Prime Minister we could, and then I stuck my neck out and said, though it's not my business, I think we should, and she instantly shot back, 'Why do you say that?' Well, I said, if we do not, if we don't do something really positive, if we're not entirely successful, and still worse if we do nothing, then we shall never lift our heads up again and we shall be living in a third-class country.[16]

13 Allied Tactical Publication (ATP)-33(A) *NATO Tactical Air Power* (Brussels: NATO Military Agency for Standardization, 1980); ATP-27(B), *Offensive Air Support* (Brussels: NATO Military Agency for Standardization, 1979); David J. Stein, *The Development of NATO Tactical Air Doctrine, 1970-1985* (RAND Corporation, 1 January 1987).

14 TNA: AIR 10/5589: AP 1300 RAF Manual of Operations, Fourth Edition, 1957, AL2 Feb 1963, p.67.

15 ATP-27(C)/AJP-3.3.2 *Air Interdiction and Close Air Support*, (Brussels: NATO Military Agency for Standardization, 1999), p.1–1.

16 Stephen Prince, 'British Command and Control in the Falklands Campaign', *Defense & Security Analysis*, 18:4 (2002), pp.333–49 (p.337).

Faced with an existential threat to Britain's place in the world and, to her at the time, unpopular government, Thatcher took Harold Macmillan's advice to form a war cabinet to avoid the lack of strategic direction of the Suez campaign of 1956, and as previous British wartime prime ministers David Lloyd George, Winston Churchill and Clement Atlee had done, and which John Major would do in 1990 for the Gulf War. Notably Thatcher's War Cabinet included her leading party opponent Francis Pym, no one from the Treasury, and the CDS as military advisor.[17] The War Cabinet met at least once a day during the campaign.

The chain of command was from Mrs Thatcher's War Cabinet, through the CDS, newly empowered as the prime minister's military adviser, the Commander-in-Chief Fleet, Admiral Sir John Fieldhouse, who commanded the Task Force sent to the South Atlantic, as Commander Task Force 317 (CTF 317) from his headquarters at Northwood, to the task group and task unit commanders at sea. It is generally held to have successfully orchestrated the campaign from the strategic to the tactical, across the diplomatic, information, military, and economic instruments of national power, and from crisis response to conflict as described in today's UK *Defence Doctrine*.[18] Examples include the Task Force's departure just three days after the decision to send one, the gradual escalation through the repossession of South Georgia and the *Black Buck* Vulcan raids on Port Stanley airfield, and the change of rules of engagement to allow the submarine HMS *Conqueror* to sink the Argentine cruiser ARA *General Belgrano*. Jonathan Band was Fieldhouse's flag lieutenant during the campaign, and twenty years later when First Sea Lord judged that the chain of command had worked well.[19] The official Naval historian Stephen Prince makes a similar assessment.[20]

The decision to send 10 RAF Harrier GR3s from No. 1 Squadron based at RAF Wittering as attrition reinforcements for the 20 Sea Harriers initially available to the Task Force was a further example of political will, as heavy Sea Harrier casualties were expected. Furthermore, the Harrier GR3s were modified to carry the new AIM9L Sidewinder missiles, for air-to-air combat, and for carrier deck landings.[21] As it was, by the time the first six Harrier GR3s transferred from the SS *Atlantic Conveyor* to HMS *Hermes* in the South Atlantic from 18 to 20 May, no Sea Harriers had been lost in air combat and so the Harrier GR3s flew only two air defence sorties on 19 May before being dedicated to the offensive air support role.[22] The Harrier GR3s were modified to take the RN's 2-inch rocket pod as their 68mm SNEB rocket pod was

17 Lawrence Freedman, *The Official History of the Falklands Campaign*, Government Official History Series (London: Routledge, 2005), Volume ii, p.26.
18 Ministry of Defence, Joint Doctrine Publication (JDP) 0–10 *UK Defence Doctrine*, 6th edn (Shrivenham: Development, Concepts and Doctrine Centre, 2022).
19 Vice Admiral Sir Jonathan Band, 'British High Command during the Falklands Campaign', Badsey, Havers, and Grove (eds) *The Falklands Conflict Twenty Years on: Lessons for the Future*, pp.30–9 (p.32).
20 Prince, 'British Command and Control in the Falklands Campaign'.
21 Jordan and Shields, 'In at the Deep End', p.113.
22 Squire, 'Harrier Operations – No 1 Sqn', pp.103–4.

Harrier GR3 XZ997 (Flight Lieutenant Rochfort) following a landing accident on HMS Hermes, Falklands Campaign, 21 May 1982, still armed following an unsuccessful armed reconnaissance sortie over San Carlos. (RAF Museum: P032382)

not cleared for carrier use. They were subsequently modified during the campaign to carry the ALE-40 chaff and flare dispenser, an improvised self-protection radar jammer, and, just days before the Argentine surrender, one aircraft was modified to take the AGM-45A Shrike anti-radiation missile for the destruction of enemy air defence radars and others for the 1000lb Paveway laser-guided bomb (LGB). While the Shrike was not used, the Paveway was, as explained later.[23]

Furthermore, it was a political imperative to maintain public support at home and force the diplomatic pace. That drove the decision to land at San Carlos before control of the air had been secured and to order Thompson to fight a battle he did not want to capture Goose Green.[24] Thompson later noted, 'there was one key player missing from the chain of command: a three-star operational commander' in theatre who would have protected him from political and four-star interference.[25]

Joint theatre command

Contrary to popular opinion, Rear Admiral Sandy Woodward, commanding the carrier task group as Commander Task Group (CTG) 317.8, did not command

23 Jordan and Shields, 'In at the Deep End', pp.113–14, pp.121–22.
24 Andrew M. Dorman, Michael D. Kandiah, and Gillian Staerc (eds), The Falklands War: [Seminar] Held at the Joint Services Command and Staff College (JSCSC), Watchfield Wiltshire on 5 June 2002 (London: Centre for Contemporary British History, 2005), p.55.
25 Julian Thompson, *No Picnic*, p.16.

the surface Task Force; Fieldhouse did. Furthermore, Fieldhouse's Flag Officer Submarines, Vice Admiral Herbert, commanded a second, submarine, Task Force 324. Fieldhouse's air commander was Air Marshal Sir John Curtiss, also at Northwood, commanding the RAF's maritime group, No. 18 Group, which when the crisis started was expected be the RAF's main contribution. Curtiss was the RAF's only three-star group commander and he had a uniquely broad operational experience starting on Halifaxes in 1944, flying transports in the Berlin Airlift, night fighters in the 1950s, serving with the V-Force, and latterly commanding RAF Brüggen and the RAF Staff College.[26] Fieldhouse asked for Major General Jeremy Moore, Chief of Staff to the Commandant General Royal Marines, to be his Land Force advisor and commander, and to remain at Northwood until a second brigade deployed.[27] Nominally Moore took over as Commander Land Force Falkland Islands (CLFFI) from 22 May, the week the Harrier GR3s arrived, although he was then sailing south on the liner SS *Queen Elizabeth II* with unreliable and insecure communications.[28]

Initially there were three task group commanders in the South Atlantic: Woodward, Commodore Michael Clapp, Commodore Amphibious Warfare (COMAW), commanding the amphibious assault group as CTG 317.0, and Thompson commanding the Landing Force as CTG 317.1. Band later paraphrased their roles as: Woodward would get them there and protect them; Clapp would land them and Thompson would fight them to Port Stanley.[29] Fieldhouse ordered Woodward, as the senior, to arbitrate amongst the other task group and unit commanders.[30] Thompson wrote that 'Woodward, who is often incorrectly described as the Task Force Commander, seemed to take upon himself, as the senior naval officer present, the job of being in overall command' and these tensions were apparent from when Woodward, Thompson and Clapp first met at Ascension Island.[31] Prince defends Fieldhouse's decision to retain command as he had little choice because of the poor communications capabilities of the warships in the South Atlantic.[32]

Air command and control

The absence of a theatre joint or air commander caused friction when No. 1 Squadron was switched to offensive air support. According to NATO doctrine, normally the

26 TNA: AIR 41/95: 'Narrative of RAF Operations during 1982', Operation Corporate (Falkland Islands Conflict) Air Historical Branch (RAF), 1988, p.1–6.
27 Band, 'British High Command during the Falklands Campaign', p.32.
28 Major General Julian Thompson, 'Brigade Command in the Falklands 1982', *The British Army Review*, 143:5 (2007), pp.8–16 (p.9).
29 Band, 'British High Command during the Falklands Campaign', p.32.
30 Admiral J.D.E. Fieldhouse, *Recorded in the London Gazette, No. 49194, 13 December 1982* (London: HMSO, 13 December 1982), p.16010.
31 Julian Thompson, *No Picnic*, pp.16–17.
32 Prince, 'British Command and Control in the Falklands Campaign', p.340.

air component commander would exercise operational control and apportion effort between components, retaining control of defensive and offensive counter-air operations, and air interdiction to isolate the battlefield, and assign aircraft to the land commander for offensive air support. CAS on the battlefield in close proximity to friendly forces was integrated with their fire and movement by Tactical Air Control Parties (TACPs) comprising Forward Air Controllers (FACs). Experienced TACPs were pulled from I (British) Corps in Germany to be attached to the Landing Force brigades, and subsequently battalions, to do this. Offensive air support as we have seen also included battlefield air interdiction, which in contrast to air interdiction, was used to attack targets nominated by the Land Component, normally in Central Region by corps commanders, and which did not require the integration that CAS demands. The land commander therefore required a staff to coordinate offensive air support with the air commander.

In the Falklands Campaign, however, Curtiss controlled RAF operations flown from the UK and Ascension only and not those flown from the Task Force itself, and had no senior subordinate with the Task Force. Thus Woodward, a submariner, had to depend for air advice on the captains of the carriers *Hermes* and *Invincible*. Their expertise was air defence and not the other air power roles employed in the conflict, notably the GR3 offensive air support. The British carriers were seen as the Task Force's centre of gravity, and the main threat to them was Argentine air attack.[33] The Task Force's air operations were configured for air defence flown by the Sea Harriers, which Woodward controlled, delegating control to the captain of *Hermes*, Captain Linley Middleton RN, a former Fleet Air Arm fighter pilot. As No. 1 Squadron was initially deployed to reinforce the Sea Harriers they were understandably placed initially under Woodward's control. On switching role No. 1 Squadron was nominally assigned to the COMAW Clapp for the landings and subsequently to CLFFI, Thompson and then Moore, for the fight to Stanley. Yet Woodward and Middleton continued to task No. 1 Squadron, notwithstanding their assignment to COMAW and CLFFI, direct from the ship's staff to individual aircrew, and not through the squadron commander, Squire, as would happen in air force operations. Worse, Squire and his flight commanders and attached Central Tactics and Trials Organization (CTTO) GR3 weapons expert, Squadron Leader Peter Harris, were routinely overridden.[34] Thus there were three sources of tasking: Woodward's staff, the ship's staff and the forces ashore, without any formal allocation of effort by quantity or time.

Thus, when Squadron Leader Ron Elder visited the Falklands for two weeks from 25 June, spending three days on *Hermes*, to do a hasty assessment for the RAF's tactics centre of excellence, CTTO, he reported that Woodward as CTG 317.8, through *Hermes*, had retained control of No. 1 Squadron throughout the conflict, although given their role they should have been tasked by CLFFI after the landings. All attack

33 Shields, *Air Power in the Falklands Conflict*.

34 TNA: AIR 20/13191: 'A worm's eye view', Sqn Ldr P Harris, CTTO/25/18/1/Ops, Operation *Corporate* (Falklands Conflict): Report and Debriefs.

planning and tasking was conducted on *Hermes* although she had no attack planning facilities as she was configured as an air defence carrier. There was no Tactical Air Control Centre to prioritise and task air requests. All aspects of tasking were handled by a single ship's officer. The Carrier-Borne Ground Liaison Officer was misemployed in another role on Woodward's staff. Instead, the Harrier GR3s, with two holding five minutes' cockpit readiness on *Hermes*, were often spontaneously tasked against low-value targets from patchy air requests for support rather than targeting high-value targets based on reconnaissance, including their own tactical air reconnaissance, had they been allowed to do any. According to Elder's report there seemed to be no one in the tasking chain who understood the need to prioritise air requests, targets and tasking or weapon to target matching.[35] As a result, as Beetham, the Chief of the Air Staff, subsequently observed, 'there was no properly constituted OAS [offensive air support] plan.' Beetham wanted to deploy an air commodore as an offensive air support advisor, but this was unacceptable to the RN as he would have outranked the carrier captains.[36]

As already indicated, Captain Middleton, whose long experience as a RN Fleet Air Arm pilot included flying Sea Hawk attack missions at Suez in 1956, was a cause of friction for No. 1 Squadron from the moment they landed on *Hermes*. When the first four Harrier GR3s landed on *Hermes* at 1500 hours on 18 May, Middleton ordered them airborne that evening, before their few groundcrew had arrived to fix unserviceabilities or align head-up displays and inertial navigation systems. After intervention by Squire and much discussion they were stood down. On another occasion Woodward overruled Middleton when he tried to prevent two replacements for a shot-down aircraft being tanked from Ascension, calling it an RAF publicity stunt.[37]

Woodward used Middleton as his air advisor, but Middleton did not seek advice, and in any case Woodward's nominated Harrier GR3 advisor, Squadron Leader Sid Morris, was sent ashore to run the forward operating base at San Carlos.[38] This was declared operational on 30 May and used from 5 June, mainly by Sea Harriers for Quick Reaction Alert, and there were only 17 GR3 movements because of poor communications.[39] Middleton was said to be furious when the parameters for the loft profile were signalled by CTTO allowing the first successful British use of LGBs in action on 13 June.[40] Curtiss' chief of staff, Air Vice-Marshal George Chesworth, cites the blocking of signals from No. 18 Group to No. 1 Squadron, the 'exasperating lack of appreciation of air power's value against high priority targets' and told the AHB 'Middleton didn't like the RAF.'[41]

35 TNA: DEFE 56/182: CTTO/25/18/3/Ops Sqn Ldr Elder Report on Air Operations during the Falkland Islands Conflict dated 4 August 82, 1982, pp.19–20.
36 TNA: AIR 41/95: 'Narrative of RAF Operations during 1982', p.1–10.
37 Jordan and Shields, 'In at the Deep End', p.121.
38 TNA: AIR 20/13044: FI Transcripts AHB, 1984, Squire, pp.2–5.
39 TNA: AIR 41/95: 'Narrative of RAF Operations during 1982', p.7–17.
40 Private correspondence.
41 TNA: AIR 20/13044: FI Transcripts AHB, Chesworth, p.4.

Yet, there was a well-established air-land integration set up in 3 Commando Brigade, but it struggled because the Clansman HF combat net radio links to the ships were so unreliable. The No. 1 Squadron aircrew had discussed FAC procedures with the 3 Commando Brigade Air Liaison Officer (ALO) and its TACPs while sailing south on SS *Atlantic Conveyor*.[42] Furthermore, the 5 Infantry Brigade TACPs were attached from I (British) Corps in Germany where they will have worked with RAF Germany Harriers. Initially the HQ 3 Commando Brigade ALO was based in the Support Arms Coordination Centre on Fearless and after the landings went ashore with the (Field Artillery) Fire Support Coordination Centre. Here the intent was for the ALO to prioritise the air requests from the Brigade's four TACPs. The failure of the HF sets forced them to use the teleprinter Defence Communications Network strategic communications using Flash messages.

From 30 May with the arrival of Moore as CLFFI, Wing Commander Fred Trowern, an offensive air support expert, took on the offensive air support tasking role coordinating the requests from the two subordinate brigades.[43] Curtiss had selected Trowern as Moore's air advisor from the Joint Warfare Staff at nearby Latimer. Trowern was initially based on *Fearless* with Moore although on 11 June joined Headquarters 3 Commando Brigade 'on a mountain top' to get better communications. Although the TACPs and ALO teams were properly constituted, and although LFFI equated to a division and Trowern had developed offensive air support procedures based on ATP 27(B), Trowern was on his own, had to cover 24/7 and also had responsibility for the forward operating base.[44] Moore's 'report of proceedings' made one mention of air-land integration, it being hampered by poor communications, and had in any case only wanted a squadron leader as air adviser whereas Beetham wanted an air commodore and Curtiss a group captain.[45] Moore admitted his headquarters was hurriedly assembled and lacked the benefit of any work up, but he believed it performed well, and any future two-star headquarters should be formed from Commando Forces rather than an Army divisional HQ, which would have been well versed in air-land cooperation with a dedicated and trained staff. As the AHB narrative notes, with the lack of planning on *Hermes,* the lack of a Tactical Air Control Centre and poor radio communications, it is remarkable there were any offensive air support operations.[46]

42 TNA: AIR 41/95: 'Narrative of RAF Operations during 1982', p.7–7.
43 'Fred Trowern, Fighter Pilot Who Helped Develop the Hawker Harrier and Went on to Play a Key Role in the Falklands War', *The Telegraph*, 2 April 2019.
44 TNA: AIR 20/13044: Trowern interview; TNA: WO 305/6479: 'Land Forces Falkland Islands: Standing Operating Procedures', SOP 101.
45 TNA: ADM 201/276: Falklands Conflict: Report on Proceedings of Forces under the Command of Major General J Moore, 1982; TNA: AIR 20/13044: FI Transcripts AHB, 1984.
46 TNA: AIR 41/95: 'Narrative of RAF Operations during 1982', pp.7–15.

Counter-air

The evidence is Woodward and Middleton gave a high priority to offensive counter-air, often spontaneously. Overall, there were forty-five high-level missions and fifteen low-level attacks on Stanley airfield by Vulcans, Sea Harriers, and Harrier GR3 using loft and lay-down plus 2000 rounds of naval gunfire which caused little physical damage and was unable to prevent Argentine C-130 flights. Of these, GR3s flew nine high and low-level attacks against Port Stanley runway. In addition, there were three attacks on air strips that damaged some aircraft but did no worthwhile damage to the strips. While the first Harrier GR3 attack mission was a three-ship air interdiction attack on a fuel dump at Port Howard on 20 May, the second was against a possible helicopter landing site near Mount Kent.

The priority Woodward and Middleton gave to spontaneous offensive counter-air missions caused friction. For example, according to the RAF's AHB Narrative, on 23 May a Harrier GR3 four-ship attacked the airstrip at Dunnose Head with BL-755 Cluster Bomb Units (CBUs) and 1,000lb retarded bombs, tasked by *Hermes*, following armed reconnaissance by two pairs on 21 May. The sortie was delayed because Clapp had a short notice request to attack Pebble Island. This was overruled by Woodward, although he admitted at the time No. 1 Squadron were assigned to Clapp but directed that any tasking for the Squadron must be cleared by Middleton.[47] Two days later three GR3s attacked Peeble Island airstrip destroying several Pucaras already knocked out by the Special Air Service (SAS).

Middleton's authority extended as far as attack profile and weapon selection, as they were selected by the ship before the pilots were briefed, despite the lack of expertise. On 24 May there was a dispute between Middleton and Squire over attack profiles for an attack on Port Stanley airfield. The Squadron flew Squire's planned laydown attack for accuracy when Middleton had wanted loft to reduce risk. The squadron realised after the attack that the bombs had been loaded on Hermes fused at 40 milliseconds for loft, not the laydown attack profile flown.[48] There were subsequent, ineffective, loft attacks on Port Stanley airfield on 25, 26 and 27 May, as the Goose Green battle started.

Whereas on 31 May, when supposedly under CLFFI's control for the march to Stanley, two Harrier GR3s holding cockpit readiness for CAS armed with rockets and guns, were suddenly tasked to attack '4 x Swept-wing aircraft at Stanley – possibly Étendard.' The crews were briefed, by the recently shot-down and subsequently rescued Squadron Leader Bob Iveson, in the cockpit as Middleton would not let them out to replan, forcing them to use an attack profile used previously on 24 May. Both aircraft canopies and both the leader's drop tanks were damaged by ground fire and the No 2 suffered a bird strike. The possible Étendard turned out to be Aermacchis.

47 TNA: AIR 41/95: 'Narrative of RAF Operations during 1982', p.7–20.
48 TNA: AIR 41/95: 'Narrative of RAF Operations during 1982', p.7–21; TNA: AIR 20/13191: 'Harris Report', p.8.

The pilots of No. 1 (F) Squadron on SS *Atlantic Conveyor* during Falklands Campaign, 1982. Wing Commander Peter Squire is second right. To the left of him are: Squadron Leader Pete Harris, Flight Lieutenants Jeff Glover, Mark Hart, John Rochfort and Tony Harper. To the right of him is Squadron Leader Bob Iveson. Sitting in front is Squadron Leader Jerry Pook. (RAF Museum: P032429)

Harrier GR3, Falklands Campaign, 1982 at the Forward Operating Base, San Carlos armed with RN 2-inch rockets for CAS. (RAF Museum: P032385)

The normally dispassionate AHB Narrative thought No. 1 Squadron were fortunate to avoid major loss.[49]

Air intelligence and tactical air reconnaissance

The immediate post-campaign reporting is damning about the lack of air intelligence and reconnaissance on which to base offensive air support. Just four low-level tactical reconnaissance missions were flown, two looking for Exocet launchers and two for enemy ground forces. The centres for the collection and dissemination of intelligence for the Task Force were at Northwood, onboard *Hermes* with CTG staff, aboard *Fearless* with COMAW and the Landing Force and later CLFFI. Expecting to be employed in the air defence role, No. 1 Squadron deployed without its Army Ground Liaison Officer (trained in offensive air support) and squadron intelligence officer.[50] Elder's report noted that detailed intelligence was particularly sparse for offensive air operations.[51]

Furthermore, there was no coordinated, pre-planned tactical air reconnaissance programme in support of land operations. According to Harris, the RAF's Harrier GR3 lead weapons expert, there was no air reconnaissance before the landings or along the line of advance to Goose Green. In the absence of any reconnaissance tasking expertise until the arrival of CLFFI's staff, Harrier GR3 reconnaissance sorties were flown too high for their F95 cameras or too low for the GR3 reconnaissance pod with its five cameras capable of horizon-to-horizon coverage. Furthermore, the two photographic interpreters on each carrier could only cope with the product from one to two Harrier GR3 reconnaissance pods per day, were not tasked to provide immediate air reconnaissance advice and were located some distance from the No. 1 Squadron operations room.

Targets detected on reconnaissance using cameras were then not subsequently attacked. For example, a 3 Commando Brigade request on 26 May for air reconnaissance of Argentine positions west of Stanley was not tasked until 9 June. The reconnaissance was along the forward line of own troops (FLOT) was finally flown on 10 June, yet a line of 23 Jeeps detected were not attacked for a further six hours, by which time they had moved. Furthermore, intelligence from Special Forces was not made available.[52] The Sea Harriers were tasked to take photographs on an opportunity basis on return from combat air patrol. Eventually intervention by OC 1 Squadron enabled four (CTTO reports two) Harrier GR3 reconnaissance sorties to be flown which then enabled targets to be attacked.[53]

49 TNA: AIR 41/95: 'Narrative of RAF Operations during 1982', p.7–13.
50 TNA: DEFE 71/528: Report on Air Operations During the Falkland Islands Conflict. With Map, 1982. Data supporting Elder CTTO Report.
51 TNA: DEFE 56/182: Elder CTTO Report, p.4.
52 TNA: AIR 20/13191: 'Harris Report', p.6.
53 Squire, 'Harrier Operations – No 1 Sqn', pp.4–6, p.106.

Harris summarised the lack of air reconnaissance by stating 'had more air reconnaissance sorties been flown earlier in the conflict, numerous high-value targets would undoubtably been found which could have subsequently been tasked for air attack, artillery bombardment or naval gunfire support.' He felt the lack of understanding of air reconnaissance could have had 'disastrous consequences' if the Argentine force had been stronger.[54]

Armed reconnaissance

In the absence of intelligence, reconnaissance and planning, armed reconnaissance seemed to be the fall-back option with 11 two-ship missions flown compared to just two tactical air reconnaissance and seven CAS missions. NATO defines armed reconnaissance as 'an air mission flown with the primary purpose of locating and attacking targets of opportunity, … and not for the purpose of attacking specific briefed targets.' Elder heavily criticised them in his report, stating:

> Eleven armed reconnaissance missions were flown, as pairs. Most targets were acquired late and often more that more than one re-attack was required. One GR3 was lost on a re-attack: the pilot ejected safely and was captured. It is questionable whether AR [armed reconnaissance] sorties achieved anything of major value. With a few exceptions, targets were not high-value and probably did not justify the exposure of costly aircraft and crew in a profile which is tactically unsound and has a reduced probability of success over pre-planned attacks.[55]

Thus, on 21 May Flight Lieutenant Jeff Glover was shot down by ground fire, wounded, and captured, having taken off as a singleton expecting FAC controlled CAS over San Carlos only to be re-tasked for armed reconnaissance over West Falkands for which he had no maps.[56] He was flying alone because his leader's aircraft was unserviceable. Captured by the Argentines, Glover was released on 8 July.

Air interdiction

Elder thought the four missions classed as air interdiction missions were the most successful missions flown by Harrier GR3 because they were pre-planned, multiple aircraft tasks using extant tactics from Germany, planning to saturate defences,

54 TNA: AIR 20/13191: 'Harris Report', p.6.
55 NATO Standardization Office, *AAP-06 NATO Glossary of Terms and Definitions (English and French)*, Edition 2020 (Brussels: NATO Standardization Office, 2020), p.14; TNA: DEFE 56/182: Elder CTTO Report, p.23.
56 TNA: AIR 20/13044: FI Transcripts AHB.

using different desired mean point of impacts to minimise risk from self-damage and attacking from different directions. The CBUs had good effect and there was no need to re-attack.[57] The air interdiction missions would have been so defined because there was no requirement to coordinate with ground forces, although on at least one occasion the Port Howard missions aircraft were controlled by a special forces' FAC.

Battlefield air interdiction

Twenty Harrier GR3 missions, all flown by pairs, were classed as battlefield air interdiction. These were essentially pre-planned CAS, although not under the control of an FAC. They were flown using the full suite of Harrier GR3 weapons: CBUs, retard and delay action 1000lb bombs, 2-inch rockets and 30mm cannon. None of the attacks were particularly effective because the targets, normally a grid reference, were difficult to acquire and were well dug-in and camouflaged. For example, on 30 May, 10 sorties were flown in support of the land force's move towards Stanley although no targets or activity were seen at the briefed grid references.[58] Sorties were flown against requested grid references and against targets at Moody Brooke identified by tactical air reconnaissance on 9 June.

Close air support

There were just seven tasked CAS missions, normally by pairs of Harrier GR3s. The perception of their effectiveness varies greatly. The GR3 CAS was conducted in the face of the Argentine air defences and in daylight. The Argentines had a mix of surface to air missiles system, including one state of the art Roland system, a range of AAA from 20mm to 40mm, including radar-controlled twin 35mm AAA subsequently used by the RAF.[59] The most potent threat to the Harrier GR3 was small arms fire from either side. By the time of the Argentine ceasefire, the six surviving Harrier GR3s (one was lost crash landing) were all damaged by small arms fire.[60]

On 27 May Iveson was shot down by 35mm AAA on his fourth re-attack trying to locate the target, a 105mm gun providing CAS to 2 Para at Goose Green. According to the mission report poor communications with the FAC meant the two Harriers orbited the Initial Point (IP) at 8,000ft, 'giving away all element [sic] of surprise'.[61] Unable to find the gun, the CBUs were dropped on a line of troops and the jets continued to reattack, looking for the gun, and strafing enemy positions in the general area. In this case

57 TNA: DEFE 56/182: Elder CTTO Report, p.22.

58 TNA: AIR 41/95: 'Narrative of RAF Operations during 1982', p.7–24.

59 Wing Commander Mike Fonfe, *The Falklands Guns: The Story of the Captured Argentine Artillery That Became Part of the RAF Regiment* (Barnsley: Frontline Books, 2023).

60 TNA: DEFE 58/270: AOIC CTTO Report November 1982, p.12.

61 TNA: DEFE 71/528: Elder CTTO Report Annexes, MISREP 3M02 dated 26 May 1982.

the 3 Commando Brigade ALO was acting as FAC because the 2 Para FAC, a 50-year-old squadron leader, had been medically evacuated with exhaustion. Iveson escaped and evaded and was recovered three days later. Two hours later another two-ship led by Squire was unable to detect the target and did not drop any weapons. The decisive CAS attack on 28 May cited in the introduction was by Squire and Flight Lieutenant Tony Harper delivering CBUs and Pook firing 2-inch rockets. Captain Kevin Arnold, of 148 Battery, Royal Artillery, was the FAC.[62] The subsequent government white paper called it 'a timely strike considerably helped the progress of the paratroopers [*sic*].'[63]

The advantage of LGBs were their accuracy, the aircraft did not have to overfly the target area, and as the FAC illuminated the target the pilot did not have to acquire it while under fire and flying at 'ultra low-level', meaning less than 100ft. As Squire later noted, the full potential of LGBs with which the Harrier GR3 had been hurriedly fitted could not be used until the day before the ceasefire when the FACs had the laser target markers in place. One factor was the loss of twenty-one lives in an earlier Sea King crash including Flight Lieutenant Garth Hawkins, RAF Regiment, the 22 SAS FAC, and the only RAF fatality of the conflict, with his SAS Laser Target Marker team and equipment. The loss of expertise and equipment meant that laser target marker LGB missions in the Stanley area under the guidance of SAS forces were not possible. [64] Attempts on 30 and 31 May to use the GR3s' Laser Ranger Marked Target Seeker system to self-designate failed because it was incompatible with the LGB.[65]

Finally, from 11 June, the tactical air control of close air support clicked. The GR3s were now equipped with the ALE-40 chaff and flare dispenser. As previously mentioned, a tactical air reconnaissance of the FLOT was flown on 10 June. Trowern moved to his 'mountain top' with HQ 3 Commando Brigade where he could coordinate the air requests of both brigades, each using a separate tactical air request net, and issue prioritised and properly formatted air tasks in accordance with ATP-27(B). In doing so, Trowern, counter to Elder's report and the AHB Narrative, in Harris' words, took 'absolute control of the GR3s when it became apparent that aircraft were damaged during attacks against low priority targets because of spontaneous targeting.'[66] Furthermore, FACs with laser target markers were now in place to allow the use of the LGBs, an achievement given the conditions and bulky equipment. A first LGB attack using laser target markers was flown on 10 June but communications were lost with the FAC and, unable to communicate a time on target, the LGBs were jettisoned.

The first successful British use of LGBs was on 13 June when four LGBs were delivered from thirty-degree loft profiles at 5.2 and 3.7 kilometres from the target,

62 Jordan and Shields, 'In at the Deep End', p.120.
63 TNA: AIR 41/95: 'Narrative of RAF Operations during 1982', p.7–24.
64 TNA: AIR 41/95: 'Narrative of RAF Operations during 1982', p.7–19.
65 TNA: AIR 41/95: 'Narrative of RAF Operations during 1982', p.7–24.
66 TNA: AIR 41/95: 'Narrative of RAF Operations during 1982', p.7–13; TNA: AIR 20/13191: 'Harris Report', p.6.

1000lb laser guided bomb carried under of RAF Harrier GR.3 during Falklands Campaign, 1982. (RAF Museum: P032403)

according to CTTO. Two missed because of incorrect designation and two hit Argentine troop concentrations on Tumbledown and Mount Kent. Squire believed this demonstration was one of the factors that swayed the Argentine decision to surrender, although there were of course many others.[67] Thus Major John Kiszely, commanding the Left Flank Company, 2nd Battalion Scots Guards, may have been witnessing the LGBs, when as a lieutenant general twenty years later he wrote of the importance of air superiority:

> At company level, its benefit was crucial not only to our ability to manoeuvre but in its effect on morale – ours and the enemy's. Seeing 1,000-pound bombs crashing into Tumbledown was almost as psychologically significant to us as it was to them, even if these bombs killed no one; the side capable of delivering such a big bang looked to be the bookies' favourite.[68]

67 Squire, 'Harrier Operations – No 1 Sqn', p.106; TNA: DEFE 58/270: AOIC CTTO Report, 19 November 1982 , p.24.
68 Lieutenant General J.P. Kiszely, 'The Land Campaign: A Company Commander's Perspective', in Badsey, Grove, and Havers (eds), *The Falklands Conflict Twenty Years on: Lessons for the Future*, pp.99–108 (p.106).

The importance of tactical air control and reliable and effective communications is exemplified by events on 14 June. Trowern rejected two low-value air requests from 5 Infantry Brigade and instead selected two air requests more suitable for LGBs to target: an enemy HQ and a gun battery position on Sapper Hill. He was then able to call off the attack just two minutes before the time on target when it appeared that the enemy were about to surrender. The tactical air control of Harrier GR3 CAS was now working.

Conclusions

With hindsight, it seems remarkable after the British Army's experience of the Second World War that such little use was made of the 10 Harrier GR3s to provide CAS to such a lightly-armed British Landing Force. As the chapter has shown, when used effectively as at Goose Green and on the final battles around Stanley, CAS, whether delivering the lethal CBUs or the new LGBs, could be decisive. Instead as the AHB Narrative records: 'the RAF view at all levels from CAS [Chief of the Air Staff Beetham] to the two wing commanders most closely involved [Squire and Trowern] was that the air war in the Falklands area, other than AD [Air Defence], was not properly organised.'[69]

Furthermore, although the CTTO reports are written mainly from the perspective of operating the GR3 rather than the effectiveness of CAS, Elder's view of the utility of CAS was based on the friction he had found and had concluded a theme redolent of the RAF in 1918 as outlined in earlier chapters:

> CAS only has a place as a last resort if either the enemy is about to over-run or by-pass a position when out of range of organic fire support, or when massive casualties might be inflicted without air support. Re-attacks [*sic*] should only be considered if the target has particularly high priority.[70]

There were mitigations for the lack of CAS. When Curtiss received a copy CTTO's November 1982 final report, which drew on Elder's report and cited twenty other post operation reports, he objected to its inaccuracies which he said failed to meet CTTO's normally objective standard and requested the Vice Chief of the Air Staff, Air Marshal Sir Peter Harding, withdraw it. Curtiss objected to criticism of the joint command arrangements for air support in theatre stating they were hurriedly improvised and the requirement for air-land integration was initially unforeseen, as the AHB Narrative recognises.[71] Furthermore authority for offensive air support was not transferred from Woodward to CLFFI because of the loss of the SS *Atlantic Conveyor* and its impact on the establishment

69 TNA: AIR 41/95: 'Narrative of RAF Operations during 1982', pp.1–10.
70 TNA: DEFE 56/182: Elder CTTO Report August 1982, p.24.
71 TNA: DEFE 58/270: AOIC CTTO Report, 19 November 1982 , p.24.

of the forward operating base. Curtiss also acknowledged there should have been a wing commander air staff officer on *Hermes* to help with the ground attack and reconnaissance planning.[72] Moreover, as this chapter demonstrates, Woodward, able to task the GR3s until the final few days of the conflict, prioritised offensive counter-air, often spontaneously.

The air power historian Peter Gray warns about learning lessons from what he calls an idiosyncratic campaign.[73] Yet, one idiosyncrasy is that whereas in other case studies in this book, air forces are often the reluctant providers of CAS and it is the land forces who are 'drugged on bombs' as Marshal of the RAF Lord Tedder put it,[74] in the Falklands it seemed to be the reverse. The efforts of No. 1 Squadron to provide CAS were restricted because of the reasons Curtiss outlined, and also because of Woodward and Middleton's prioritisation of counter-air, and unreliable communications. Furthermore, the archival evidence supports Pook's later account of inter-service differences which added to the friction. Rather than demanding CAS, Moore as CLFFI seemed unaware of its absence as an issue. Moreover, contrary to the initial CTTO report and the AHB Narrative, Woodward did not control the GR3s throughout, as Trowern wrested control for CLFFI from 11 June. The combination of tactical air reconnaissance, Trowern's tactical air control, functioning air/land communications, the coordination of air requests and air tasking and the use of laser target markers for LGBs enabled effective CAS at the end of the campaign.

Squire hinted that the Services at the time were not well prepared for joint 'interaction'.[75] Yet the NATO CAS procedures used for air-land operations were commonplace in Central Region and well practiced. Trowern told the AHB the only officers who understood employing offensive air support in the Falklands were RAF and special forces, but that the doctrine for its use was right.[76] Once again, as other chapters highlight, the hard-won lessons of CAS had to be relearnt. *The Falklands Campaign: The Lessons* (Cmnd. 8758) called for 'examination of the need for a properly constituted Joint HQ in the UK to command OOA [out of area] operations together with the creation and tasking of a 2-star joint HQ to command such operations overseas.'[77] This, almost twenty years later, led to the institutionalisation of jointery in the 1998 Strategic Defence Review.

72 TNA: DEFE 58/270: Air Cdre Neville, 'AOIC CTTO Report', 19 November 1982; TNA: DEFE 71/653: Operation Corporate: Lessons Learned, Curtiss to Harding (VCAS) 10 January 1983.
73 Air Commodore (Ret'd) Dr Peter Gray, 'Air Power: Strategic Lessons from an Idiosyncratic Operation', in Badsey, Havers, and Grove (eds), *The Falklands Conflict Twenty Years on: Lessons for the Future*, pp.253–64.
74 Tedder to Portal, 25 Oct. 1944, in Arthur Tedder, *With Prejudice: The War Memoirs of Marshal of the Royal Air Force Lord Tedder* (London: Cassel, 1966), pp.605–6.
75 Squire, 'Harrier Operations – No 1 Sqn', p.109.
76 TNA: AIR 20/13044: FI Transcripts AHB.
77 Great Britain Ministry of Defence, *The Falklands Campaign: The Lessons*, Papers by Command (Great Britain. Parliament); Cmnd. 8758 (London: H.M.S.O, 1982).

11

Close Air Support in Afghanistan – an RAF Tornado Perspective

Gus Macdonald

Introduction

Prior to 2001, close air support (CAS) in Western air forces had been a specialised mission for specific aircraft types, and was considered to have been in decline.[1] Between 1945 to 1990, the CAS mission had tended to rise and fall in prominence as Cold War proxy-wars erupted worldwide.[2] CAS is considered to have peaked during the Korean war, despite the US Fifth Air Force having only allocated 13 percent of total sortie tasking in support to the US Eighth Army.[3] The US Marine Corps (USMC) CAS allocation stood at 36 percent at the same statistical period during October 1952.[4] This waxing and waning of CAS importance, set against doctrinal priorities, was largely responsible for the lack of development and indeed the subordination to tactical support with which the CAS role was held. For the UK, NATO and the US, operations in Afghanistan would reveal the requirement for the CAS mission in support of smaller force deployments and had implications for the effectiveness of future force numbers which were then being considered. The strategic circumstance confronted in Afghanistan therefore played an important role in driving doctrinal development. The need for this development in the role of CAS, which was long

1 Rebecca Grant, 'The Clash About CAS' *Air Force Magazine* (Jan. 2003), p.56; Christopher Bolkcom and Kenneth Katzman, 'Military Aviation: Issues and Options for Combating Terrorism and Counterinsurgency' (Washington, DC: The Library of Congress: Congressional Research Service, 2005), p.6.
2 Colonel Melvin L. Greene, *Close Air Support: Proud Past, Uncertain Future*, Air War College Research Report (Maxwell AFB, AL: USAF Air University, 1988), p.21.
3 Allan R. Millett, 'Korea, 1950–1953' in Benjamin Franklin Cooling (ed), *Case Studies in the Development of Close Air Support* (Washington, DC: USAF: Office of Air Force History, 1990), p.384.
4 Grant, 'Clash About CAS', p.56.

overdue, was exposed by the operational and political environment the coalition found itself in 2003.

Operation Anaconda

Any consideration of the UK CAS experience in Afghanistan must consider the US CAS experience in the opening stages of operations there as it places the CAS role in the evolving mission of the International Security Assistance Force (ISAF). The lessons drawn from US operations in 2002 offer guidance to the considerations and experiences of the increased UK participation in 2006–9.

Operation *Anaconda* opened as a 1200-person operation. It was expected to encounter only light resistance and it was expected it would secure many prisoners. However, the operation quickly encountered fierce resistance and was able to secure little by way of organic fire support.[5] Given the nature of Afghan terrain it was not logistically viable to attempt to move heavy guns into theatre, reducing the role and capability of the Fire Support Teams (FSTs). The lack of artillery support increased the prominence and requirement for the CAS mission at a time when the strongly-placed defensive positions of Al Qaeda resulted in a deluge of CAS requests.[6] Compounded by a lack of preparation at Combined Air Operations Centre (CAOC) level, this resulted in something resembling a free-for-all in terms of tasking.[7] A USAF report on the conduct of Operation *Anaconda* conceded that the coordination of the Air Component in controlling air strikes was 'left far more to chance, and the efforts of a few individuals.'[8]

At the height of operations, more than 200 fire support coordination measures (FSCM) were in place, further complicated by the demand for no-fire zones from other US government agencies. In what would become the norm for combined counter-insurgency and peace support operations (PSO) in the region, conflicting requirements complicated the airspace apportionment and CAS request system.[9] Equally disturbing from the air-land integration (ALI) perspective was the traditional notion of support fire priorities for the engaged US soldiers, who understandably preferred organic fire support, starting with the smallest calibre weapon at their disposal, that is, mortars of varying calibres, then artillery, and Apaches, and then Fast Jet.[10] For

5 Rebecca Grant, *Operation Anaconda: An Air Power Perspective* (Washington, DC: Headquarters USAF, 2005), p.15–8.

6 John J. McGrath, *Fire for Effect: Field Artillery and Close Air Support in the US Army* (Fort Leavenworth, KS: Combat Studies Institute Press, 2010), pp.150–1.

7 Grant 'Clash About CAS', p.56.

8 Grant, *Operation Anaconda,* p.39.

9 Richard L. Kugler, Michael Baranick, Hans Binnendijk, *Operation Anaconda: Lessons for Joint Operations* (Washington, DC: National Defense University, Center for Technology and National Security Policy, 2009), p.vi.

10 Grant, 'Clash About CAS', p.57.

US forces in combat on the ground, the battles being fought were not what had been planned for. As a result, from the tactical to the operational level, the support and command and control (C2) structures were initially unfit to effectively coordinate and were then subject to rapid adaptation 'on the hoof'.[11]

Further complicating the ability to increase the CAS delivery process was a lack of technology to extract target location coordinates of the correct quality to deliver weapons in GPS mode.[12] C2 problems, for controlling both airspace and asset allocation, were typified by operations in March 2002, when the newly-forward deployed USAF Fairchild Republic A-10 Thunderbolt II attack aircraft conducted successful CAS missions in support of pinned-down forces. Pulling up from one pass, an A-10 came within three hundred yards of an orbiting US Army Boeing AH-64 Apache attack helicopter gunship and later, the A-10s were surprised when US Navy McDonnell Douglas F/A-18 Hornet multirole combat aircraft dropped weapons underneath them.[13] This example emphasises the inherent danger in uncoordinated attacks in close proximity not only to the enemy forces, but equally when uncoordinated with friendly forces; crews were forced to make hurried and informal risk assessments under extreme pressure to deliver weapons. What was apparent to the crews involved was a glaring lack of coordination and communication between participating aircraft and the C2 elements charged with their safe separation. At best, an attack would be broken off due to the lack of coordination, causing unwanted delay in the delivery of munitions to troops in contact with the enemy. At worst, two coalition aircraft could be lost, with the associated rescue mission burden and the loss of credibility to a scrutinising public and media.

The US experience of Afghan operations between 2–16 March 2002 provided a range of lessons which would be incorporated into both Afghanistan and Operation *Iraqi Freedom* in 2003. The importance of the central role of liaison staff between Land and Air Components was re-emphasised; the importance of planning and rehearsal of Air and Land Components was noted and the theatre-specific structure of C2 was addressed to ensure that apportionment and airspace control was more robust.[14] On a positive note, the utility of air assets was extended in the CAS role during Operation *Anaconda*, particularly the utility of the USAF's Rockwell B-1B Lancer and Boeing B-52 Stratofortress strategic bombers. As strategic bombers, these aircraft are capable of round-the-globe operations to extend the reach of US airpower, while being nuclear weapon capable; as such, their use had never been considered in the tactical CAS arena of Low Intensity Conflict (LIC). The term 'strategic' has regularly been extended to include many capabilities but in terms of their utility in Afghanistan and beyond, these aircraft successfully fulfil the core air power attribute of ubiquity, notably height, speed and reach, whilst also fulfilling the inherent jointness of air

11 Kugler, Baranick & Binnendijk, 'Operation Anaconda', p.22.
12 Grant, *Operation Anaconda,* p.39.
13 Grant, *Operation Anaconda*, p.79.
14 Grant, *Operation Anaconda,* p.79.

power which sits at the heart of UK Air Power doctrine.[15] Pressure to minimise the logistical and physical footprint, and consequently the force protection requirement which comes with in-theatre aircraft deployment, was greatly assisted by the use of these assets as well as US Navy carrier-borne aircraft. Notably the loiter times of the B-1B and B-52, equipped with an advanced designation pod, a large munitions load, and utilising the Joint Direct Attack Munition (JDAM), a GPS-guided precision weapon, afforded the land units increased overwatch time.[16]

UK operations in Afghanistan

UK forces had been operating in Afghanistan prior to 2006, when ISAF forces brought increased troop numbers to the region. Support for ongoing operations in Iraq also required an increased level of ALI and the means to produce increasing numbers of Forward Air Controllers (FACs) to deliver the CAS mission to the supported land forces. Dressler asserts that Afghanistan quickly became one of the most difficult missions for the UK; despite great efforts and sacrifices, the limited and thinly spread combat forces were simply not equipped to tackle an insurgency that controlled most of Helmand province.[17]

For the UK, many of the problems of outdated ALI doctrine had been noted from the experience of Operation *Telic* in Iraq in 2003. Success in *Telic* depended upon the deployment and integration of fast-moving light forces, highly mobile armoured capabilities and CAS.[18] A lack of training and adequate doctrine resulted in many air power lessons learnt in Normandy during the Second World War having to be relearnt by British forces.[19] While control of the air did not present a problem in Afghanistan or Iraq, the command and control aspects between air and land bore many historical weaknesses, namely a lack of cohesive doctrine, tactics and training.[20] Additionally, the lack of assets dedicated to the CAS role was deemed insufficient by participating UK land forces.[21] Insufficient assets to fulfil the CAS role is a long-

15 Ministry of Defence, *Joint Doctrine Publication 0-30, UK Air Power*, 3rd edn (Shrivenham: Development, Concepts and Doctrine Centre, 2022), p.3
16 Richard Kugler, *Operation Anaconda in Afghanistan: A Case Study of Adaptation in Battle* (Washington, DC: National Defense University, Center for Technology and National Security Policy, 2007), p.195.
17 Jeffrey Dressler, *Counterinsurgency in Helmand: Progress and Remaining Challenges* (Washington DC: Institute for the Study of War, 2011), p.11.
18 Director General Corporate Communications, *Operations in Iraq: First Reflections* (London: MOD, 2003), p.19.
19 Ian Gooderson, *Air Power at the Battlefront: Allied Close Air Support in Europe 1943–45* (London: Cass, 1998), pp.227–8.
20 Gooderson, *Air Power at the Battlefront*, pp.227–8.
21 Wing Commander H. Smyth DFC, RAF, 'From Coningham to Project Coningham-Keyes: Did British Forces Relearn Historical Air-Land Cooperation Lessons During Operation "Telic"?', *Defence Studies*, 7:2 (2007), pp.258–86 (p.275)

standing complaint from soldiers and reinforces the preference for organic support wherever possible. However, the 'Clear, Hold, Build' strategy employed in 2006 produced a dramatic upsurge in Troops in Contact (TIC) situations and a consequent increase in demand for CAS. The unplanned TIC scenarios increased the risk of both fratricide and collateral as individuals under pressure attempted to coordinate support.

The FACs, or Tactical Air Control Parties (TACPs), which formed the link to land forces were also embedded in the FSTs from the Royal Artillery, and the Special Forces Support Group (SFSG) which assisted UK SF teams in both Iraq and Afghanistan prior to 2006. FAC training within the UK is delivered by the Joint Forward Air Controller Training and Standards Unit (JFACTSU) which remains the only NATO and US Joint Services accredited schoolhouse in UK Defence to train FACs.[22] Perhaps the most difficult test for JFACTSU was the pressing requirement to provide sufficient FACs for both theatres at relatively short notice, which produced an output of around 100 FACs per year.[23] Given the training requirement in terms of live-drop aircraft serials, and the increased numbers of students needed to supply the rolling six month brigade deployments, the decision to support the increased ISAF involvement in 2006 produced a strain on delivery of the training output of JFACTSU.

FACs, and the TACPs which they form, play a central and critical role in the link between air power and land forces. Such increased responsibility in balancing the safety of friendly troops against the risk of disproportionate response gave rise to the term 'strategic corporals' in Afghanistan. Viewed positively, such a description can be seen to infer the blurring of operational and tactical responsibilities; through the decentralisation of control to the empowered FAC can positively influence the desired effect. In doing so they can potentially direct air strikes against high-value targets without the need to recourse which might otherwise delay the process and allow their escape. Viewed negatively, however, the 'strategic corporal' in Afghanistan had the capacity to inadvertently direct air strikes against civilians. Targeting errors of this kind risked inflaming political sensitivities not to mention the humanitarian issue of civilian casualties.

Another important link between air and ground forces which deployed in 2006 was the Joint Fires Cells (JFC) from 1 Battery, Royal Artillery, which comprised a mortar cell, a TACP, and attack helicopter liaison officer with an ISTAR representative collocated in order to provide company-level Joint Fires support.[24] In a similar approach to that of the North Africa campaign in 1942, the ability to collocate fire support and to host the various specialisations within one arm of the C2 chain, allowed for faster coordination and decision-making.[25] Importantly, the JFC was able

22 RAF Leeming, Joint Forward Air Controller Training and Standards Unit (JFACTSU) <https://web.archive.org/web/20140528121931/http:/www.raf.mod.uk/rafleeming/aboutus/jfactsuhome.cfm>, accessed 29 Apr. 2024.

23 RAF Leeming, JFACTSU.

24 Gary Wilkinson, 'Joint Fires in the Contemporary Operating Environment – An Afghanistan Case Study', *The Journal of the Royal Artillery*, 134:1 (2007), pp.27–31 (p.31).

25 John Terraine, *The Right of The Line: The Role of the RAF in World War Two* (Barnsley: Pen & Sword, 2010), p.377.

to call upon the utility of the improving deployed precision artillery. The JFC was able to coordinate more than 475 fire missions which employed the 105mm Light Gun in 'Danger Close' conditions inside 150m.[26] The multinational deployment of rocket artillery included the use of the M-142 High Mobility Artillery Rocket System and the eventual deployment of the Guided Multi Rocket Launched System, which increased the organic fire support out to 40km.

Operations in Afghanistan, and subsequently for the more generic conduct of counter-insurgency or PSO, have not generally required a Fire Support Coordination Line (FSCL) as the situation for the counter-insurgency forces is a relatively static one, and often well within the range of organic fire support. The use of 'kill boxes' has been the preferred option for the coordination and deconfliction of close air and organic fires and was a development of 'kill box CAS' as incorporated by the RAF Panavia Tornado GR4 crews in *Telic* – a lesson learned from the USMC.[27] A kill box is a three-dimensional area reference (a box) that enables coordination and control and facilitates rapid attacks. It combines traditional aspects of both an Airspace Control Measure (ACM) and FSCM, used to facilitate the expeditious air-to-surface attack of targets.

The use of the kill box in Afghanistan permitted CAS missions to be executed in the often restricted and crowded airspace around the main operating bases and patrolling areas. Further enhancing the flexibility of the kill box is the ability to subdivide the apportioned area into smaller keypads and to stack friendly assets in allocated height blocks. The norm was to place the smallest sound footprints, often with the best optical capabilities, at the base of the stack. Unsurprisingly, these tended to be the Remotely Piloted Aircraft Systems (RPAS) (synonymous with Uncrewed Aerial Systems and Uncrewed Aerial Vehicles), and above them came turboprops with Fast Jets and even B-1Bs at the top. This permitted the subdivision of likely enemy positions and of congested airspace areas into multiple user areas. For a standard overwatch mission, the stack would be allocated in vertical blocks, one thousand feet apart as a minimum. Should a live drop be required, the controlling authority and the JTAC would close off height blocks to permit weapon releases through the lower blocks. Kill box flexibility has been well adapted to the counter-insurgency environment and has extended its use beyond the FSCL and air interdiction (AI) description in current CAS doctrine. Furthermore, the capability of new technology has blurred the distinction of organic support, AI and CAS missions as the range of precision surface fires now extends to almost 70 kilometres.[28] On a cautionary note, what can appear a favourable range for organic fire could, in the often collateral-prioritised situation as found in Afghanistan, present an increased risk; a precision shell fired at its

26 Wilkinson, 'Joint Fires', p.31.

27 Sebastian Ritchie, 'The RAF in Operation *Telic*: Offensive Air Power, March – April 2003' *Air Power Review*, 18:3 (2015), pp.30–45 (p.35); Sebastian Ritchie, *Royal Air Force Command and Control, 1982–2014* (London: UK MoD, Air Historical Branch, 2022), p.122.

28 David Ralston and Patrecia Hollis, 'PGM Effects for the BCT Commander,' *Fires: A Joint Professional Bulletin for US Field & Air Defense Artilleryman* (2009), pp.22–7 (p.24).

extended range has no self-destruct capability. Conversely, a Paveway IV (PWIV) or Brimstone Dual Mode Seeker (DMS) missile, released from Tornado GR4 aircraft, or Eurofighter Typhoon multirole combat fighter, could be guided away from its pre-programmed target by use of the dual laser facility. This capability was used on several occasions during operations where civilians appeared in the vicinity of targets post weapon release. With collateral concerns a top priority, such flexibility maintained the utility of CAS above organic support at extended ranges in Afghanistan.

Incidents of fratricide in Afghanistan remained a source of tension between coalition forces as they attempted to direct CAS in multinational operations. Combat Identification, despite advances in technology, still remains a problem for CAS. In Afghanistan and the other enduring CAS operations, poor situational awareness in conducting the attacks is invariably the root cause of civilian casualties and fratricide. An example of this difficulty occurred in 2011, where two US soldiers were killed in a blue-on-blue strike by a Hellfire missile, fired from a US General Atomics MQ-1 Predator Uncrewed Aerial System. In this case, a combination of poor situational awareness by the ground commander and the decision to continue an attack when there were doubts as to maintaining combat identification of 'who was who' by the Predator crew, caused the friendly fire.[29] This incident demonstrates the importance of restraint, considering any doubt. Where this restraint is not maintained, amid the pressure to deliver CAS despite a lack of Positive Identification, air strikes can often have wider undesirable effects. Cool heads are required by all concerned in the delivery of weapons in counter-insurgency operations.[30] For the soldier or TACP on the ground and being shot at, this often proved difficult to maintain, and frequently the aircrews were the critical link in ensuring adherence to the Rules of Engagement, the proportionality, and the critical requirement for precision to minimise the inherent risks. All this needs to be achieved under a tight time constraint and in an often rapidly changing combat engagement. The fierce fighting between UK forces and Taliban in 2006 was in part a result of the British 'Platoon House Strategy', where small troop numbers attempted to control specific hotspots of insurgency, including Sangin and Musa Qalah.[31] Media reporting was marked by a leaked letter to the British press which declared the RAF support to be 'utterly, utterly useless', following a near blue-on-blue engagement.[32] While the cause of the potential fratricide was the error of the pilot in

29 Christine Boshuijzen-Van Burken, 'Ethics and Technology', in Désirée Verweij, Peter Olsthoorn, and Eva van Baarle (eds), *Ethics and Military Practice* (Leiden, The Netherlands: Brill, 2022), pp.67–82, <https://doi.org/10.1163/9789004512474_007>; Alexis Madrigal, 'Drone Kills 2 US Soldiers in Friendly-Fire Incident' *The Atlantic* (11 Apr. 2011) https://www.theatlantic.com/technology/archive/2011/04/drone-kills-2-us-soldiers-in-friendly-fire-incident/237142/> accessed 29 Apr. 2024.

30 Peter Lee, *Reaper Force: Inside Britain's Drone Wars* (London: John Blake, 2018).

31 Theo Farrell and Stuart Gordon, 'COIN Machine: The British Military in Afghanistan', *RUSI Journal*, 154:3 (2009), pp.18–25 (p.20).

32 BBC News, 'Major calls RAF support "useless"', *BBC News* (22 Sept. 2006), <http://news.bbc.co.uk/2/hi/5371392.stm> accessed 28 April 2024.

their effort to support the entrapped land forces, the operational direction of placing insufficient forces with limited logistical supplies into such a contested region reveals the link between inappropriate doctrine and the negative effect which can result. This incident reveals as much about the unrealistic troop numbers allocated to hold the platoon houses as well as the tempting targets they became for Taliban attack, but it also serves to highlight the associated increasing risks associated with TIC situations.

NATO doctrine notes the main causes of fratricide as misidentification of targets, target location errors, target or friendly locations incorrectly transmitted or received, and the loss of situational awareness by terminal controllers, CAS aircrew, or C2 agencies.[33] From experience, it remained a source of stress for all concerned that TACPs and aircrew alike were required to convert passed coordinates into useable coordinate data, posing two serious problems. Firstly, and potentially most seriously, the conversion of any data runs the risk of input errors to the munition in use. From personal experience in 2009, the software utilised in the Tornado GR4, required target coordinates to be entered, converted to a datum acceptable to the weapon software and compared back to the original datum. The scope for possible error increased through each process, and the time required to verify each stage of the process increased the time required to deliver the effect. Software developments quickly overcame the need for conversion; however, an agreed and doctrinally ratified datum common to all participating coalition partners would have improved delivery times and accuracy while decreasing the risk of error.

The perception that technology automatically delivers the best solution is not always correct in operations; while RPAS and Fast Jet targeting pods can now provide a higher quality video output both to the crews and to other linked users, the imagery is not always perfect in fidelity, requiring judgment and other intelligence inputs to form acceptable target identification. Mitigation of target coordinates, for example, is now incorporated into CAS doctrine by a requirement only to pass target information as coordinates, while friendly forces are passed as a range and bearing from the target location to minimise the risk of inadvertently inputting a friendly position. The need for defined approaches is necessary because of the risk of errors occurring in combat situations. In Operation *Enduring Freedom* the only fratricides that occurred in the major combat phase were incidents where US aircrews entered friendly rather than enemy coordinates into GPS guided JDAMs. One such example occurred when a US FAC inadvertently passed his location and was attacked, killing three soldiers; this type of error occurred on a further three documented occasions.[34] Reducing fratricides

33 ATP-3.3.2.1(E) Version 1, *Tactics, Techniques and Procedures for Close Air Support and Air Interdiction* (NATO HQ, Brussels: NATO Standardization Office, 2019), p.1–8.

34 Michael Binney, 'Joint Close Air Support in the Low Intensity Conflict', Unpublished Thesis (Naval Postgraduate School, 2003), pp.26–7; Sean P. Larkin, 'Air-to-Ground Fratricide Reduction Technology: An Analysis', Unpublished Thesis (Command Staff College, Marine Corps University, 2005), pp.12–5; Phillip S. Meilinger, 'Fratricide', *Air and Space Forces Magazine* (Jan. 2013), <https://www.airandspaceforces.com/article/0113fratricide/>, accessed 28 April 2024.

depends on both air and ground forces being familiar and practicing with targeting procedures. Such procedures, alongside technological advances which provide better information sharing and connect air and ground forces to the same picture and accompanying established prioritisation of air strikes in response to urgent requests, are essential to safeguard against fratricides.[35]

Alongside fratricide, the unintended deaths of civilians remained a politically major issue for the coalition, whose counter-insurgency objectives could not be met without the moral component. In 2011, aerial attacks remained the tactic that caused the most civilian deaths by Pro-Government Forces. During 2011, 187 civilians were killed in aerial attacks, a nine percent increase compared to 2010, when 171 civilians died in air strikes. The rise in civilian deaths from air strikes in 2011 accounted for 44 percent of the total civilian deaths caused by Pro-Government Forces in that year. The increase in civilian deaths occurred despite reduced numbers of aerial operations by ISAF/Operation *Enduring Freedom* using fixed or rotary-wing aircraft (from 1,816 in 2010 to 1,675 in 2011).[36] Such statistics reveal the ongoing incidences of poor target identification and situational awareness, which produced disproportionately negative effects on the overall political strategy. Ironically, winning the engagement did not deliver victory in the overall counter-insurgency and PSO campaign and CAS played a disproportionately significant role in the statistics. At the tactical level, Taliban forces sought to engage Pro-Government Forces in areas where civilian casualties were likely, as a form of both defence and attack, knowing the political significance of any coalition errors.[37] Despite the known limitations and risks, CAS remained fundamental to the collation 'small footprint' in Afghanistan and CAS support in all of its forms (kinetic and non-kinetic) ensured the minimum number of ground forces could achieve the task. As always, the CAS role carried a constant element of risk which remained outweighed by the operational gain it delivered.

The requirement to conduct CAS operations in a counter-insurgency environment such as Afghanistan placed an increased emphasis on collateral damage mitigation. As a result, smaller GPS and laser guided munitions have become the pressing requirement in all counter-insurgency operations. The RAF's British Aerospace Harrier GR9 strike aircraft which deployed in 2006 assumed the CAS role with a variety of weapons in their typical aircraft fit, which included Enhanced Paveway II (EPII), a GPS/laser capable 1000lb bomb, as well as low and high drag unguided 1000lb bombs and rockets. They were also equipped with the Sniper Advanced Targeting

35 Joe Pappalardo, 'Afghanistan Taught U.S. "Hard Lessons" In Close Air Support,' *National Defense*, 90:621 (2005), pp.62–3 (p.63).

36 United Nations Assistance Mission in Afghanistan (UNAMA), *Protection of Civilians in Armed Conflict* (Kabul: UNAMA, 2011), p.24.

37 Colin Tucker, 'The Efficacy of Airpower in Counterinsurgency', *Security Studies*, 31:2 (2022), pp.218–50 <https://doi.org/10.1080/09636412.2022.2065926>; Susan Allen, Sam R. Bell, and Carla Martinez Machain, 'Air Power, International Organizations, and Civilian Casualties in Afghanistan', *Armed Forces & Society*, 49:4 (2023), pp.1048–60 <https://doi.org/10.1177/0095327X221100780>.

Pod (ATP), a third generation ATP which produced improved image quality both in TV and Infra-Red (IR) modes. The ability to positively identify fleeting targets was greatly increased with the incorporation of such technology. Thus, in the CAS environment the pilot is required to assess the situation and select the best weapon available, with collateral concerns always a priority. Traditional unguided munitions could still be utilised but were prone to errors which an intolerant counter-insurgency environment would not permit. Technology would drive improvement in the flexibility of weapon utility. The main drawback for EPII deliveries stemmed from a lack of programmability once airborne. Fuse settings were made on the ground, effectively setting the detonation delay for the bomb for an entire sortie. While such an omission might seem insignificant, the flexibility of being able to programme a weapon while airborne offered increased collateral safety though the ability to delay detonations and thus reducing the blast spread of the weapon. The current drive is to carry ordnance of minimal collateral effect, as provided by the US 250lb Small Diameter Bomb (SDB); the SDB requirement was for compactness to allow greater payload delivery. Such weapons offer the added benefit of being lighter allowing greater payloads; by comparison, a USAF F-15E Strike Eagle can carry up to 12 SDBs, being able to fully programme the weapons in terms of fusing and profile, and dual GPS or laser guidance.[38]

The RAF operated the Tornado GR4 and the General Atomics MQ-9 Reaper (RPAS) in the Afghanistan CAS roles. The Tornado GR4, developed from the GR1 which first entered service in 1982, was conceived as a short-range tactical nuclear strike and AI system. Tornado crews, pre-2003, conducted minimal CAS training, and the training syllabus developed for the Tornado GR Force reflected the need to remain current and qualified across a wide range of traditional AI roles, as well as the multitude of weapon systems the aircraft could employ. The requirement to fulfil many different roles in both air-to-air and air-to-ground is a common issue for NATO partners, who must remain current in a variety of roles with a variety of aircraft types and at ever-increasing development and procurement costs.[39]

Evolving tactics, techniques and procedures

Operations in Iraq in 1991 had revealed the gap which existed in tactics, techniques and procedures (TTPs) for precision-guided munitions within the RAF Tornado force, requiring the use of aging Hawker Siddeley Buccaneer aircraft to provide the

38 Boeing, 'Defence Space and Security: Small Diameter Bombs', < https://www.boeing.com/content/dam/boeing/boeingdotcom/defense/weapons-weapons/images/small_diameter_bomb_product_card.pdf >, accessed 29 Apr. 2024.

39 Trevor Taylor, Cost of Combat Air Power, in John Andreas Olson (ed), *Routledge Handbook of Air Power* (London: Routledge, 2018), p.284.

Destroyed Iraqi Army T-55 or T-62 tank rear/right three-quarter view partially dug-in. RAF Tornado GR1/GR4s were used for interdiction in both Gulf Wars. (RAF Museum: X003-7116/0238)

target laser marking facility for the RAF.[40] Integration of LGBs would continue post-1991, but overall the RAF continued to train its Tornado crews in the traditional use of unguided munitions for the majority of its roles – outdated Cold War doctrine proved hard to change in a period described by Alistair Byford as a 'doctrine holiday'.[41]

During this period, RAF doctrine began to evolve along more common lines and in sync with US methods. This was the result of acknowledging the need to move away from delivering 'dumb' weapons at ultra-low level, and of a broader requirement to operate in less contested airspace. These lessons had emerged from the experience of enduring operations in Iraq No-Fly Zone operations and in the conflicts in Bosnia and Kosovo.[42] To cater for the technology development of smart weapons, the RAF upgraded the Tornado GR1 to the GR4, being capable of delivering GPS guided munitions, with the significant ability to 'communicate' with the weapon while airborne in order to update delivery profiles and target locations. This was a

40 Paddy Teakle, 'No Ordinary Job, A Personal Perspective', *Air Power Review*, 21:2 (2018), pp.130–45 (p.139).

41 Alistair Byford, 'Operation Granby and the Dawn of Precision in the Royal Air Force: A Personal Perspective', *Air Power Review*, 21:2 (2018), pp.146–60 (p.149).

42 Sebastian Ritchie, *The Royal Air Force and UK Air Power over Iraq and Kosovo, 1997–2000* (London: UK MoD, Air Historical Branch, 2022).

A Royal Air Force Tornado GR4 sets out on an early morning sortie from Kandahar airfield in Afghanistan. Crown copyright 2021 <http://www.nationalarchives.gov.uk/doc/open-government-licence/>. (MOD: 45151494)

significant step, accenting the incorporation of newer GPS technology into the inventory. The introduction of Enhanced Paveway GPS guided munitions now overcame the all-weather requirement which had limited LGB operations in Kosovo. Given sufficiently accurate target location coordinates, blind deliveries by day and night could be achieved.

For Operation *Telic* in 2003 the RAF Tornado GR4 Force (TGRF) had upgraded smart weaponry including Storm Shadow cruise missiles, PWII and PWIII GPS weapons. *Telic* reinforced the need for a Tornado Force capable of operating in the contested and congested airspace of modern High Intensity Conflict. However, the quick war resulted in an emerging PSO and counter-insurgency environment for which 1000lb and 2000lb GPS bombs were broadly unsuitable. The LIC environment, which was to be the main deployment requirement for the TGRF in the coming years, required limited collateral and maximum flexibility in any kinetic attack.

On arrival in theatre in July 2009, the Tornado GR4 deployed with the newly-procured PWIV bombs. PWIV offered complete airborne programmability both in the selectable impact angle and the delay fusing. Further technological improvements came in the form of digital downlink capabilities. Traditional CAS required the FAC to describe the terrain and target location through ground features which the aircrews could visually acquire. Once both pilot and FAC established a common visual reference point, the FAC would guide the pilot onto the target location through a series of references. The entire 'talk on' could take anything from two to five minutes, or longer if both were unable to positively identify a common feature during a 'talk on'. Given the necessity for speed of delivery, and that the FAC would invariably be the subject of incoming small arms fire, the risk of misidentification was increased along with the time from a request for CAS to the delivery of the required effect. Technical innovation improved the acquisition process through the development and rapid deployment of the Remotely Operated Video Enhanced Receiver (ROVER) system.

Aircraft equipped with ATPs capable of transmitting their Full Motion Video to a man-portable terminal now allowed the TACPs and FACs deployed on the ground to verify the proposed target and to control the 'talk on', reducing the time required from an aircraft arriving on station to the release of a weapon.

Perhaps the biggest step forward in terms of innovative technology applied to LIC and counter-insurgency in Afghan saw the Tornado GR4 deploy into the region with an adapted DMS Brimstone missile. The updated Brimstone missile allowed for laser designation against static and moving targets and, as it retained the original anti-armour warhead of the original Brimstone missile, it possessed useful small collateral properties. By way of self-defence improvements, a new spectral IR flare capability was installed, and provided in-cockpit indications and alarm of incoming IR threats while simultaneously being capable of fully automatic flare deployment. The ability to not only track potential targets moving at speed, but to quickly conduct an attack on them while they were mobile, was a notable increase in capability for the TGRF; gone was the requirement to stop the target with munitions in order to fix it in one location for a second attack – now a GR4 crew could permanently neutralise a fast-moving ground target with one DMS Brimstone missile, all the while tracking its movement.

During the later stages of the Afghanistan CAS mission the US utilised more than two hundred RPAS in worldwide operations, while the RAF had purchased 10 Reaper RPAS.[43] The UK's Reaper fleet began the armed-ISR mission in May 2008 making the UK the largest user of the Reaper after the US, at the time.[44] Reaper was primarily intended to be utilised as an ISR platform, with extended loiter times in the region of 18 hours. Such extended capability, coupled with the ability to datalink via the ROVER system to JTACs on the ground, reinforced the utility of the RPAS in the Afghan theatre and offered a CAS capability with the armed employment of PWIV and Hellfire missiles.

The utility of RPAS has generated rapid technological development in the aircraft and armament industries, where a variety of RPAS came into operation, including the leased Hermes 450 system operated by the British Army. Additionally, the British Army ordered the delivery of more than 50 Watchkeeper RPAS, operated by the Royal Artillery.[45] The reality of such an increase in the number of RPAS in theatre was the increased congestion of already limited airspace to coordinate and deconflict the permanent overwatch which such systems allowed, against the variety of air activity which was conducted in support of operations. In reality, the abundance of air assets, from hand-launched RPAS through the gambit of air assts to traditionally strategic assets such as the B-52, placed an ever-increasing reliance on safe separation of aircraft in congested hotspots. The downside was a resulting reduction in flexibility because

43 Tim Ripley, *Air War Afghanistan: NATO Air Operations from 2001* (Barnsley: Pen & Sword, 2011), p.125.

44 Ripley, *Air War Afghanistan*, p.132.

45 Ben Moore, 'Army's new Watchkeeper drone to patrol Wiltshire skies', *BBC News* (24 Feb. 2014) <http://www.bbc.co.uk/news/uk-26320927>. Accessed 28 Apr. 2024.

A RAF Reaper UAV (Uncrewed Aerial Vehicle) is pictured taxiing at Kandahar Airfield, prior to a mission in the skies over Afghanistan. Crown copyright 2021, <http://www.nationalarchives.gov.uk/doc/open-government-licence/>. (UK MOD: 45151487)

The aircrew for a No. 31 Squadron, Royal Air Force Tornado GR4 scramble to their aircraft at Kandahar airfield in Afghanistan to support troops on the ground in Helmand Province. Crown copyright 2021. <http://www.nationalarchives.gov.uk/doc/open-government-licence/>. (UK MOD: 45157228)

of the need to deconflict. Friendly losses in counter-insurgency and LIC operations, regardless of whether they are the result of enemy action or mid-air collision, present NATO coalition partners with political damage on a scale which can produce strategic impact on operations. This is evidenced by the 2006 RAF Hawker Siddeley Nimrod MR2 crash in Afghanistan, with the loss of 12 lives, the effects of which saw the withdrawal of the type from service and radical review of military flight safety in the UK. In such campaigns, flight safety compliance will always take priority, and Afghanistan posed some unique challenges both in terms of terrain and climate to air support. With mountain ranges bordering Pakistan and towering over Kabul, the challenge of providing overwatch day and night often proved nugatory. Weather extremes also required constant awareness by aircrews; air-to-air refuelling often became an extended challenge, fighting the turbulent air currents generated by the combination of terrain and climate. In such conditions, even the simplest of tasks became infinitely harder.

Training for CAS

It is worth remembering that the Tornado was originally conceived as a nuclear strike attack and Air Interdictor, designed to punch across the Forward Line of Own Troops (FLOT) at ultra-low-level to deliver a tactical nuclear weapon on Warsaw Pact targets. CAS was never an envisioned role for Tornado and its crews. The eventual upgrades to the airframe resulted in a multi-role capability which still favoured high intensity conflict. CAS, as a role, remained one of many missions the Tornado Force could carry out, and the key to ensuring crews were able to operate immediately on entering the Afghan theatre of operations was training. A typical work-up to deploying was a mix of live flying, often live strafe with the 27mm Mauser cannon on a weapons range, and a lot of simulator training. As part of the GR4 improvements the Tornado simulator was upgraded to a full visual, fixed platform dome. The simulator led all software improvements and crews were able to experience all the accumulated lessons from previous operations in the CAS role.[46]

An additional and essential element of training was the experience of truly hot and high operations; Kandahar sat over 3000ft above sea level, with summer temperatures regularly exceeding 40 degrees centigrade in the summer. While the Tornado GR4 had upgraded software and weapons, the same could not be said of its engines and overall performance – designed to fly supersonic at 100ft over the north German plains, the engines lost power quickly at height and this remained a constraint throughout the aircraft's long service. TGRF crews, trained to deal with engine failures on the Kandahar runway and, more critically, just after take-off. Weapons training, Rules of Engagement (ROE) adherence and application, airborne decision making and aircraft emergencies, were combined into every simulator sortie. Every sortie was an

46 Author's personal experience.

examination, and failure was not a considered option. Pre-deployment also required legal briefs and where possible, liaison with the army units who would be deploying at the same time. From a personal perspective, effective airborne decision making was the single most important factor for crews and formations operating in Afghanistan, born as it was from the knowledge of the ROE and the tactical situations which crews routinely found themselves in. Out-of-hours availability was serviced by Ground alert CAS (GCAS) at Kandahar, where aircraft and crews sat on 30-minute readiness to fly. GCAS was shared between the USAF at Kabul and the RAF at Kandahar.

Conclusion

For five years the Tornado GR4 Force supported RAF Fast Jet CAS operations in Afghanistan. The distillation of experience was transferred directly into operations in Syria and Iraq from 2014 until the Tornado GR4 retirement in 2019. Afghanistan proved to be a dramatically beautiful country to view from the air; ironically, the same topography which highlighted its beauty also made it one of the most dangerous places to operate at night and in bad weather. In terms of CAS doctrine, Afghanistan served to reinforce the broader lessons already understood by all who operated there. As is always the case, doctrine and the TTPs which are developed from it, form a basis for live operations which must then be adapted to the theatre of operations; in this case Afghanistan and Operation *Herrick* (the UK operation in Afghanistan) was no exception, with the introduction of PWIV and DMS Brimstone reinforcing the need to adapt new weaponry into theatre operations within weeks of their entering the TGRF inventory. The topography of the landscape did much to dictate the terms of engagement, and the lessons relearned on Operation *Anaconda* flowed into the TTPs which were adopted and adapted in the decade which followed. Afghanistan and Operation *Herrick* produced air-minded soldiers and land-minded airmen who were well versed in the CAS role, as well as its limitations.

12

Close Air Support in Global South Conflicts: The Nigerian Military Experience, 1967–2022

Samuel Oyewole

Introduction

Studies on air power and close air support (CAS) for surface forces in military strategies and operations have evolved over a century with limited attention, recognition and reference to the experiences and perspectives of many countries (small, medium and regional powers) in the Global South, especially those that do not pose direct threats to the dominant powers in international politics. This development has created hegemonic perspectives of this subject based on the experiences of leading military powers globally, such as the USA, the USSR/Russia, the UK, France, Germany, Italy, Israel and few others. Consequently, the experiences of most countries in the Global South are marginalised and underestimated in CAS and air power literatures. This development tends to alienate students of defence, air and space power, and security studies in the Global South, as the subject is usually reduced to abstract issues and mere foreign affairs in this part of the world.[1]

The so-called 'Global South perspectives' in CAS and air power studies are associated with many challenges. Most of what has appeared as Global South perspectives on the subject are mere reflections of Global North scholars on the leading military powers from the Global North and their experiences in Global South conflicts. In most cases, therefore, literature on military interventions – and their attendant employment of CAS and air power – of the USA and its allies in Vietnam, Iraq, Somalia, Afghanistan, Libya, and Syria, as well as the British and French colonial and post-colonial campaigns in Africa and Asia, are advanced as not only being

1 Samuel Oyewole, 'Air Power Capabilities and Applications of African Regional Powers', Conference Paper, Royal Air Force (United Kingdom) Museum, *New Thinking in Air Power*, Air Power in the Middle East and Africa Panel, 16 Sept. 2021, <https://www.crowdcast.io/e/rafmconference2021/5>, accessed 17 Feb. 2024.

authoritative but comprehensive perspectives of air power in the Global South. In this manner, the Global North perspectives of the Global South have become the hegemonic narratives of the latter.[2]

It is against this background that this chapter is interested in the nexus between the experiences and perspectives of the Global South on CAS and air power as a contribution to relevant military and strategic studies. Drawing from the experiences of Nigeria, one of the leading military powers in Africa, this chapter seeks to provide insights into CAS of medium/regional powers in the Global South. Nigeria has deployed and engaged its military in multiple internal and external conflicts since 1960, although its use of air support can be dated back to 1967. This study examines CAS in Nigerian military capabilities, strategies and campaigns, their contributions, and challenges between 1967 and 2022. Accordingly, this chapter is further divided into seven sections, including the nature of Global South conflicts, CAS in Global South conflicts, the Nigerian military experiences, CAS in Nigerian military experiences, the challenges of CAS in Nigerian military experiences, the implications of Nigerian military experiences, and conclusion.

The nature of Global South conflicts

In geo-economic terms, the Global South is commonly referred to as the poor, less developed, or developing countries and regions of the world, which are dominantly located in the southern hemisphere, vis-à-vis the Global North. From geopolitical perspective, the Global South has been used to describe Third World and post-colonial countries, which emerged as a non-aligned bloc in the Cold War ideological rivalry

2 John P. Cann, *Flight Plan Africa: Portuguese Airpower in Counterinsurgency, 1961–1974*, Illustrated edition (Warwick: Helion and Company, 2015); Lt Col Karen U. Kwiatkowski, *Expeditionary Air Operations in Africa: Challenges and Solutions: Fairchild Paper* (CreateSpace Independent Publishing Platform, 2012); Mark A. Lorell, *Airpower in Peripheral Conflict: The French Experience in Africa*, Rand Library Collection (Santa Monica, Calif: RAND Corporation, 1989); David R. Mets, *Land-Based Air Power in Third World Crises* (Maxwell AFB, AL: Air University Press, Air University AU, 1986); Karl P. Mueller, *Precision and Purpose: Airpower in the Libyan Civil War* (Santa Monica, CA: RAND, 2015); John Andreas Olsen, *European Air Power: Challenges and Opportunities* (Lincoln, NB: Potomac Books, an imprint of the University of Nebraska Press, 2014); John Andreas Olsen (ed), *Airpower Applied: U.S., NATO, and Israeli Combat Experience* (Annapolis, Maryland: Naval Institute Press, 2017); Michael Paris, 'Air Power and Imperial Defence 1880–1919', *Journal of Contemporary History*, 24:2 (1989), pp.209–25; Paul F. Spaven, *A US Air Force Strategy for Africa*, Drew Paper; No. 7 (Maxwell Air Force Base, Ala: Air University Press, 2009); Jon Sutherland and Diane Canwell, *Air War in East Africa 1940–41: The RAF Versus the Italian Air Force*, Illustrated edition (Barnsley: Pen & Sword Aviation, 2009); David Wragg, *Fighter Operations in Europe and North Africa 1939–1945* (Barnsley: Pen & Sword Aviation, 2012); Becca Wasser and others, *The Air War Against the Islamic State: The Role of Airpower in Operation Inherent Resolve* (RAND Corporation, Santa Monica, CA: 5 February 2021).

between the capitalist West and the communist Eastern bloc. These, among other, perspectives explain the geostrategic understanding of the Global South as unstable regions, with weak state institution capacity, and a terrain for power projection and competition among superpowers and great powers. The Global South is, therefore, a geographical, geo-economic, geopolitical, and geostrategic conception that is associated with a binomial division of the world. With the exception of Australia and New Zealand, all states geographically situated in the southern hemisphere of the world form part of the Global South, which broadly cover Africa, Asia, Latin America and the Caribbean.

As the Cold War's nuclear deterrence and balance of terror froze areas of tension between the East and the West in the Global North, the Global South became an arena of power struggle, theatre of proxy war, and the major hotspot of armed conflict. The prospects of major wars between and among superpowers and great powers declined following the end of the Second World War, as the Global South became the scene of many intense and protracted local, national, transnational, and regional wars with global drivers and implications. Resentments against a colonial imposed state system, its compositions, borders, and authorities in many post-colonial states mixed with socio-economic deprivation, political alienation and instability, cultural and ideological differences, internal and external exploitation, as well as power politics at the local, national, regional and global levels have encouraged many intra, trans, and inter-national conflicts in the Global South during and after the Cold War.

One of the defining features of most Global South armed conflicts is the complexity of actors, issues, scope, scale, and period involved. Because most of the conflicts are glocalised, frontline actors are sometimes pawns in the wider geopolitical context. Considering the covert, proxy and shadow dimensions of many conflicts, their actors and drivers may not be fully determined. However, Global South conflicts often involve foreign interests, which may produce different forms of interventions, including direct or indirect military, economic, socio-cultural and political interference from regional and global players. Accordingly, most conflicts in the Global South cannot be simply reduced to one or few issues and causes, because they are usually multidimensional and multifaceted. With scope and scale that are dynamic and dependant on resilience of visible and shadow actors and their enduring interests, strategies and capabilities, armed conflicts in the Global South are usually protracted and sometimes without permanent end.

Against this background, five dimensions of armed conflicts can be observed in the Global South, although their complexity can transform them and accommodate more than one dimension at a time. First, there are limited and declining cases of inter-state conflicts in the Global South. Prominent examples are the Arab-Israel conflicts and Iraq-Iran war. Second, the Global South is dominated by intra-state conflicts, involving a state and armed non-state forces, which desire changes in their nationality, state ideology, government, policy, and socioeconomic conditions. This kind of conflict can be found almost everywhere in the Global South. Third, globalisation and weak institutional capacity of the state to protect national borders have increased the cases of transnational armed conflicts in the Global South. This is the case of the crises in the Great Lake region, Southern Africa, Mano River Basin, Lake Chad region, Sahel and Gulf of Guinea in Africa, and the spread of Al Qaeda from Afghanistan and Islamic State from Iraq. Fourth, the end of the Cold War has advanced more space for initiatives and interventions of regional players and powers in Global South conflicts. This has emboldened regional powers, such as Nigeria, to intervene directly or indirectly, politically or militarily in intra, inter, and trans-national armed conflicts in their sphere of influence. Many of these Global South interventions have been conducted within national and regional frameworks in cooperation, competition and conflicts with great powers from the Global North. Fifth, the importance of foreign interests in many Global South conflicts have necessitated great powers' interventionism. Many of these foreign interventions have been justified under mission descriptions such as peacekeeping, support for allies, international policing, coalition against aggression, global war against terrorism, and humanitarian intervention. Examples include the USA in Vietnam, the Soviet Union in Afghanistan, NATO in Libya, multilateral forces in Syria, and France in the Sahel, among others.

Within this context, the experiences of Global North powers in Global South conflicts are often presented in the extant literature at the expense of Global South perspectives, due to the asymmetric advantage of the former in global share of knowledge production.[3] Without disregarding relevant perspectives on the interests, influence, and interventions of the Global North, a genuine Global South perspective should be premised on the experience of one or more countries from Africa, Asia, Latin America and Caribbean. This is important to extract military and strategic insights from Global South experiences and perspectives. In the light of these, this chapter examines CAS in Nigerian military experiences with internal and transnational conflicts and regional interventions between 1967 and 2022.

Close Air Support in the Global South conflicts

CAS is an important component of tactical air power in modern warfare. Colonel Melvin L. 'Smoky' Greene. Jr. of the United States Air Force (USAF) described it as 'the ability of air power to place weapons exactly where and when the ground forces need them in a situation where the target selected by the ground forces is "Close to friendlies".'[4] This perspective, and many other related perspectives, reduced CAS to an offensive air operation, ignoring its defensive and non-lethal dimensions. From a broader point of view, however, the US Joint Services doctrine defines CAS as the 'air action by fixed-wing (FW) and rotary-wing (RW) aircraft against hostile targets that

3 Mets, *Land-based Air Power in Third World Crises*; Lorell, *Airpower in Peripheral Conflict*; Kwiatkowski, *Expeditionary Air Operations in Africa*; Cann, *Flight Plan Africa*.

4 Colonel Melvin L. Greene, *Close Air Support: Proud Past, Uncertain Future*, Air War College Research Report (Maxwell AFB, AL: USAF Air University, 1988).

are in close proximity to friendly forces and requires detailed integration of each air mission with the fire and movement of those forces.'[5] The objective of CAS, according to the Nigerian Air Force doctrine, is to 'provide firepower in offensive and defensive operations, day or night, to disrupt, suppress, neutralise, fix, or delay enemy forces in close proximity of friendly ground forces.'[6]

Despite the centrality of airstrike within CAS it is also necessary to consider associated air power roles including air intelligence, surveillance and reconnaissance (ISR), and transportation. As an offensive instrument, airstrike in Counter-Land Operations provides air-to-surface firepower to eliminate hostile forces and their assets, while protecting and easing the operation of the surface forces. As a defensive instrument, air power is important to improve the operational performance of friendly forces, through air ISR and guidance for the movement and strategy of the surface forces. This is also relevant to protect the surface forces and minimise casualties at the frontline. Between defensive and offensive, air transportation provides force insertion behind the enemy line, reinforcement of the frontline and evacuation, especially of the retreating, wounded and killed forces or civilians trapped, from the operational theatre.

Beyond the declining record of war in the Global North, the growing military capacities in aerial denial capabilities with the advancement in anti-aircraft technologies have made CAS more challenging in war between and among leading military powers. However, CAS has become a normal feature of great and superpower military interventions in most conflicts in the Global South, where threats to low tactical flights are limited or absent. These operations are also significant in reducing the risk of casualties – which can rapidly reduce public support for military operations in Global North countries. Moreover, interventionist military powers have popularised the use and relevance of coercive air power, including the lethal dimension of CAS in Global South conflicts.[7] These, among others, including the comparably lower experience of the Global South and inadequate research attention the limited cases have received, are responsible for the prevailing representation and projection of the experiences of the interventionist military powers from the Global North as Global South perspectives.

Despite the foregoing concern, many countries in the Global South have developed varying force capabilities for CAS with different experiences on their deployments and employments. Although there is no fixed minimum or maximum distance that must exist between surface and air forces in CAS, the experiences of many countries

5 Joint Chiefs of Staff, *Joint Publication 3-09.3 Close Air Support* (Washington DC: Joint Chiefs of Staff, 2019).

6 Nigerian Air Force, *Counter Land Doctrine*, AFM 1-CL, November 2021, <https://airforce.mil.ng/doctrines>, accessed 19 Feb. 2024.

7 Mueller (ed), *Precision and Purpose*; Olsen (ed), *Airpower Applied*; Mets, *Land-based Air Power in Third World Crises;* Lorell, *Airpower in Peripheral Conflict*; Kwiatkowski, *Expeditionary Air Operations in Africa.*

in the Global South show the possibility of close and distance air support. A number of scenarios are evident in CAS discourse in the Global South, from both the Global North and South perspectives. First, there are cases where air power and CAS is absent, with surface-reductionist operations and visible aspiration for close or distance air support, or air-reductionist operations. For many small and medium nations in the Global South with little or no air power capabilities, military operations are synonymous with the deployment and operations of the ground forces. On the other hand, air-reductionist operations are rooted in coercive air power theory, which contentiously assumes that air operations can independently win a war or achieve a given strategic objective.[8] Such operations are commonly associated with limited political will and military objectives that underscore unwillingness to deploy ground forces to a conflict theatre by some regional powers in the Global South and most often the interventionist great and superpowers from the Global North. This is most evident in the air campaigns by NATO in Libya, and the US military operations in Somalia and Sahel.

The second scenario is one-sided operations, which are typical of surface or air dominated operations, or disarticulated air and surface operations. In this case, surface-reductionist is different from surface-dominated operations, considering that air support is absent in the former and inadequate or minimal in the latter. This is the case of many military operations of most medium and leading regional or sub-regional powers in Africa, Asia and Latin America. Air-dominated operations also feature limited ground forces in support of massive air campaigns by some regional powers in the Global South and most often the interventionist powers from the Global North. However, there are cases of disarticulated campaigns, with little or inadequate and sometimes competing and conflicting air and ground operations. This is evident in many military operations of some leading and most medium regional powers in the Global South.

The third scenario is balance or adequate force deployment and employment of air power and CAS. Although this appears to be an ideal situation, some of the leading military powers around the world have developed relevant capabilities that brought some of their operations close to this reality. The experiences of great and superpowers from the Global North, and leading military powers from the Global South, such as China and India, have dominated perspectives on what ideal air power entails. However, many regional powers in the Global South have also displayed the possibility and prospects of balance force deployment and employment of air power and CAS in some of their limited military operations. Hence, Nigeria and many other regional powers in the Global South can offer alternative perspectives and experiences on the realities of CAS. Motivated by the need to protect surface forces and enhance their firepower and operational effectiveness, CAS has become a notable feature of the Nigerian military operations. In this case, Nigerian military experiences between 1960 and 2022 cover the three scenarios under review.

8 Robert Pape, *Bombing to Win: Air Power and Coercion in War* (Ithaca, NY: Cornell University Press, 1996); Daniel Byman, Matthew Waxman, and Eric V. Larson, *Air Power as a Coercive Instrument* (Santa. Monica, CA: RAND Corporation, 1999).

The Nigerian military experience: why and how it matters

Before a close examination of CAS in Nigerian military experiences, there is a need to examine what the experiences entail and why they matter. To start with, why does Nigeria's military experiences matter? Or why should we care about Nigeria's military experiences? From a general point of view, there is a notable shortage of African experiences and perspectives in the global and Global South discussions on CAS, and generally air power, military and strategic studies. This is a notable gap that an insight into the Nigerian military experiences might fill. Moreover, the rise of other sources of power have returned the world to a multipolar system, with competing interests in Nigeria, Africa and the rest of the Global South. This development has raised the importance of the experiences and perspectives of countries like Nigeria. It has equally changed the dynamics of Western preference for African solutions to African problems from hegemonic lukewarm and withdrawal to competition for engagements. This has created room for countries like Nigeria to project regional power in cooperation with Western and other powers. In this case, Nigeria tends toward pro-Western defence, security and foreign policies, although it adopted a non-aligned posture in Cold War and post-Cold War global power politics and retains beneficiary relations with non-Western powers, such as China and Russia.

From a specific point of view, Nigeria possesses considerable experiences in internal, trans-national and regional conflicts and attendant military operations. Nigeria has an enduring history of internal conflicts and military operations. Since its independence in 1960, Nigeria has had numerous armed conflicts, which have directly or indirectly claimed millions of lives. Ten of thousands lost their lives in several political conflicts, some of which attracted military response in the first six years of Nigeria's independence.[9] Prominently, the Biafra (old Eastern Region) secessionism and federal military response led to a thirty months of civil war, which claimed over two million lives in Nigeria between 1967 and 1970.[10] Amidst these, Nigeria raised its military strength from 9,980 troops in 1965 to 271,050 troops in 1971.[11] Thereafter, a series of lower intensity conflicts of ethnic, religious, ethno-religious, regional and political natures claimed hundreds of thousands of lives in Nigeria, despite the military response in

9 Okwudiba Nnoli, *Ethnic Politics in Nigeria*, 2nd ed. (Enugu, Nigeria: Pan African Centre for Research, 2008); Gbeke Adenuga, Amos Olajubu, Samuel Oyewole & J. Shola Omotola, 'Ethno-religious Conflicts and the Challenges of National Security in Nigeria's Fourth Republic', *South African Review of Sociology*, 53:2 (2023), pp.130–49. DOI: 10.1080/21528586.2023.2233462.

10 Eghosa E Eghosa, Ebere Onwudiwe, and Rotimi T Suberu (eds), *The Nigerian Civil War and its Aftermath* (Ibadan, Nigeria: John Archer, 2002).

11 Samuel Oyewole, 'Civil-military Relations: Conflict and Cooperation between Military Bases and Host Communities in Nigeria', *African Security*, 13:4 (2020), pp.353–79; Institute of International Security Studies (IISS), *The Military Balance* (London: IISS, 1970–1975); Central Intelligence Agency (USA), 'Nigeria: Armed Forces', National Intelligence Survey Publications (1973).

many cases. Since the turn of the twenty-first century, however, Nigeria has witnessed the proliferation of sophisticated armed groups and trans-nationalisation of many internal conflicts.

Nigeria became a major of hotspot of transnational armed conflicts, especially in the last two decades. Since 1999, the advocacies for environmental justice by ethnic minority groups in the oil producing Niger Delta region of Nigeria degenerated into militancy and criminal violence, which have fuelled transnational crises, including maritime insurgency, piracy and armed robbery in the Gulf of Guinea. For this purpose, Nigeria constituted a Joint Task Force in 2003, with over 30,000 troops in 2016, to address the internal dimension of this crisis, and raised its naval strength from 7,000 (2001–2006) to 25,000 personnel (since 2020) to address the transnational and regional dimension of the crisis.[12] Recognised as the deadliest terrorist group in 2014–2015, Boko Haram and its Islamic State evolved from Nigeria to become the biggest transnational crisis in the Lake Chad region.[13] Nigeria's war against Boko Haram has witnessed the increase in military deployment from 5,000 in 2011 to over 50,000 troops in 2020, and the formation of a Multinational Joint Task Force (MJTF) with Chad, Cameroon, Niger and Benin.[14] Nigeria has deployed troops across the country and along the borders against local and transnational armed banditry in a series of campaigns that have become intensive since 2018.[15]

Nigeria is one of the regional powers with a record of external military interventions. It is the most populous African country with the largest economy and is one of the leading military powers on the continent. Since its peace support operations in the Congolese Civil War (1960–1964) shortly after independence, Nigeria has become the leading African contributor to various peace-keeping initiatives globally, regionally

12 Samuel Oyewole, 'Flying and Bombing: The Contributions of Air Power to Security and Crisis Management in the Niger Delta Region of Nigeria', *Defence Studies*, 18:4 (2018), pp.514–37; Samuel Oyewole, 'Suppressing Maritime Piracy in the Gulf of Guinea: The Prospects and Challenges of the Regional Players', *Australian Journal of Maritime & Ocean Affairs*, 8:2 (2016), pp.132–46.

13 Samuel Oyewole, 'Boko Haram: Insurgency and the War against Terrorism in the Lake Chad Region', *Strategic Analysis*, 39:4 (2015), pp.428–32.

14 Temitope B. Oriola, Freedom O Onuoha, and Samuel Oyewole (eds), *Boko Haram's Campaign of Terror in Nigeria: Contexts, Dimensions and Emerging Trajectories* (London: Routledge, 2021); Freedom C Onuoha and Samuel Oyewole, 'Anatomy of Boko Haram: The Rise and Decline of a Violent Group in Nigeria' *Al Jazeera Centre for Studies* (2018) <https://studies.aljazeera.net/en/reports/2018/04/anatomy-boko-haram-rise-decline-violent-group-nigeria-180422110920231.html>, accessed 17 Feb. 2024.

15 Folahanmi Aina, John Sunday Ojo & Samuel Oyewole, 'Shock and Awe: Military Response to Armed Banditry and the Prospects of Internal Security Operations in Northwest Nigeria', *African Security Review*, 32:4 (2023), pp.440–57. DOI: 10.1080/10246029.2023.2246432; John Sunday Ojo, Folahanmi Aina and Samuel Oyewole (eds), *Armed Banditry in Nigeria: Evolution, Dynamics and Trajectories* (London, Palgrave Macmillan, 2024).

and sub-regionally.[16] It gained international attention for its military engagements in the Liberian Civil War (1989–1997) and Sierra Leonean Civil War (1991–2002), as well as in Chad, Sudan, Mali and the Gambia, among others. Between 1990 and 2018, Nigeria deployed 732,305 troops for peacekeeping in different war-torn African countries, accounting for 13 percent of the total intra-regional military deployment.[17] These, among other, cases provide the background for CAS in Nigerian military experiences.

CAS in the Nigerian military operations

The Nigerian military experience with CAS has been shaped by relevant capabilities, strategies and campaigns. Nigeria inherited a colonial army, with distant origins in Glover's men of 1863, and a marine force that was converted to a navy in 1956. Shortly after independence, Nigeria realised the need for an air force, as its army contingent deployed for peacekeeping in DR Congo in 1960 had to rely on foreign air power for transportation. The Nigerian Air Force (NAF) had its origin in 1962 and was formally established in 1964. Beyond air transportation, the civil war (1967–1970) raised the need for rapid advancement in Nigeria's air capabilities for coercive air power and CAS. As of 1970, the NAF had 3,000 personnel, 33 combat aircraft – including three medium bombers, 12 ground-attack aircraft, 18 armed trainers and 10 helicopters – as well as three transports and some communications and liaison aircraft.[18]

During Nigeria's civil war, both the federal and the secessionist forces employed air power in their campaigns. Although the war was dominated by ground forces, the contribution of the air forces was significant in their limited ways. The most visible contribution of air power to the war was in the areas of transportation and ground attacks. Many air raids were recorded on both sides, with presentations that show limited operational coordination beyond few cases. Among such exceptions are the Nigerian military operations at Okigwe on 21 September 1968. As described by Major-General Madiebo, Commander of the Biafran Army, 'the significance of the use of air support by the enemy was that it was always a clear indication of a long drawn-out major move…'[19] Equally, Frederick Forsyth, a former BBC correspondent on the war, recognised CAS by the NAF in the endurance of the Nigerian Army contingent that was encircled by Biafran Army without supply in Owerri between

16 Alexander Ogomudia (ed), *Peace Support Operations, Command and Professionalism: Challenges for the Nigerian Armed Forces in the 21st Century and Beyond* (Ibadan, Nigeria: Gold Press, 2007).

17 Samuel Oyewole, 'Military Capabilities of Regional Powers in Africa: Nigeria and South Africa in Comparative Perspective,' in Olusola Ogunnubi and Samuel Oyewole (eds), *Power Politics in Africa: Nigeria and South Africa in Comparative Perspective* (Newcastle: Cambridge Scholar Publishing, 2020).

18 IISS, *The Military Balance* (London: IISS, 1970).

19 Alexander A. Madiebo, *The Nigerian Revolution and the Biafran War* (Enugu, Nigeria: Fourth Dimension Publishing, 1980), p.284.

MiG-15 as supplied by the USSR to the Nigeran Air Force in the Civil War. (RAF Museum: PC94/202/7)

February and March of 1969.[20] These, among other, cases show the relevance of CAS in Nigeria's civil war. However, air power tends to be limited in the general picture of the war. This is perhaps due to our understanding of the conflict which has instead been shaped by shortage of needed materials, and narratives and writing styles of army-dominated accounts.[21]

After the civil war, the NAF devoted its attention to capacity building, as an attempt to address notable challenges. A shortage of well-trained personnel led to the recruitment of mercenary pilots from abroad whilst a Western embargo forced the country to approach the Soviet Union and its allies for weapon supply. The post-war federal government diversified sources of weapons and training of personnel, as it pursued a radical foreign policy (especially between 1975 and 1979) and beneficiary relations with both the East and the West. As of 1991–1992, when Nigeria became involved in the Liberia and Sierra Leone crises, its air force had 9,500 personnel, 95 combat aircraft and 15 armed helicopters, many of them in worrisome serviceable conditions.[22] At that point, it was challenging for NAF to maintain its 37 old fighters, including six MiG-21MF, four MiG-21U, 12 MiG-21B, 15 Jaguar (12 SN and three BN), as well as 15 Bo-105D attack helicopters, and two F-27 armed maritime reconnaissance aircraft. The major platform that assured the firepower of NAF were the 21 Alpha Jets acquired in the 1980s.[23]

20 Frederick Forsyth, *The Making of an African Legend: The Biafra Story* (London: Penguin, 1977), p.143.
21 General Olusegun Obasanjo, *My Command: an account of the Nigerian civil war, 1967–1970* (Ibadan, Nigeria: Heinemann Educational, 1980); Madiebo, *The Nigerian Revolution and the Biafran War*.
22 IISS, *The Military Balance, 1991–1992* (London: IISS, 1991).
23 IISS, *The Military Balance, 1991–1992*; IISS, *The Military Balance, 1980–1981* (London: IISS, 1980); IISS, *The Military Balance, 1981–1982* (London: IISS, 1981).

Air power and CAS played important role in the Nigerian-led Economic Community of West African States Monitoring Group (ECOMOG) military interventions in Liberia and Sierra Leone. Although a frontline account by a Nigerian National Television Authority's (NTA) correspondent on the Liberian war identified NAF in the joint operational environment, it was silent on CAS and air power.[24] However, other accounts have identified NAF's contribution in capabilities and operations. For instance, Nwolise noted that NAF deployed four Alpha Jets, C-130s, and Super Puma Helicopters among other platforms, which were central to strategic and tactical airlift, ISR, search and rescue or destroy, and CAS in the operational theatre.[25] However, air power and CAS were more salient in available accounts of the Nigerian military campaigns in Sierra Leone. One of the Nigerian Army Commandants in Sierra Leone, Brigadier General Adeshina proudly wrote about Operation *Race to Makeni* in March 1998:

> Some twenty minutes after the commencement of the advance, two Alpha Jet fighter planes joined us in the operation which I codenamed – Race to Makeni. Throughout the advance, the fighter jet gave us cover from the air and kept us updated about everything happening in our front. It was quite delightful watching the operation at this stage.[26]

The foregoing position is supported by the personal account of retired Air Commodore Balogun on the Nigerian air war in Sierra Leone. It described the well-coordinated air and ground operations that led to the successful attacks and recovery of the Sieromco and Rutile Mines in January 1995, during the first military intervention. At the later intervention, CAS played a significant role in the recovery of the Nigerian embassy from the rebel forces as well as attacks against the insurgent-occupied parliament building and the capturing of the state house in Freetown, Sierra Leone, in early February 1998.[27] CAS was further evident in a series of search and rescue missions of the NAF for the trapped, encircled and missing friendly ground forces in different locations at different times during the Sierra Leone war in 1998.[28] In one of its armed reconnaissance in support of ground forces, the NAF fighters also intercepted and neutralised hostile air platforms that might have endangered friendly forces. These,

24 Segun Aderiye, 'ECOMOG Landing', in M.A. Vogt, *The Liberian Crisis and ECOMOG: A Bold Attempt at Regional Peace Keeping* (Lagos, Nigeria: Gabumo, 1992).

25 Osisioma B.C. Nwolise, 'The Nigerian Armed Forces in Joint and Combined Operations in Peace Support Missions: The Liberian Experience', in Alexander Ogomudia (ed), *Peace Support Operations, Command and Professionalism: Challenges for the Nigerian Armed Forces in the 21st Century and Beyond* (Ibadan, Nigeria: Gold Press, 2007), pp.109–10.

26 R.A. Adeshina, *The Reversed Victory: Story of Nigerian Military Intervention in Sierra Leone* (Ibadan, Nigeria: Heinemann Educational, 2002), p.39.

27 A.A. Balogun, *Nigerian Air War in Sierra Leone: From the Cockpit of Aggressor 08* (Abuja, Nigeria: Balinger Concepts, 2017), pp.42–50.

28 Balogun, *Nigerian Air War in Sierra Leone: From the Cockpit of Aggressor 08*, pp.42–50.

among other, instances provide relevant insights into the rich experience of the Nigerian military with CAS in its Sierra Leonean campaigns.

Despite the effective employment of CAS in support of ground forces in the late 1990s, the NAF was confronted by serious crises in the wake of the twenty-first century. Fifteen years of uninterrupted military rule with anti-air force sentiments among senior and ruling army officers, Western sanctions against Abacha's brutal regime, major military interventions in Liberia and Sierra Leone, poor economy management and maintenance culture crippled the Nigerian military capacity in air power and CAS during this period. Nigeria finally returned back to civil rule in 1999 and wound down its regional military interventions in the early 2000s. Although the NAF had an establishment of 9,500 personnel with 91 combat aircraft and 15 armed helicopters in 2000, the inventory was only 50 percent serviceable.[29] Without major intervention, however, this trend continued till the rise of the Niger Delta crisis. Hence, toward the peak of Niger Delta militancy in 2006, the 84 combat-capable aircraft owned by the NAF were either non-operational or waiting for repair.[30] This partly explains the reason for the limited utility of CAS and air power in the war against Niger Delta militancy.[31]

Nigeria's war against oil militancy and criminal violence in the Niger Delta region and the attendant maritime piracy in the Gulf of Guinea raised the need to revive its military air power and CAS capabilities and strategies. The NAF became part of military-led JTF against militants in 2003 and have featured together with the Nigerian Navy aviation in anti-piracy naval policing of the Gulf of Guinea. Although they are limited in the general picture of the campaigns, air power and CAS are most visible in the theatre between 2004 and 2016. CAS made few, yet significant, headlines in the campaigns against the Niger Delta Peoples Volunteers Force (NDPVF) in 2004 and 2006, and the Movement for the Emancipation of Niger Delta (MEND) in 2006 and 2009.[32]

One of the remarkable stories of CAS against oil militancy was the campaign that neutralised the Niger Delta Liberation Force (NDLF) between late 2010 and early 2011. John Togo, one of the commanders of the defunct MEND, rejected a federal government amnesty in 2009 and established a notorious NDLF, which among other encounters with the military repelled and neutralised 14 gun boats of a joint ground-sea operation, from where seven soldiers and an anti-terrorist policeman were killed and 17 other injured on 17 November 2010. After months of joint operations with CAS, however, aerial bombardment of the militant camp near Warri in Delta State on 22 May 2011 killed many NDLF's fighters and inflicted a serious injury on its

29 IISS, *The Military Balance* (London: IISS, 2000).
30 IISS, *The Military Balance* (London: IISS, 2006).
31 Oyewole, 'Flying and Bombing'.
32 Samuel Oyewole, 'Struck and Killed in Nigerian Air Force's campaigns: Assessment of Airstrike Locations, Targets and Impacts in Internal Security Operations', *African Security Review*, 30:1 (2021), pp.24–47.

leader, who ordered the disbandment of its force before his death two days later.[33] Responding to the hijacking of the *Energy Centurion* off the coast of Lome, Togo on August 28, 2012 and siphoning of 3000 of its 56,000 tonnes of gas cargo, NAF also provided CAS for ground and naval operations that neutralised one of the biggest uncovered pirate sanctuaries in the Gulf of Guinea, located in Igbokoda, Ondo State, Nigeria. CAS equally featured in similar joint operations against pirate sanctuaries in Robot and Okpoko creeks in the Niger Delta in June 2014.[34]

Beyond the Niger Delta crisis, Nigeria also witnessed the rise of lethal Boko Haram insurgency and armed banditry, which necessitated military deployment and operations that require CAS. Between 2013, when the war against Boko Haram became full-blown, and 2023, Nigeria raised its air force personnel strength from 10,000 to 18,000 and from 54 combat capable aircraft and 11 armed helicopters to 62 combat capable aircraft, 27 armed helicopters and three heavy armed drones.[35] In addition to this quantitative increase, the serviceability of different platforms operated by NAF also significantly increased. Amidst these changes, the Nigerian Army has also established an aviation wing that is equipped with drones and helicopters. Accordingly, air power and CAS have featured prominently in the war against Boko Haram and its Islamist Caliphate as well as various armed bandit groups in Northern Nigeria and beyond. As of February 2015, NAF had flown a total of 5,390 operational missions against Boko Haram, with 2,648 for ground attack, 1,479 for airlift, and 1,443 for ISR.[36] Many of these ground attack and ISR missions were conducted in close support of ground operations.

CAS has featured in multiple ways in the war against Boko Haram and its Islamic State, including in ground operations which had the aim of neutralising their fighters, sanctuaries, and assets, and regaining occupied territory. Hundreds of insurgents were killed in a combined operation by NAF and the ground troops that advanced in three companies in the Sambisa Forest on 28–29 March 2014. CAS was critical to the campaigns that recovered about 20,000 square miles of Nigeria's territory occupied by the insurgents, especially between 2014 and 2016. On 8 March 2015, for instance, Buni Yadi and Buni Gari, among other communities in Yobe State, were recovered by an air supported ground formation, following two days of a series of airstrikes around the Niger–Nigerian border, in an operation that killed over 200 insurgents.[37] In January 2016, CAS featured in offensive counter-insurgent operations in

33 Oyewole, 'Flying and Bombing', p.17.
34 Oyewole, 'Suppressing Maritime Piracy', p.140.
35 IISS, *The Military Balance* (London: IISS, 2013); IISS, *The Military Balance* (London: IISS, 2023).
36 Samuel Oyewole, 'Making the Sky Relevant to Battle Strategy: Counterinsurgency and the Prospects of Air Power in Nigeria', *Studies in Conflict & Terrorism*, 40:3 (2017), pp.211–31.
37 Oyewole, 'Making the Sky Relevant to Battle Strategy: Counterinsurgency and the Prospects of Air Power in Nigeria', p.222.

Embraer T-27 Tucano entered service with the NAF in 2020; seen here is a T-27 of the Brazilian Air Force. (RAF Museum: P022143)

Ajigin, Asaga, Bitta, Damasaka, Dure, Gadzama, Gulumba Gana, Mada, Kumshe, Ngwalimiri, Takwalla, Tumbun Gin, Sigel, Yajiwa and other communities.[38]

Since 2018, Nigeria's war against armed banditry has also featured CAS and air power. A coordinated air and ground operation in Dumburum Forest, Zamfara state, rescued 80 hostages and arrested six bandits in February 2019. As of 8 October 2021, CAS was involved in a series of joint operations that rescued 187 hostages from various armed bandit groups in Zamfara state alone. On 19 October 2021, CAS also featured in a joint operation that neutralised over 50 armed bandits around Saulawa, Farin and Ruwa areas of Birnin Gwari, Kaduna State.[39] In these, and other, cases NAF has provided the ground forces with CAS in search, rescue, destroy and sweep operations in the wars against armed banditry and insurgency. In many cases, air support paved the way for ground forces, and provided close overhead and backup in theatre of operations. Close and distance air support through transportation is also relevant in force evacuation, insertion, and reinforcement at the frontline.

Against this background, the Nigerian military has recorded varying degrees of operational, tactical and strategic successes due to the important role of CAS. Nevertheless, many other operations have raised concern on the availability, adequacy and effectiveness of CAS in Nigeria's wars against armed banditry, Boko Haram terrorism and insurgency, and its Islamic Caliphate/State. While Nigeria has recorded a growing utility of CAS, its inadequacies and challenges in military operations cannot be ignored in its experiences and perspectives.

38 Oyewole, 'Making the Sky Relevant to Battle Strategy: Counterinsurgency and the Prospects of Air Power in Nigeria', p.223.

39 Samuel Oyewole, Folahanmi Aina and John Sunday Ojo, 'Wings over Flies: Air Campaigns against Armed Banditry in North West Nigeria', *RUSI Journal*, 167:4–5 (2022), pp.92–103, p.100.

The challenges of CAS in Nigerian military operations

The Nigerian military has experienced a series of challenges in its deployment and employment of CAS in various campaigns. Absence and inadequate utilisation of CAS or distance and delay in air support for ground forces have gravely affected many operations of the Nigerian military, including in the wars against Biafra, Niger Delta militants, pirates, Boko Harm and armed bandits as well as interventions in Liberia and Sierra Leone. As identified earlier, NDLF killed and injured many ground forces in absence of CAS on November 17, 2010. Without CAS, the army contingent in Baga repelled and forced Boko Haram insurgents to withdraw in the early hours of January 3, 2015, but failed in the face of reinforced siege of this and neighbouring communities later that day, leading to the death of 2,000 people, destruction of 3,700 buildings, and displacement of tens of thousands. The Nigerian Army lost Baga, Bama, Chibok, Gwoza, Konduga, Katarko, and other major towns that made up the 20,000 square miles occupied by Boko Haram between 2013 and 2015 mainly or partly due to absence and inadequacy of CAS.[40]

The absence and inadequacy of CAS in Nigerian military engagements cannot be disconnected from issues of operational environment, strategy, funding and capabilities. In 286 operational sorties between 25 December 2015 and 29 January 2016, for instance, NAF maintained air presence for 536 hours 21 minutes (22.3 of the 36 days) with 316,637.5 litres of aviation fuel, which amounted to N60.3 million.[41] While this may appear impressive, it does not account for the complex terrain where the Nigerian military recently operated, with multidimensional threats and concurrent operations at multiple fronts. In the asymmetric warfare in which the Nigerian military has mostly been involved, the ground forces have maintained a stretched presence across major cities, towns, villages, and roads. It is, therefore, challenging to always maintain adequate CAS for all ground forces in all places. Moreover, the Nigerian budget for NAF aircraft fuel declined from N1.86 billion in 2013 to N749.9 million in 2016.[42] Around the same time and thereafter, NAF has increased in personnel strength and assets, although they are inadequate to ensure sufficient, required, timely, regular or permanent air presence in all the battle spaces.

Interagency differences have also accounted for absence and inadequate CAS in many Nigerian military operations. Aside from the Defence Headquarters in Abuja, Nigeria did not have a unified in-theatre military command for its war against Boko Haram in the north-east prior to 2015. Besides, many accounts of the Nigerian military experiences in the Civil War, Liberia and Sierra Leone Wars, and the war against Boko Haram have shown that many operations were planned and executed by the ground forces with little or no consideration, consultation or regard for the role of air

40 Oyewole, 'Making the Sky Relevant', p.223
41 Oyewole, 'Making the Sky Relevant', p.221.
42 Federal Government of Nigeria, *Budgets* (Abuja, Nigeria: Budget Office, 2013) p.11; Federal Government of Nigeria, *Budgets* (Abuja, Nigeria: Budget Office, 2016).

power or CAS.[43] Some of these accounts also indicate that some of the jointly planned and executed operations were not properly coordinated and executed. Again, delay in arrival and untimely withdrawal of air cover are also notable in some Nigerian military operations. Some of these exclusive ground and disarticulated air-ground operations ended tragically, sometimes at the cost of the lives of personnel on the ground and civilian population. It is not surprising that the Nigerian Army and Navy now maintain in-house aviation wings.

Prominent among the factors that are responsible for disarticulated CAS in Nigerian military operations is communication gap. The inadequate capacity of the Nigerian military in air-ground communication contributed to the limit of CAS in the Civil War (1967–1970). Air Commodore Balogun (Rtd.) also documented a number of joint operations that were called off or poorly executed due to inability to establish radio contact with the ground forces at critical moments in the Nigerian military intervention in Sierra Leone.[44] One such tragic experience was recorded in the war against Boko Haram at the Sambisa Forest on 29 March 2014, where three companies of ground troops were receiving air cover. However, after Alpha Jets providing air cover had exhausted their ammunition, the units were ordered to withdraw. This message was only received by two of the companies. The final company, believing they were still receiving air cover and were to hold their position, were isolated and attacked with 20 soldiers killed in the encounter.[45]

The enemy's ground fire is another major threat to CAS in Nigerian military operations. Concerning the NAF in the Civil War, Forsyth noted that 'Very rarely have aircraft been used in conjunction with ground forces, or against Biafran ground forces. When they have, the bombers have preferred to fly very high out of small-arms range and drop their bombs at random, which means that they usually fall in the bush.'[46] This concern endured in the recent war against Niger Delta militancy, Boko Haram insurgency and armed banditry. On 11 September 2014, Boko Haram brought down a NAF jet, captured the pilot and later beheaded him with a video posted online to deter the air campaign.[47] Again, armed bandits downed a NAF combat aircraft on 18 July 2021, although the pilot was later rescued in a joint operation.[48] However, the growing adoption of guided munitions by NAF and space support for its air power have increasingly improved precision airstrike even at high altitude.[49]

43 Forsyth, *The Biafra Story*; Adeshina, *The Reversed Victory*; Balogun, *Nigerian Air War*; Oyewole, 'Making the Sky Relevant'.
44 Balogun, *Nigerian Air War*, p.26, p.45.
45 Oyewole, 'Making the Sky Relevant', pp.224–5.
46 Forsyth, *The Biafra Story*, p.264.
47 Oyewole, 'Making the Sky Relevant', p.225.
48 Oyewole, 'Wings over Flies', p.101.
49 Samuel Oyewole, *Utilitarianism in Outer Space: Space Policy, Socioeconomic Development and Security Strategies in Nigeria and South Africa* (Charm: Springer, 2024) pp.102–4; Oyewole, 'Struck and Killed'.

Location of bases, pattern of deployment and general operational preparedness or readiness are also responsible for distanced and delayed air support in Nigerian military operations. There are indications that some platforms used in the war against Boko Haram in the north-east are based in distant locations, such as Mina and Jos. This move became expedient after the Boko Haram attack against the 79 Composite Group Air Force Base in Maiduguri, Borno State on 2 December 2013, when about 20 personnel and 25 insurgents were killed and two helicopters and some staff quarters were burnt.[50] This informed the decision of the NAF to establish special forces for base, force protection and an independent air-ground operation capacity. However, distanced and delayed air support are negative indications of CAS and air power in Nigerian military readiness and preparedness. Accordingly, air support only arrived several hours after the ground forces were overran and civilian populations were decimated by Boko Haram in many locations, such as Chibok, Dapchi, Gwoza and Bama between 2014 and 2016.[51]

Politics, procurement, corruption, maintenance, professionalism, training and reliance on mercenary are equally challenging in Nigerian military operations. In almost all the reviewed cases of Nigerian military campaigns, the tactical and strategic prospects of the operations were undermined by their political arrangements.[52] Nigeria also suffered Western arm embargos at the peak of the Biafran, Sierra Leonean and the Boko Harams wars.[53] Weapons procurement and prosecution of major operations by the Nigerian military have been riddled by corruption. These factors have accounted for poor maintenance, which is further complicated by the occasionally questionable levels of professionalism of the military. Shortages of well-trained personnel was also evident during the civil war, given the challenges of training Nigerians on previously-acquired German aircraft and how newly-acquired Russian aircraft were mostly crewed by Egyptian and other mercenaries.[54] Despite the decades of advancement in Nigerian military capacities, it also collaborated with some rebel groups and mercenaries in Liberia and Sierra Leone, and recently in the war against Boko Haram. These, among other, issues are notable challenges that have undermined the adequacy and efficiency of CAS and the Nigerian military in operations.

50 Oyewole, 'Making the Sky Relevant', p.225.
51 Oyewole, 'Making the Sky Relevant', p.225.
52 Forsyth, *The Biafra Story*; Adeshina, *The Reversed Victory*; Balogun, *Nigerian Air War*; Oyewole, 'Making the Sky Relevant'; Oriola, *Boko Haram's Campaign*; Onuoha, 'Anatomy of Boko Haram'; Oyewole, 'Civil-military Relations'.
53 Forsyth, *The Biafra Story*; Adeshina, *The Reversed Victory*; Balogun, *Nigerian Air War*; Oyewole, 'Making the Sky Relevant'; Oriola, *Boko Haram's Campaign*; Onuoha, 'Anatomy of Boko Haram'; Oyewole, 'Civil-military Relations'.
54 Michael I. Draper, *Shadows: Airlift and Airwar in Biafra and Nigeria, 1967–1970* (Aldershot, Hampshire: Hikoki, 2000).

Conclusion and implications

Despite the numerous experiences of countries in the Global South and the potential relevance of their narratives and perspectives, studies on CAS, air power and military remain dominated by the experiences and perspectives of the Global North. Accordingly, this chapter provides insights into Global South perspectives, drawing from Nigerian military experiences. Armed conflicts in the Global South have generally witnessed deployment and employment of close or distance air support in the operations of national, regional and global military powers. Amidst these, most operations of small and medium militaries are between surface-reductionist or dominated and disarticulated air support; regional military powers often strive to transcend surface-dominated or disarticulated air support to balance force arrangement and employment and air-domination, while interventionist super and great powers mostly from the Global North often represent air-reductionist or domination and an assumed ideal balance of CAS employment.

The Nigerian military experience with CAS provides a fresh perspective on the subject in the Global South conflicts. It shows the situations and possible scenarios of regional powers in Africa and others in the Global South. The Nigerian military has employed CAS in the Biafran, Liberian, Sierra Leonean, Niger Delta, anti-piracy, Boko Haram and anti-banditry campaigns since 1967 with remarkable progress, impacts and challenges. These campaigns are a reflection of internal, transnational and regional conflicts and military operations, which are prevailing features of Global South crises. As evident in this chapter, CAS is important to ISR, real-time situation awareness, force protection, as well as search, rescue, destroy, and sweep missions in Nigerian military operations. Nevertheless, the Nigerian military has also experienced inadequate, distanced and delayed air support in many operations, due to issues with funding, operational environment, capabilities, preparedness, location of bases, pattern of deployment, strategy, communications, politics, corruption, procurement, training, and force outsourcing.

The implications of Nigerian military experiences are multidimensional. For Nigeria, various challenges of CAS have caused long wars and unnecessary suffering and losses in different operations, while its employment and effectiveness have contributed to the military advancement of tactical and strategic objectives. For the Global South, this chapter raises the need to assess details, similarities and differences in experiences. For countries below Nigeria in military power, that is, small and medium states in the Global South, there are possible similarities in the experienced political, policy, strategic and operational linkages, especially in internal security operations. Nigeria's peers, that is, other comparable regional powers, have a high likelihood of shared commonalities and similarity in experiences and challenges in internal, transnational and regional operations. For countries above Nigeria, that is, emerging global powers from the South, these and related experiences can be cross-examined for guidance and shared similarities, especially in external engagements. Finally, the Nigerian and other related experiences on the subject are relevant for the great and superpowers of the Global North, especially in relations to the geopolitics and geo-strategy of Global South conflicts, military interventions and aids.

Against this background, this chapter observes the overriding need for the Nigerian civil and military authorities to improve relevant political, policy and strategic frameworks for CAS and related military planning, capabilities, preparedness, strategies, coordination and operations in its ongoing and future force deployments and employments. Beyond Nigeria, more research efforts are equally required to understand Global South experiences on CAS, air power and military studies. Accordingly, there is a need to assess details, similarities, and differences in experiences across different categories of conflicts, military operations and countries. This is important to develop robust Global South perspectives on the subject; learn, unlearn and relearn what works, when, where and how, as well as identify, borrow and adapt relevant lessons. The Global North, especially the Western powers, also need to gain a better understanding of the Global South conflicts and military operations, their dynamics, prospects and challenges, the inherent national, regional and global interests and actors, and the geopolitical consequences.

13

Conclusion

Harry Raffal and John Alexander

Introduction

This collection of case studies has considered important aspects of close air support and the integration of air power on the battlefield from the First World War to the modern day. Close air support remains a critical element of operations and, employed effectively, it can play a decisive role on the battlefield. It is, however, a capability which is accompanied by challenges which can reduce its potential effect. Many of these challenges are inherent and there are, therefore, reoccurring themes within the collected case studies. The importance of doctrine and tactics, as well as the need to establish effective inter-service cooperation and reliable communication, are demonstrated in examples from the First World War to the modern day. When achieved, the integration of air power on the battlefield can provide fire power to ground forces whilst allowing for rapid and responsive flexibility to changing operational circumstances. The visible and effective application of air power through close air support can result in ground forces demanding the prioritisation of this capability. As the case studies demonstrate, this is a specific challenge that air forces are required to overcome. Demands for visible applications of air power are often at the expense of the greater tactical effect air forces can achieve through strikes beyond the battlefield to interdict the enemy.

A final theme emerging from the book is that close air support first requires air superiority in the area of operations. Within a contested environment, where an adversary's air force or ground-based air defences remains able to contest air superiority, air power can achieve only a limited impact on the battlefield. Close air support is not, therefore, assigned the priority within a phased air campaign but must instead follow a counter-air phase to ensure the necessary air superiority. This operational reality can cause inter-service friction when ground forces are in operation and perceive their air force as being absent because of the lack of close air support. The themes of the military effectiveness of close air support, the relative value to the battlefield of different offensive air power capabilities – principally between interdiction and close air support – and of the need for air superiority, are apparent from the case studies in this work. These themes can also be identified in the Russian invasion of Ukraine, demonstrating that even as technology advances, doctrine, tactics and inter-service cooperation remain enduring issues of close air support.

Realising the utility of close air support

As the collected case studies highlight, close air support can have a decisive effect on the battlefield. Close air support's potential lies in the ability to provide rapid, responsive and flexible fire support to ground forces. The integration of air operations with the fire and movement of ground forces, in order that attacks can be delivered in close proximity to those forces, rests upon effective communication, training and procedures.[1] Maintaining the techniques and procedures which allow the theory and doctrine of close air support to be manifested in operations is difficult. Outside of operations, inter-service capabilities tend to atrophy. The aircraft and munitions that deliver close air support can help shape its effectiveness, but technology cannot compensate for the absence of air-land integration, inter-service cooperation and mutual trust.

The psychological value of close air support

The case studies in this work demonstrate that the principal value of close air support is not the destruction and physical impact on enemy forces or equipment. Although close air support can provide a physical effect, this is less than the benefit produced through psychological effect, the suppression, neutralisation or demoralisation of enemy forces on the battlefield. Providing such support also has, as Field Marshal Montgomery recognised in the Second World War, positive value for the morale of friendly ground forces. As the case studies show, whether on the battlefields of the First World War or those of the twenty-first century, the concentrated use of air combat power on the battlefield can neutralise or suppress hostile forces, even where these are not destroyed. This is an enduring aspect of close air support, whether ground-strafing, unguided rockets or bombs, or precision-guided munitions (PGMs). As Vesey Holt demonstrates, the mobile warfare that emerged in the final twelve months of the First World War benefitted from direct support by aircraft, but the destruction they achieved was less than the demoralisation they caused. Meech and Terry's case studies introduce the value of air support in responding to threats to ground forces, attacking targets that are hidden to ground troops but visible to aircraft

1 Following NATO definition at *AAP-06 NATO Glossary of Terms and Definitions (English and French)*, Edition 2020 (Brussels: NATO Standardization Organization, 2020), p.26.

or beyond the immediate reach of organic fire support. These operations also demonstrate the need for concentration of force to achieve decisive results from air support for ground forces. The same theme emerges in the Japanese invasion of Malaya; the physical effect achieved against ground forces by the IJAAS was less than the psychological – the suppression of artillery in coordination with the Japanese Army offensive and the demoralisation of British forces. On the battlefields of the Falklands, Afghanistan and Nigeria, the benefit of integrated air support is shown to be not the physical destruction of the enemy but its morale effect and the suppression and neutralisation of hostile forces.

The psychological effect of close air support is not limited to its effect on hostile forces. As the case studies demonstrate, the expectation of receiving air support is an important aspect of air-ground cooperation. As Alexander discusses, Montgomery was conscious that the morale of troops could be negatively affected where air support was not visible. He therefore ensured that within Eighth Army the wider effectiveness of air power was disseminated. Troops received details of the air support being undertaken as well as the important role of air interdiction to the battlefield and efforts were made to explain to them why this air support might be occurring out of sight. The importance of visible close air support is identified by Alexander's case study of the Falklands conflict in 1982. During the Battle of Goose Green close air support was provided by three RAF Hawker Siddeley Harrier GR3s. The Harriers delivered a timely attack on Argentine gun positions which were firing on British troops at 2000 metres and 'turned the tide of the battle'. Alexander's case study distils the underlying point still further when discussing subsequent close air support in the Falklands, described as being almost as significant psychologically in favour of friendly forces as it was against Argentine troops.

The mental strain and emotional challenge to aircrew of close air support operations is an aspect little discussed in the wider historiography. The experiences of No. 46 Squadron, as discussed by Terry, provide ample evidence that the nature of these operations can 'shatter' the mental health of aircrew. However, the wider challenge of how air forces return personnel from a combat to non-operational environment would benefit from greater exploration. This is also true for Uncrewed Aerial System (UAS) operators who have been engaged 'remotely' in close air support.[2] Returning personnel to the relative banality of the 'real world' outside of combat operations requires effective people management. Ensuring personnel have a space between operations and normality provides an opportunity to 'decompress'.[3] This space also provides the time to reform a sense of identity at a normal baseline – something that can be fragmented by the traumatic experience of providing close air support. This is particularly the case when traditional informal means of adjusting, such as the squadron mess bar,

2 Peter Lee, *Reaper Force: Inside Britain's Drone Wars* (London: John Blake Publishing, 2018).

3 Greg Taylor, 'Supporting operations in Afghanistan from Cyprus', *Ministry of Defence*, 11 Jan. 2011. <https://webarchive.nationalarchives.gov.uk/ukgwa/20130103062302>;<https://www.gov.uk/government/news/supporting-operations-in-afghanistan-from-cyprus>

are increasingly less valuable. Similarly, the emotional management of the aircrews' families is an under-discussed aspect of combat operations. Aircrews who know their families are supported can focus on operations with less concern. As well as improving the wellbeing of personnel such support translates into personnel capable of making better decisions. Improving the wellbeing of personnel can lead to enhanced combat effectiveness in close air support.[4]

Deliberate and decisive

Requests for close air support can be divided into two categories: deliberate and dynamic. Deliberate pre-planned requests, within the primary cycle of operations, can permit the achievement of detailed air-land coordination to suppress or neutralise an adversary's ground forces. Pre-planned fire support will often be best met not by air power, but by a ground force's organic fire support. Where accuracy, long-range or counter-battery fire are considerations for a ground commander, close air support may prove the best means of delivering fire support and enabling ground operations. Close air support also provides a flexibility in that aircraft can observe and immediately strike targets hidden to forces on the ground.

Close air support typically derives from immediate requests to meet unexpected needs on the battlefield, often of an emergency nature. Ground forces requesting immediate air support can receive fire support from on-call air missions as well as through the diversion or dynamic re-tasking of scheduled air missions. Even within pre-planned missions, air power can rapidly respond to changes in operational circumstances to rapidly provide firepower to the immediate point of requirement. During the First World War, as Meech highlights, the change from trench to mobile warfare led to artillery struggling to maintain contact with forward troops and the battlefield. Direct support from aircraft was, however, valued for more than the compensatory effect that was provided in the absence of artillery. Aircraft over the frontline provided a flexibility in fire support as they were rapidly able to adjust to changes observed on the battlefield.

Close air support, to be decisive, must meet requests from ground forces for fire support with rapidity. As the respective case studies on air support in the First World War demonstrate, delays in the provision of air strikes greatly diminished their effectiveness as a form of fire support for ground troops. An important feature of the counterattack patrol operations of 1918 was their rapidity, combined with responsiveness. Examining close air support in the Falklands, Alexander established that the RAF's pre-planned armed reconnaissance sorties in the Falklands could be repurposed to deliver effective fire support because of operational circumstances observed from the air and in response to fire support requests from ground

4 Air Marshal Ian McNicoll, 'Operations – Kosovo', *Journal of the Royal Air Force Historical Society*, 80 (2023), pp.60–74 (p.67).

forces. Such responsiveness typifies how air power can be effectively integrated on the battlefield. In contrast, in Malaya, rigid pre-specified targets provided to the RAF's initial offensive sorties deprived the aircrew of flexibility thereby reducing the potential integration of air power within the ground force's defensive operations.

Richards' discussion of the use of aerial field artillery, and the ground force's desire to have immediate call on air power in coordinated support of their operations, underscores these same points. Oyewole's exploration of the NAF's experience of close air support further highlights the importance of rapidity. Across various campaigns, distance and delay in the application of air power in support of the battlefield and ground forces gravely affected operations of the Nigerian military. This led to increased investment in combat attack helicopters and light attack aircraft to improve the speed at which close air support can be provided. The rapidity of close air support therefore remains crucial to the effective application of air power on the battlefield.

Immediate requests for close air support need to be balanced between rapidly responding to the request and the effectiveness of the support that can be brought to bear. On-call or re-tasked air-ground operations can enable the dynamic execution of close air support to respond to, or to exploit, a time-critical situation. Nonetheless, the capabilities of an air platform, its weapons load, and the threat being faced should all be considered in conjunction to its proximity and potential speed of reaction. As part of close air support requests, it is important to identify where a delay in receiving effective fire support will be preferable to tasking nearby air assets which are less appropriate for the mission profile. Ground forces requesting close air support whilst under fire will frequently prioritise speed of response over a judicious appraisal of the most effective fire support asset capable of responding.

As MacDonald highlights, the British Army's experience of receiving close air support from coalition air forces in Afghanistan demonstrated difficulties where calls for air support were rapidly met. The pressure on ground units led Forward Air Controllers (FACs), now joint terminal attack controllers, situated with them to seek rapid fire support. The nearest air asset, and not necessarily the most effective for the required support, was therefore often prioritised. This prioritisation of rapidity over effectiveness could then result in frustrations because the requested support encountered difficulties in reducing a threat which might have been better suited to an alternative, more effective, air platform.

Throughout the history of close air support there is a tendency for air forces to believe that ground forces had become addicts of air power. In the Second World War, within campaigns in which one side had gained air ascendancy to a degree sufficient for its aircraft to routinely provide fire support, ground forces frequently become reliant on receiving tactical air support. This was the case even when the ground forces possessed organic fire support solutions. During the 1944 liberation of north-west Europe, Tedder observed to Portal that ground forces had been 'drugged with bombs' and that it was 'going to be a difficult process to cure the drug addicts – particularly since the troops are undoubtedly getting pretty tired.'[5] Organic fire power is a crucial aspect of close combat, and it is where ground units should dedicate considerable resource and planning to achieve maximum lethality and effect. Routine requests for fire support by ground forces continue to be most effectively met by drawing on organic artillery or mortars. Nonetheless, air forces can rapidly deliver concentrated fire support against a specific target that can have a decisive effect on close quarter fighting.

The Second World War shows that, during operations, ground forces can become doped on air power. Outside of combat operations, however, there is the risk that ground forces neglect how air operations can best support the ground campaign. In comparison to an artillery barrage, the munitions of fighter jets can appear limited in their relative fire support value. In 2023, Major General Colin Weir, Chief of Staff of the Field Army and previously the General Officer Commanding 1st (United Kingdom) Division, predicting how the British Army '*Will* Fight in 2026' made no reference to close air support or the means to leverage air power in close combat. Weir's focus was, instead, on improving the lethality and concentration of the Army's organic fire support, and ensuring that fire power could be sustained and decisive.[6] A recurring theme in the history of close air support is the trend for ground forces, in peacetime, to neglect the role of air power, and concentrate instead on the predominant role of organic fire, and fire potential. This theme emerged in the Falklands and, as Alexander demonstrates, the right doctrine can be in place, but it is of little use if the officers in theatre do not understand how offensive air support should be employed. A similar theme emerges in the Malayan Campaign; the Indian Army had developed experience of air-land integration on its North-West Frontier but as Raffal notes, the inexperienced officers in theatre had not received sufficient instruction or training to take advantage of the experience that had been gained. Prior to the Japanese invasion of Malaya, the British Army (which included substantial India and Australian forces) concerned over its own shortage of artillery, believed 'close support bombing' was a necessary element of defence. A shortage of aircraft in Malaya, however, led the British Army to assume such support could not be relied upon and that fire support would need to be provided by artillery. Little work was therefore done to test how air-ground cooperation would be achieved in practice as opposed to theory. As Raffal highlights, Percival subsequently identified serious shortcoming in the combined headquarters operations room that had been established. The combined headquarters failed to ensure effective communication but was not conducive to collaborative planning between the respective staffs. The experience of Malaya ultimately demonstrates that collocation is not sufficient where it is not underpinned by mutual understanding and trust at a personal level.

5 Tedder to Portal, 25 Oct. 1944, in Arthur Tedder, *With Prejudice: The War Memoirs of Marshal of the Royal Air Force Lord Tedder* (London: Cassel, 1966), pp.605–6.

6 Major General Colin Weir, 'No One Said it Would be Easy … How We *Will* Fight in 2026', *British Army Review*, 183, Summer 2023, pp.6–10 (p.10).

Effective instances of close air support find that the forces involved have developed sufficient trust in their counterparts in the other service to know that their needs are safeguarded. This trust needs good inter-service cooperation, but it is easy to overlook the importance of individual relationships. Alexander's discussion of inter-service tensions in the Falklands starkly demonstrates that the value of combined operations can be undercut when cooperation and trust do not exist between in-theatre forces and individual commanders. When the commanders of each service have an appreciation of the balance required to achieve the operational objectives of the wider campaign, effective inter-service integration can occur. The air-land relationship is essential in ensuring the respective capabilities of each force are seamlessly combined to achieve joint operational objectives.[7] The difficulties Montgomery overcame in North Africa to achieve air-land integration were as much around relationship management, as they were coordination, collocation of headquarters, and appropriate tactics. Montgomery was also fortunate in receiving willing cooperation from his counterparts in the air force. Where this multilateral cooperation does not occur, air power, and in particular close air support, cannot achieve maximum effectiveness.

Preparing for Close Air Support

Close air support cannot be improvised. It is a capability which requires training, preparation and coordination between air and ground forces. As MacDonald highlights, during 2006, the training of FACs was placed under severe strain because an upsurge in operations in two theatres placed a greater demand on the single accredited UK training facility. This occurred as a new strategy in Afghanistan produced an increase in the number of unplanned troops-in-contact operations, whose nature involved higher risks of fratricide and civilian casualties. As Terry notes, the absence of training, procedures and effective techniques heightened the risk of fratricidal attacks occurring when aircrew were called on to undertake ground strafing. These attacks were, however, not integrated. MacDonald's case study notes the extent to which the risk of fratricidal attacks is heightened when dynamic requests for air support are made but which lack effective coordination within ground operations. In contrast, the German battle flights preparation for the March 1918 offensive included practice for ground attacks in support of storm troops to maximise their fire power effect and reduce casualties from fratricide.[8]

Regular joint training permits aircrew and air controllers to internalise the practices and procedures needed to realise doctrine on the battlefield whilst developing the communication skills on which effective cooperation depends. Training programmes

7 Seb Cox, 'The Air/Land Relationship – An Historical Perspective 1918–1991', *Air Power Review,* 11:2 (2008), pp.1–11.

8 John R. Cuneo, 'Preparation of German Attack Aviation for the Offensive of March 1918', *Military Affairs*, 7:2 (1943), pp.69–78 <https://doi.org/10.2307/1983066>.

also enhance the understanding of how air platforms, their munitions and supporting technology can effectively achieve close air support. The performance of RAF and RAAF squadrons in Malaya in cooperation with ground forces demonstrates that in the absence of training it is difficult, if not impossible, to realise air-land integration. In the First World War, the Tank Corps received effective support where practice had facilitated procedure and cooperation. As Alexander's case study identifies, Montgomery identified the importance of combined training, but he was an outlier. As Macdonald notes, this experience was replicated in 2006 during RAF operations in Afghanistan. When time or funds are limited, single-service capabilities can often receive greater priority and focus and cooperation can be neglected until operations re-expose the underlying need for joint training and procedures.[9]

For close air support to be effective, air and ground forces need to jointly train and develop both a doctrine and methodology for close air support operations. Peacetime technical training cannot, however, replicate the immediacy and urgency of combat. Shaping practice establishes the means of planning close air support operations, air-ground communication, and trust between the services. This preparation needs to extend to operational planning. As MacDonald observes, in Operation *Anaconda* the battle that the Coalition fought against the Taliban was not what had been initially planned for, and the support structures proved unfit to effectively coordinate close air support and required rapid adaptation. Command and control problems extended to control of both the airspace and asset allocation.

A recurring theme in the historiography of close air support is that lessons learnt in the previous war are quickly forgotten in the retrenchment of peace and the prioritisation of service, rather than inter-service, capabilities.[10] The techniques for close air support were being evolved and developed by the RAF in 1918. The value of these experiences was then reinforced through cooperation with ground forces across the Empire in the inter-war period.[11] As Alexander demonstrates in discussion of Montgomery's developing understanding of air power, these experiences did influence British Army doctrine and thinking. Nonetheless, the wider value of these experience was lost, despite the work of air power theorists such as Sherman and Slessor, because the lessons they offered were not prioritised in policy or training. During the Second World War, British military operations suffered across different theatres before, in 1942, the RAF and Eighth Army began to consistently integrate air ground operations. Integrated inter-service cooperation was neglected again after the Second World War. The inherent challenges of close air support in combat re-emerged in the Falklands and, as MacDonald discusses, did so again thirty years on during British operations in Afghanistan. As Richards and Oyewole respectively demonstrate, the

9 Harvey Smyth, 'Air–Land Integration' in John Andreas Olsen (ed), *Routledge Handbook of Air Power* (London: Routledge, 2018), p.157.

10 Benjamin J. Cooling, 'Conclusion' in *Case Studies in the Development of Close Air Support* (Washington, DC: Office of Air Force History, USAF, 1990), p.543.

11 David Omissi, *Air Power and Colonial Control* (Manchester: MUP, 1990).

lack of integrated cooperation and practice in peacetime affected air-ground operations of both a global superpower and an African regional power.

These examples demonstrate the importance of command and control within close air support. In Afghanistan, and more widely in counter-insurgency operations, the use of 'kill boxes' has been the preferred option for the coordination and deconfliction of air and organic fire support. Macdonald discusses how the expeditious air-ground attack of targets is enabled in a restricted and crowded airspace through this means of command and control. This is facilitated by technology, both communication and asset tracking.

Communication and Close Air Support

Communication between ground and air forces is an essential feature of close air support operations. Close air support is characterised by the proximity of air strikes to friendly forces. In the absence of effective communication, the combination of this proximity, the brief targeting window that is often available to aircrew providing close air support and the frequently confused ground situation in combat can result in errors in targeting. Such errors reduce the fire support contribution to ground forces and can lead to fratricide. This risk is further compounded where multiple air assets are in simultaneous operation as pilots and controllers are forced to manage a congested and complicated airspace above the battlefield. Ground forces need to be able to communicate positional information regarding their own location and the location of enemy positions, as well as update aircrew on the tactical battlefield picture. Where this is achieved, aircrews are better able to interpret the target they are being directed onto by ground controllers. This results in increased accuracy, a higher probability of destroying the target, and a reduction in risk to friendly forces. Communication between air and ground forces also allows for adjustments to intended fire support missions where the tactical situation is in flux and positions are changing rapidly. The flexibility and responsiveness of close air support is one of the reasons it is highly valued by ground forces, but these aspects depend on accurate communication.

As Meech notes, joint coordination of operations required good communications and, in many situations, the relevant headquarters needed to be collocated or at least close to each other. As Terry demonstrates, where this was lacking, strafing of friendly troops was not uncommon, even when a clear firing line could be established. Collectively, the First World War case studies demonstrate the value of planning, tactical air control systems, coordination, and communication. Alexander's discussion of Montgomery draws the theme of communication and control out further whilst the importance of both pre-planned and immediate air support also clearly emerges. In Malaya, 1941–42, despite the collocation of headquarters, delays in communication and coordination resulted in the RAF's pre-planned operations being based on target intelligence which was typically out of date. Until relatively late in the battle these air support operations were not afforded the flexibility to adapt their targets and provide immediate support against opportune targets.

As McDonald demonstrates, communication between controllers and aircrews is essential for the success of close air support missions. In Afghanistan, communication enabled aircrew to understand the operational situation, maintain the established rules of engagement, and operate close air support with reduced risk to friendly forces and civilian casualties. Aircrew were also able to provide ground forces with updates on their operational status, their remaining weapon loadout, and report any movements or tactical developments they observed. The importance of communication is further illustrated by Oyewole. Where Nigerian air and ground forces achieved effective communication, fratricide and civilian casualties were minimised. Oyewole also demonstrates that where air-ground communication fails, ground forces can sufferer considerable combat losses. As with all aspects of close air support, communication depends on recurring training and the habitual refreshment of practice and techniques. This training is only effective where it is inter-service in nature, and where the skills on which close air support is dependant are optimised for the complexities of the battlefield.

Precision Guided Munitions and Close Air Support

As PGMs have been introduced into the inventories of air forces, the accuracy of close air support strikes has been greatly increased. This has in turn transformed the destruction and physical effects that close air support can achieve whilst simultaneously decreasing the risk of fratricide and civilian casualties. PGMs also allow beyond line-of-sight targeting, with munitions being guided to their targets either by laser designation from another aircraft or from a ground controller or GPS. As well as reducing the need for aircrew to visually observe, identify, verify, and attack a target, PGMs greatly increase the ability of an air force to satisfy all-weather 24-hour tasking demands. Guided munitions allow for aircraft to make stand-off strikes thereby reducing the vulnerability of aircraft to ground-based enemy air defences without compromising on accuracy or destructive effect. As Alexander discusses, during the Falklands conflict the use of laser-guided bombs, the day before the Argentine forces requested a ceasefire, allowed accurate airstrikes on troop concentrations without flying directly over the frontline. The use of this stand-off capability greatly reduced the exposure of the aircraft to anti-aircraft artillery fire and shoulder-launched surface-to-air missiles. Advances in these munitions have significantly increased the stand-off distance that aircraft can provide air strikes against hostile forces in contact with, or close proximity to, friendly forces. Current technology allows a pre-programmed autopilot flight profile from release of the PGM on into the target area. These autopilot profiles are selected to optimise the attack conditions for different target types maximising the delivery of the munition's payload. In turn, this affords each close air support strike to achieve the maximum desired effect, whether that is physical destruction or, if operating in extremely close proximity to friendly forces or civilians, suppression of enemy forces.

PGMs also allow for post-launch abort. As McDonald notes, in Afghanistan an important characteristic of close air support in counterinsurgency was the ability to abort an attack post-launch if civilians entered an area. The introduction of blast profile munitions has, in conjunction with PGMs, further reduced the risk of close air support attacks resulting in losses to friendly forces or civilian casualties. The effectiveness of air munitions, combined with the ability to post launch abort, meant that close air support was often favoured within the campaign over organic fire support. Nonetheless, air strikes remained the tactic that caused the greatest number of civilian deaths by coalition forces. Close air support played a disproportionate role in these civilian casualties. In counter-insurgency operations there therefore exists a tension between the small in-theatre footprint permitted by close air support and the extent to which these operations can undermine the political strategy by producing casualties. The latter risk being recognised by insurgent forces, who typically choose to engage in areas where civilian casualties will occur. As McDonald discusses, technology is only one layer in effective close air support and the advantages of precision are negated where tactics, techniques and procedures are lacking.

Aircraft and Close Air Support

An air force's ability to effectively provide close air support rests upon the capability of its aircraft, and the extent that these can support well-developed doctrine, techniques and practices. As the case studies identify, close air support is only viable once an air force achieves air superiority. However, operating a phased air campaign requires that an air force either has sufficient mass to field single-purpose air superiority and attack aircraft, or has multi-role aircraft with sufficient flexibility to successfully meet various operations within the campaign. As the collected case studies demonstrate, air forces typically find themselves reliant on aircraft that can both contest air superiority and fulfil ground-attack roles. During the Second World War fighter-bombers came to fill an important role in Allied air-ground operations.

As Pyke discusses, the value of fighter-bombers such as the Republic P-47 was their flexibility. Having secured air superiority, the P-47 was able to switch to direct support of the ground campaign. The ability to deploy a relatively high-munitions load within a robust airframe, capable of sustaining considerable damage, and able to make accurate low-level attacks provided a psychological effectiveness against ground targets. The aftermath of the Second World War saw a retrenchment in close air support as air forces prioritised capabilities which were not inter-service in nature. This coincided with the introduction of jet-engined fighter aircraft with aerodynamically sophisticated designs. The subsequent experience in Korea and Vietnam was that these single-role fighter aircraft, operating at increasingly high speeds, had evolved away from characteristics which were favourable for ground attack.[12] To undertake close air support aircraft required survivability when operating over areas of heavy fire and needed to be able to accurately target hostile forces in close proximity to friendly forces. The case studies considering the First World War also emphasise the need for survivability for aircrew to effectively undertake ground attack.

The introduction of the Fairchild A-10 Thunderbolt was designed to provide an airframe with survivability and around a weapons load optimised for the close air support role.[13] The evolution of ground-based air defences means, however, that the US Air Force now regards the A-10 as unable to operate in a contested environment.[14] Reflecting a recurring trend in the history of close air support, the US Air Force has favoured aircraft with the flexibility to be incorporated into a phased air campaign. Multi-role combat aircraft such as the McDonnell Douglas F/A-18 Hornet and Lockheed Martin F-35 Lightning II provide the ability to strafe, although with a lower-calibre cannon, and they can offer stand-off precision strikes but most importantly they can be used to contest air superiority. As Richards discusses, the development of attack helicopters offers ground forces the 'flying artillery' that specialised attack aircraft might otherwise be required to fulfil. In peer-on-peer warfare, the flexibility and high-performance characteristics of multipurpose aircraft makes them of greater overall value in a phased campaign – in which close air support is provided once air superiority is won and enemy air defences are suppressed.

The increasing cost of multi-role combat aircraft does, however, pose a problem for air forces seeking to deploy these aircraft in close air support operations. As the case studies demonstrate, close air support involves aircraft operating in combat situations where losses are probable. If the cost of the aircraft involved makes losses prohibitively expensive then air forces will be unable to afford to offer close air support operations to ground commanders outside of all but the most permissive air environments. This trend is heightened when the increased cost of airframes reduces the overall size of the air force. The experience of the RAF in Malaya, although based on obsolescent rather than exquisite aircraft, demonstrates that where air forces lack sufficient strength to absorb losses, they restrict operations in support of the ground forces. This calculus is necessary to ensure that the striking power of an air force is not diminished to the extent that further operations cannot be provided.

The concentration of capabilities within a reduced number of airframes, reduces the ability of the commander to divide capabilities across the battlefield. The F-35A can

12 Alan R. Millett, 'Korea, 1950–1953', in Benjamin J. Cooling (ed), *Case Studies in the Development of Close Air Support*, p.362; John J. Sbrega, 'Southeast Asia', in Benjamin J. Cooling (ed), *Case Studies in the Development of Close Air Support*, p.444.

13 George M. Watson, 'You Can't Keep a Good "Hog" Down: The Curious Saga of the A–10 Aircraft', *ITEA Journal*, 31:2 (2010), pp.165–8 (pp.165–7).

14 Air Force Chief of Staff Gen. Charles Q. Brown, House Armed Services Committee, 'Fiscal Year 2023 Budget Request of the Department of Defense for Fixed-Wing Tactical and Training Aircraft Programs', < https://www.congress.gov/event/117th-congress/house-event/114697>, accessed 28 Apr. 2024.

carry a greater load than earlier generation aircraft, with a close air support mission weapon profile featuring over 8000kg of air-to-ground ordnance, and with the potential to deliver them more accurately.[15] But dedicating an aircraft against a target means that a much larger proportion of the available air strike is being assigned, reducing potential influence and outcomes elsewhere on the battlefield.

The utilisation of UAS can offset the effects of this air power scarcity. The cost of UAS, both their procurement and operational costs, are significantly lower than modern manned aircraft. At the most advanced end of the UAS spectrum, remotely piloted medium-altitude, long endurance aircraft, such as the General Atomics MQ-9B Protector RG, have procurement costs comparable to a crewed aircraft. Their operational costs are, however, far lower when calculated based on the flight hours that this type provides. Smaller UAS, including low-cost commercial systems, can also offer a fire power effect on the battlefield. Combined with effects from rotary and fixed-wing aircraft the incorporation of UAS offers the prospect of close air support evolving further.[16] The importance of maximising air assets through coordinating their operations will, however, remain current.

Counter-insurgency operations in Afghanistan and Iraq led to air assets being required on station around the clock to provide fire support as and when requested. Larger UAS therefore came to play an important role in the assets called on to meet the ground forces' requirements for close air support. UAS possessing high endurance but with only limited speed, and altitude capabilities and limited countermeasures, can achieve success supporting units in combat in counter-insurgency campaigns and in conflicts without a dense layer of air defences. The flight hours spent providing close air support during counter-insurgency operations, and the reduction in the structural life of the airframe of the air assets providing this capability, pose a challenge to air forces which have seen their air fleets decrease in the past 30 years. UAS can, however, significantly reduce requirement for fixed- and rotary-wing aircraft to fulfil the close air support role. In conventional conflict, where neither side achieves control of the air, UAS will suffer high loss-rates. If there is sufficient supply and production capacity, however, these losses can be endured; a situation significantly different to one where personnel are being lost. The increased use of UAS for close air support in conventional conflicts, also allows manned aircraft to be used to achieve air superiority and undertake longer-range strikes. Operating a balanced force in the close air support role, therefore allows air forces to maximise their potential combat effectiveness.

15 Major Jules 'Hay' Hurst, 'Small Unmanned Aerial Systems and Tactical Air Control', *Air Space Power Journal*, 33:Spring 2019 (2019), pp.19–33 (p.23).

16 Viktoriya Fedorchak, *The Russia-Ukraine War: Towards Resilient Fighting Power* (London: Routledge, 2024), p.103.

Air power beyond the battlefield

Close air support is planned and executed at the tactical level. However, the allocation of air assets occurs at the operational level and close air support is one component of the wider air operations undertaken in support of a joint campaign directed at achieving a strategic objective. Close air support therefore requires a consideration of wider air power capabilities.

Although close air support can achieve decisive effects, frequently other air operations will have a greater critical influence on the ground campaign. A frequent theme within the individual campaigns considered in this book is that ground commanders may find greater benefit in the air force interdicting the adversary as opposed to their undertaking close air support. Within UK and NATO doctrine four air power roles are identified – control of the air, attack, mobility, and intelligence, surveillance, and reconnaissance (ISR). Within the attack role close air support and interdiction are both a subset of counter-land operations.[17] Interdiction targets the adversary's ground forces – including command and control, lines of communication and logistics – behind the battlefield, and these operations do not require detailed integration with friendly forces. The lack of immediate effect on the battlefield must be weighed with its potential for greater strategic and operational level effect.

Air interdiction operations derive their effect by striking identified or anticipated targets in an operational area based on intelligence. These operations are coordinated with the wider joint operational plan and are designed to facilitate the ground commander achieving strategic objectives. During 1944, Operation *Strangle* demonstrated the effectiveness of applying tactical air power to disrupt logistics and to interdict the movement of supplies and reinforcements along the lines of communication behind the battlefield. Pyke discusses how, by prioritising these objectives, the operation aimed to achieve an operational level outcome in support of the wider joint campaign than would have been possible by applying air power in direct support of troops on the frontline. The interdiction attacks on the Axis forces, and the cumulative effect on their logistics and supplies, subsequently facilitated the rapid advance of Allied ground forces.

As part of the air operations contributing to the ground campaign, close air support and interdiction frequently compete for the same assets. Pyke draws out the importance of this point when discussing Slessor's willingness to make full use of the flexibility of air power to achieve the strategic objectives of the wider campaign. Ground forces suffering losses and in need of immediate respite will, however, rarely welcome interdiction strikes no matter the strategic benefits these might bring in the future. Delivered at range, out of sight of units on the frontline, with non-instant effects on the frontline, and drawing on resources that could otherwise have met a commander's request for close air support, it is not difficult to understand why interdiction operations are met with antipathy. The results of interdiction are also hard to quantify, making it difficult for air

17 Joint Doctrine Publication 0-30 *UK Air and Space Power*, 3rd Ed (Shrivenham: Ministry of Defence, 2022).

forces to demonstrate the value to ground commanders. Montgomery recognised that close air support and interdiction attacks were complementary parts of the counter-land campaign and welcomed a balance in the operations. It should be recognised, however, that the air forces supporting Montgomery were of sufficient size that one capability was not employed to the exclusion of the other. Particularly in a contested air environment, however, interdiction often offers better rewards for both air and ground forces than close air support. Lukasik's case study of Sherman, and the development of American attack aviation, demonstrates the overlap between air support for the battlefield and the wider use of air power. Sherman's writing noted the peculiar vulnerability of railroads, the pressure that could result on the enemy's forward troops if their lines of communication were attacked and the advantages of attacking troops and artillery outside of field positions. Although Sherman stressed the importance of aviation support for the army, he also recognised the principle of concentration, and the employment of the air force must not be solely guided by conditions surrounding the use of ground troops. As Richards' case study explores, the US Army's experience in the Korean War, and subsequently in Vietnam, left it unsatisfied with the US Air Force's concentration. In the absence of control, the US Army came to believe that the targets of most value to the ground campaign would not be prioritised, and the centralisation was solely at the expense of prioritising close air support. MacDonald's case study brings the continuing challenges of concentration into the twenty-first century. The use of FACs in Afghanistan allowed for concentration to be maintained whilst affording flexibility of control. The use of such 'strategic corporals' provided a rapidity that would otherwise have been lacking. It was not, however, cost free and delegation to those in the field and under fire had the capacity to inadvertently direct air strikes against civilians. In exploring this issue MacDonald highlights a unique issue within delegated control within counter-insurgency. Such delegated control, taken to extremes, also risks diluting concentration against targets beyond the battlefield, and preventing air forces prioritising targets of strategic importance.

In the counter-insurgency operations of Afghanistan there were not sufficient interdiction targets to reduce the air power available for close air support. As Oyewole shows, however, in Nigeria the counter-land air operations comprised several aspects, with close air support being provided along with strikes on bases and supplies. In Malaya, in 1942, the Japanese Army suffered their greatest losses to air attacks when their road movements were observed and attacked. However, interdiction attacks often leave the air force open to criticism of their being absent. Ground forces value the immediacy of close air support and the extent to which it can destroy or neutralise hostile forces firing or manoeuvring against their own operations. It is also a visible manifestation of air power and, clearly connected to their own operations, the tactical results are readily discernible. Where inter-service cooperation and trust are lacking interdiction operations, and the resulting absence of close air support, can lead to friction occurring between air and ground forces.

For ground forces the absence or delay of fire support for any reason is a point of frustration. The multi-role nature of air assets can result in their being assigned to other missions and not being available for close air support. The centralisation of air assets to ensure that they are being used to their greatest military effect, and that they are not available to ground commanders in the same decentralised fashion as field artillery, has been a recurring source of tension within the history of close air support. As Richards observes, the lack of trust between the US Army and Air Force regarding the provision of air power to support battlefield operations led the former to develop the attack helicopter to meet their fire support needs.

Air forces often prioritise interdiction over close air support because these operations to possess greater military effectiveness in the context of the wider conflict. Deep strikes can provide a greater cumulative effect against the adversary than close air support. Within the close air support decision-making process for pre-planned operations, an appraisal needs to be made as to whether air delivered fire support is the most effective employment of air power. Air interdiction strikes are an important tactical contribution to the battlefield, and frequently compete for the same air resources as close air support.

Air superiority

Throughout the work, the importance of control of the air is identified as an essential factor. Where air forces can operate unopposed, they are able to maximise the effect of close air support. In contested air space, air forces are often unable to achieve the concentration needed to decisively influence the battlefield.

The importance of air superiority can frequently result in close air support being a lower priority for air forces than those operations which will subsequently provide the uncontested air environment in which close air support can be conducted. Air and ground forces need to have developed sufficient trust that the air campaign can achieve control of the air, and that operations will then shift to ensuring the best outcome for the ground commander's operational objectives. The mutual inter-service trust required in a phased air campaign can be difficult to achieve. Despite the success achieved by the IJAAS, its air operations in Malaya were criticised for prioritising air superiority. As part of a phased air campaign, however, once their primary aim was achieved the IJAAS undertook air-ground attacks before reverting to control of the air when RAF fighters based in Singapore began to contest air superiority. The respective case studies on the First World War again highlight that close air support is effective only once control of the air is secured. The case studies also demonstrate that although the absence of enemy fighters permitted operations, surface-to-air fire remained a danger. Sherman recognised control of the air as the 'principal element of the air situation' and Montgomery recognised the primacy of air superiority as the enabler for success of the ground campaign.[18]

18 William Carrington Sherman, *Air Warfare* (New York, NY: The Ronald Press, 1926), p.121.

Many of the resources involved in achieving air superiority are those required if ground forces are to receive close air support. The priority of the air superiority role is therefore often at the direct expense of the resources available for close air support. This example is evident from the early history of the First World War when the British employed fighter aircraft to fulfil the role of ground strafing. As Terry discusses, the lower priority afforded to ground attack in relation to air superiority affected not merely the relative resources committed to the role. Aircrew, facing heavy losses operating outside of a role for which their aircraft was designed, and with seemingly little value attached to their work, were frequently faulted for their execution of the tasks assigned. The US Army's employment of AH-64 Apache helicopters to routinely, and independently, undertake attacks against enemy forces in close friendly contact demonstrates the desire from ground forces to assure themselves of air support where they need it, and when they need it.[19] Army aviation attacks of this kind were previously termed close combat attacks, defined by the US Army as 'hasty or deliberate attack by Army aircraft providing air-to-ground fires for friendly units engaged in close combat. Due to the close proximity of friendly forces, detailed integration is required.'[20] Against non-peer adversaries, army aviation attack fire support from rotary-wing platforms can be devastating but these assets are vulnerable in a contested air environment. In the absence of control of the air, the effects of air power on the battlefield are limited.

The history of close air support is also one of aircraft being lost to ground fire, as well as their delivering effective fire support. Degrading an opponent's ground-based air defence systems is a critical aspect of campaign planning. The suppression or destruction of enemy air defence systems is critical to securing air superiority and the means to undertake further operations without meaningful interference from an adversary's forces. Where the airspace above ground forces is not 'owned', but instead heavily contested, the flexibility of air power over the battlefield, on which close air support is dependant, is reduced. Anti-aircraft artillery and man-portable air defence systems prevent aircraft loitering over the battlefield and reduce the opportunity for target identification and attack runs. This increases the likelihood of targeting errors, and in turn of fratricide and civilian casualties. It also reduces the opportunity for aircraft to undertake dynamic targeting of threats observed from the air but hidden to ground forces. Longer-range surface to air missiles can force aircraft to operate at distance from the battlefield increasing the opportunity for ground forces to conceal targets. Reviewing air strike sites in Serbia, the RAF found that a great number of targets had been decoys of a relatively unsophisticated nature.[21] Attacks from distance also require air forces to draw down a greater proportion of their PGM stockpiles or

19 Colin Powell, 'Roles and Missions Review: Steps Towards Jointness', *The DISAM Journal*, 16:1 (1993), pp.26–41 (p.33).

20 Headquarters, Department of the Army, Field Manual 3-04.126, *Attack Reconnaissance Helicopter Operations* (Washington, DC: Government Printing Office, 2007), p.1–4.

21 Air Marshal Stuart Atha, 'Operations – The Balkans and Northern Watch', *Journal of the Royal Air Force Historical Society*, 80 (2023), pp.33–47 (p.44).

accept a reduction in accuracy and point effect in their close air support. These systems also pose a threat to UAS. potentially depriving air forces of their use with a resulting loss in capability and loiter time above the battlefield. The suppression of enemy air defences has become an important part of the phased air campaign. As with air superiority missions, however, these operations can draw on the same resources required for close air support. At the outset of operations, in the absence of overwhelming numerical air superiority, ground forces are often required to make use of organic fire support until the air force has earned control of the air.

Ukraine

The Russian invasion of Ukraine is the most recent conflict capable of offering insights on the evolution of close air support, as well as confirming those enduring principles which have been indicated through the case studies offered both here and in previous works on close air support. The war in Ukraine has driven both the Ukrainian and Russian forces to adapt new tactics and technologies as they have sought to counter the challenges they have faced in providing close air support operations.

Russian forces hold an advantage in fixed-wing air assets, which has allowed them to undertake a measure of air support for their ground forces. This has, however, been restricted because the *Vozdushno-Kosmicheskiye Sily* (VKS) –Russian Aerospace Forces – lacks sufficient strength to degrade the Ukrainian Ground Based Air Defences to the extent necessary to assure the survivability of Russian air assets over the battlefield. Ukrainian Surface to Air Missiles have a range sufficient to threaten Russian aircraft operating deep within Russian-controlled air space.[22] At the outset of the Russian Invasion the VKS did not intensively prioritise a counter-air campaign to achieve air superiority. Of the 1,400 sorties that the VKS is estimated to have conducted during the initial period of the invasion, over 80 percent were made against ground targets in tactical support of Russian ground forces.[23] The VKS's prioritisation of tactical air support, combined with the Ukrainian Air Force's dispersal immediately prior to the invasion and the intersecting air defence structure adopted in anticipation of the Russian Counter-Air Campaign, resulted in the VKS failing to secure air superiority. In the contested air environment over Ukraine, the VKS lost a significant number of air assets.[24] Without survivability the VKS was subsequently unable to provide close air support to the Russian ground offensives.

22 The S–300 has a maximum range of 150km, whilst the US produced Patriot system has an operational range of 160km.

23 Sylwester Lubiejewski, 'Conclusions from the use of aviation in the first half of the first year of the Ukrainian-Russian war', *Security and Defence Quarterly*, 42:2, (2023) pp.68–104, DOI: <https://doi.org/10.35467/sdq/161959>.

24 V. Fedorchak, 'The Mass Approach in the Air War Over Ukraine: Towards identifying a critical mass', Kungl *Krigsvetenskapsakademiens Handlingar Och Tidskrift*, 1 (2023), pp.110–25 (pp.115–6).

Lacking the means to neutralise or suppress the enemy's air defences, both the Russian and Ukrainian air force's Sukhoi Su-25s have been forced to operate at critically low altitudes (10–20m) to support ground forces. As a result, the Su-25s, which were designed for direct support of ground forces on the battlefield, have had limited operational effectiveness, whilst suffering combat attrition, in contested air space. These experiences point to the benefits of multi-role aircraft capable of performing various mission types within a phased air campaign. The VKS's Sukhoi Su-34 fighter-bomber and Su-24 tactical bomber have conducted close air support but they have used stand-off capabilities, dropping glide-bombs from distances of up to 60km. The increase in survivability such stand-off weapons provide is at the expense of point effect (the gliding and correction module attached to 'dumb' bombs do allow for in-flight corrections, but these munitions lack the point accuracy of PGMs). The value of stand-off area effect close air support when achieved in coordination with ground attacks is their ability to neutralise the defensive position. In February 2024, Ukrainian defences in Avdiivka were reportedly suppressed by some 500 glide bombs. Air power, integrated with operations of the ground forces and delivered in concentration, can decisively influence the military outcome of operations.

The Russian use of glide-bombs in Ukraine stems not only from an absence of air superiority but is also due to a shortage of PGMs. The expense of PGMs is such that nations have, since the end of the Cold War, held relatively small stockpiles that are quickly expended in the event of a protracted period of high-intensity operations. In Ukraine, the Russians exhausted their stockpile of PGMs. Increasing production of PGMs relies on the capabilities of a nation's Defence Technological Industrial Base, something which is difficult to maintain in peacetime without adequate investment. The constraint of limited PGM stockpiles is not isolated to Russia. During operations over Kosovo the RAF's consumption of PGMs was a cause of concern and required urgent procurement action.[25] The political decision to fund militaries for short-campaigns, and not invest in the capability to sustain operations, means that as conflicts become protracted air forces may face decisions as to which operations – strategic, interdiction or close air support – warrant the use of a limited precision munitions. The resource requirements of sustaining close air support in a protracted conventional war indicates that, as with all military capabilities, the hidden costs of infrastructure, logistics and maintenance are a crucial component to maintaining operations.

The conflict in Ukraine has also seen conflict over the control of the electromagnetic spectrum. In a contested electromagnetic domain, a reliance on PGMs can also expose air forces to an adversary's electronic countermeasures designed to reduce the precision of the navigation system, and so reduce the point targeting and lethality

25 Comptroller and Auditor General, National Audit Office, Kosovo: The Financial Management of Military Operations, p.3. <https://webarchive.nationalarchives.gov.uk/ukgwa/20230201114112>; <https://www.nao.org.uk/wp-content/uploads/2000/06/9900530.pdf>, accessed 29 Apr. 2024

of close air support. Electronic interference can reduce the effectiveness of close air support beyond the reduction in accuracy of PGMs; any capability operating on the electromagnetic spectrum from communications to GPS tracking of air assets can be affected. This interference can inhibit command and control, detailed coordination between forces and high-situational awareness of the battlefield, leading to a loss of close air support effectiveness and an increased risk of fratricide. In the absence of control of the electromagnetic spectrum, it is also impossible to utilise UAS, and electronic warfare has proved the main means of countering the threat of UAS.[26]

UAS have become an increasingly important aspect of tactical air support in Ukraine, with both sides employing UAS to conduct battlefield air strikes. Amongst the most effective Russian UAS is the loitering munition ZALA Lancet, a one-way-attack UAS, which has been used to attack priority targets on the battlefield. The Lancet has been effective both in close air support and counter-battery attacks.[27] Ukraine has also made effective use of UAS in tactical air support of ground forces. Most notably, the First Person View (FPV) UAS. Small and manoeuvrable, with a low radar cross-section, FPV UAS are difficult to detect and have been able to penetrate contested airspace to target Russian frontline force and undertake interdiction strikes. The contribution of Ukrainian UAS operations exceeds close air support, and their wider tactical value is considerable. Ukrainian UAS ISR has provided deep strike targets for fire power assets such as the M-142 High Mobility Artillery Rocket System to degrade Russian logistics and command and control nodes.[28] UAS are not, however, an adequate replacement for the weight of explosives that can be delivered by aircraft on enemy positions in coordination with the ground offensive. Lacking close air support from fixed-wing or rotary aircraft, Ukraine's counteroffensive in 2023 struggled to break through the extensive field fortifications that Russian forces had constructed. The Ukrainian forces therefore made limited advances, despite the fire support available from artillery and the physical losses inflicted to the Russian forces occupying defensive positions. UAS do, however, offer a means to off-set a frequent cause of complaint from ground forces – their lack of control over air power resources capable of meeting their fire support needs. UAS provide ground forces decentralised asset control and a responsive capability, extending a trend which emerged from the development of attack helicopters.

26 Mykhaylo Zabrodskyi, Jack Watling, Oleksandr V Danylyuk and Nick Reynolds, 'Preliminary Lessons in Conventional Warfighting from Russia's Invasion of Ukraine: February–July 2022', *RUSI*, (Nov. 2022).

27 Sam Cranny-Evans, 'Russia's Artillery War in Ukraine: Challenges and Innovations', *RUSI: Russia Military Report* (9 Aug. 2023). <https://web.archive.org/web/20231128201708/https://rusi.org/explore-our-research/publications/commentary/russias-artillery-war-ukraine-challenges-and-innovations>, accessed 29 Apr. 2024.

28 Karolina Hird, Mason Clark, and George Barros, 'Russian Offensive Campaign Assessment' *Institute for the Study of War* (24 Jul. 2022), <https://web.archive.org/web/20220725081638>; <https://www.understandingwar.org/backgrounder/russian-offensive-campaign-assessment-july-24>, accessed 29 Apr. 2024.

Operations in Ukraine demonstrate that technological changes constantly require air and ground forces to revisit their concepts of close air support and refresh their practice to ensure the effective integration of new technologies. History demonstrates that technology forces evolutions in the tactics of close air support. The need for this adaptation has been driven in no small part by the absence of air superiority for either side. In 2022, the United States Joint Chiefs of Staff *Joint Campaigns and Operations* doctrine noted that 'Commanders should not expect air supremacy or superiority against a capable enemy.'[29] To provide air support in a contested environment requires penetrative capability. Absent of this, air forces are required to trade efficacy for survivability, or must instead prioritise the reduction of the enemy's air defence assets as a precursor to providing close air support.

Conclusion

Close air support is often considered by ground forces to be the critical capability within the air power 'attack' role. It is, however, only one aspect of how air power can affect the battlefield. Although close air support can, at times, be decisive, frequently other missions will have a greater critical influence on land warfare and ground forces. The key to all military operations remains control of the air. Effective close air support can only be consistently achieved once air forces have secured air superiority. Recent counter-insurgency operations, where there are few competing priorities for aircraft, have led close air support to be a significant aspect of military operations. Within these recent experiences, and from historical examples of close air support, the value of planning, tactical air control systems, coordination and communication to successful execution is evident. In peer-on-peer warfare, other air missions will often prove of greater value to ground forces even when they have less prominence and attract criticism for lack of direct support. Interdiction will often prove more valuable than close air support. The lack of immediate effect on the battlefield must be weighed with its potential for greater strategic and operational level effect. At the heart of all these missions is effective air-land integration. The case studies in this work show that when cooperation and coordination are achieved, close air support can be decisive.

29 Joint Chiefs of Staff, *Joint Publication 3-0: Joint Campaigns and Operations* (Washington, DC: Joint Chiefs of Staff, 2022), III–33.

Index